P9-BHW-932

Return ON

INVESTMENT

in training and performance improvement programs

Dr. Jack J. Phillips

Softcover Edition Published by

PRO*Press*

A division of
Performance Resources Organization

Phone 205.678.9700 ▪ Fax 205.678.8070 ▪ Email roipro@wwisp.com
Website: WWW.ROIPRO.COM

© 03/97 by Performance Resources Organization WB98-08 M
No part of this publication may be reproduced, stored in a retrieval system, or transmitted in any form or by any means without the
permission of Performance Resources Organization.

IMPROVING HUMAN PERFORMANCE SERIES
Jack J. Phillips, Ph.D., Series Editor

Accountability in Human Resource Management
Jack Phillips

The Adult-Learner, 5th Edition
Malcolm Knowles and Elwood Holton

Client-Driven Training
Jessica Levant

Global Transformation and Re-Engineering
Michael Marquardt

Global Trends in Training
Jack Phillips

Handbook of Training Evaluation and Measurement Methods, 3rd Edition
Jack Phillips

Human Resource Contributions to Successful Business Strategies
Edward Mone and Manuel London

The Impact of 360 Degree Feedback on Organizations
David Waldman and Leanne A. Atwater, Ph.D.

Learning in Chaos
James Hite

Measuring Learning in Organizations
David Blair and Robert Schriver

Return on Investment in Training and Performance Improvement Programs
Jack Phillips

Technology-Based Training
Serge Ravet and Maureen Layte

Gulf Publishing Company
Houston, Texas

IMPROVING
HUMAN
PERFORMANCE
SERIES

Return ON

INVESTMENT

in training and performance improvement programs

A step-by-step manual
for calculating the financial return

Jack J. Phillips

RETURN ON INVESTMENT

in training and performance improvement programs

Copyright© 1997 by Gulf Publishing Company, Houston, Texas. All rights reserved. Printed in the United States of America. This book, or parts thereof, may not be reproduced in any form without permission of the publisher.

Gulf Publishing Company
Book Division
P.O. Box 2608 ☐ Houston, Texas 77252-2608

10 9 8 7 6 5 4 3 2 1

Library of Congress Cataloging-in-Publication Data

Phillips, Jack J., 1945—
    Return on investment in training and performance improvement programs: a step-by-step manual for calculating the financial return / Jack J. Phillips.
        p. cm. – (Improving human performance in organizations)
        Includes index.
    ISBN 0-88415-492-0
        1. Employees—Training of—Evaluation—Handbooks, manuals, etc. 2. Rate of return—Handbooks, manuals, etc. I. Title. II. Series
HF5549.5.T7P434   1997
658.3'124—dc21

                                                                97-12089
                                                                       CIP

Table of Contents

Acknowledgments, ix

Preface, xi

1

MEASURING THE RETURN ON INVESTMENT: A SEARCH
FOR BEST PRACTICES 1

Basic ROI Issues and Trends, 1
ROI Strategy, 19
Versatile Applications for the ROI Process, 23
Conclusion, 24
References, 24

2

ROI MODEL 25

Preliminary Evaluation Information, 26
Collecting Post Program Data, 28
Isolating the Effects of Training, 29
Converting Data to Monetary Values, 31
Tabulating Cost of Program, 32
Calculating the Return on Investment, 33
Identifying Intangible Benefits, 34
Implementation Issues, 34
Planning for the ROI, 35
Conclusion, 38
Introduction to Case Study, 39
Case Study - Part A National Auto Products Company, 40
References, 42

3

COLLECTING POST-PROGRAM DATA 43

Sources of Data, 44
Using Follow-Up Questionnaires and Surveys, 45
Follow-Up Interviews, 60

Follow-Up Focus Groups, 61
Observing Participants On the Job, 63
Monitoring Performance Data, 66
Action Planning and Follow-Up Assignments, 68
Performance Contracts, 77
Program Follow-Up Session, 78
Selecting the Appropriate Method, 79
Summary, 81
Case Study - Part B: National Auto Products Company, 82
References, 84

4

ISOLATING THE EFFECTS OF TRAINING............................86

Preliminary Issues, 87
Use of Control Groups, 89
Trend Line Analysis, 92
Forecasting Methods, 93
Participant Estimate of Training's Impact, 95
Supervisor Estimate of Training's Impact, 99
Management Estimate of Training's Impact, 104
Customer Input of Training's Impact, 104
Expert Estimation of Training's Impact, 106
Subordinate Input of Training's Impact, 107
Calculating the Impact of Other Factors, 108
Using the Strategies, 109
Conclusion, 109
Case Study - Part C: National Auto Products Company, 110
References, 113

5

CONVERTING DATA TO MONETARY BENEFITS..............114

Preliminary Issues, 115
Strategies for Converting Data to Monetary Values, 119
Converting Output Data to Contribution, 119
Calculating the Cost of Quality, 121

Converting Employee Time, 122
Using Historical Costs, 123
Using Internal and External Experts' Input, 124
Using Values from External Databases, 125
Using Estimates from Participants, 126
Using Estimates from Supervisors, 126
Using Estimates from Senior Managers, 127
Using HRD Staff Estimates, 128
Selecting the Appropriate Strategy, 128
Accuracy and Credibility of Data, 129
Conclusion, 132
Case Study - Part D: National Auto Products Company, 133
References, 135

6

TABULATING PROGRAM COSTS...136

Cost Strategies, 137
Typical Cost Strategies, 140
Major Cost Strategies, 141
Cost Accumulation and Estimation, 144
Summary, 147
Case Study - Part E: National Auto Products Company, 147
References, 151

7

CALCULATING THE RETURN 152

Basic Issues, 153
Benefits/Costs Ratio, 154
ROI Formula, 155
BCR/ROI Case Application, 156
Other ROI Measures, 160
Utility Analysis, 161
Consequences of Not Training, 163
ROI Issues, 163
Conclusion, 166
Case Study - Part F: National Auto Products Company, 167
References, 172

vii

8

IDENTIFYING INTANGIBLE MEASURES 173

Key Issues, 174
Employee Satisfaction, 176
Employee Withdrawal, 178
Customer Service, 180
Team Effectiveness Measures, 181
Conclusion, 183
Case Study - Part G: National Auto Products Company, 184
References, 189

9

ROI AT MULTIPLE LEVELS 190

ROI at Level 1: Reaction, 190
ROI at Level 2: Testing, 195
ROI at Level 3: Skills and Competencies, 197
ROI at Level 4: Business Results, 199
Conclusion, 200
Case Study - Part H: National Auto Products Company, 202
References, 205

10

IMPLEMENTATION ISSUES 207

Planning the Implementation, 207
Preparing the HRD Staff, 215
Initiating the ROI Process, 220
Training the Management Team, 222
Monitoring Progress and Communicating Results, 226
Conclusion, 229
Case Study - Part I: National Auto Products Company, 229
References, 234

Appendix 1 235

Appendix 2 240

Index, 247

Acknowledgments

In no way has developing this book been a single-handed effort. Many individuals have helped shape the content and issues contained in each chapter. Much appreciation goes to our clients who provide us the opportunity to continue to experiment with the ROI process. Although we have had the opportunity to work with hundreds of excellent organizations and individuals, a few stand out as being very helpful in the development of the issues for this book: Toni Hodges, Bell Atlantic; Wade Hannum, Xerox; Craig Fortner, Kathy Jones, and Debi Harrel, Nortel; Joan Coggins, First Union; David Blair and Rob Schriver, Lockheed-Martin; David Soock, Canadian Tire; Bud Wurtz, NCR; Jon Friedman, Whirlpool; Terri Monroe, Baptist Health Systems; Lisa Baggett, AmSouth; Troy Barger, UPS; Rick Irwin, ComEd; Frank Ashby, Bob McCarty, and Sandra Kuhlman, Dale Carnegie; Larry Studdard, First American Bank; Ken Lowery, Ceco Building Systems; Darmidjas Darwis, Caltex Pacific Indonesia; Jan Chernick, NYNEX; and Edy Nash, Service Merchandise. Each of these individuals, in his or her own way, provided some ideas or inspiration to help develop this book.

I must also acknowledge the important work of my associates at Performance Resources Organization (PRO) who have applied this process regularly and made significant progress. My long-time colleague and officer in our company, Ron Stone, provided numerous suggestions for the book and reviewed the manuscript. Many of the techniques and strategies used in the book were developed and refined by Ron.

Most of all, I would like to thank Tammy Bush for her patience, persistence, and long hours of work to make this manuscript a reality. Her work is always exceptional and her dedication is immeasurable.

Preface

Interest in ROI

Return on investment (ROI) has become one of the most challenging and intriguing issues facing the human resources development (HRD) and performance improvement field. The interest in ROI during the 1990s has been phenomenal. The topic appears on almost every HRD conference and convention agenda. Articles on ROI appear regularly in HRD practitioner and research journals. Several books have been developed on the topic, and consulting firms have sprung up almost overnight to tackle this critical and important issue.

Several issues are driving the increased interest in, and application of, the ROI process. Pressure from clients and senior managers to show the return on their training investment is probably the most influential driver. Competitive economic pressures are causing intense scrutiny of all expenditures, including all training and development costs. Total quality management, re-engineering, and continuous process improvement have created a renewed interest in measurement and evaluation, including measuring the effectiveness of training. The general trend toward accountability with all staff support groups is causing some HRD departments to measure their contribution. These and other factors have created an unprecedented wave of applications of the ROI process.

Needed: An Effective ROI Process

The challenging aspect of the ROI process is the nature and accuracy of its development. The process often seems very confusing, surrounded by models, formulas, and statistics that often frighten the most capable practitioners. Coupled with this concern are misunderstandings about the process and the gross misuse of ROI techniques in some organizations. These issues sometimes leave practitioners with a distaste for the process. Unfortunately, ROI cannot be ignored. To admit to clients and senior managers that the impact of training cannot be measured is to admit that training does not add value or that HRD should not be subjected to accountability processes. In practice, ROI must be explored, considered, and ultimately implemented in most organizations.

What is needed is a rational, logical approach that can be simplified and implemented within the current budget constraints and resources of the organization. This book presents a proven ROI process, based on almost 20 years of development and refinement. It is a process that is rich in tradition and modified to meet the demands facing the current training and performance improvement programs.

The ROI process described in this book meets the requirements of three very important groups. First, the practitioners who have used this model and implemented the ROI process in their organizations continue to report their satisfaction with the process and the success that it has achieved. The ROI process presented here is user-friendly, easy to understand, and has been proven to pay for itself time and time again. A second important group, the clients and senior managers who must approve training and performance improvement budgets, want measurable results, preferably expressed as a return on investment. The ROI process presented here has fared well with these groups. Senior managers view the process as credible, logical, practical, and easy to understand from their perspective. More importantly, they buy into the process, which is critical for their future support. The third important group is the evaluation researchers who develop, explore, and analyze new processes and techniques. When exposed to this ROI process in a two-day or one week workshop, the researchers, without exception, give this process very high marks. They often applaud the strategies for isolating the effects of training and the strategies for converting data to monetary values. Unanimously, they characterize the process as an important contribution to the field.

Why this Book at this Time?

When examining current publications related to ROI, there is no book with a comprehensive, practical presentation on ROI, using a process that meets the demands of the three groups previously described. Most models and representations of the ROI process ignore, or provide very little insight into the two key elements essential to developing the ROI: isolating the effects of training and converting data to monetary values. Recognizing that there are many other factors that will have an influence on output results, this book provides ten strategies to isolate the effects of training, far more than any other presentation on the topic. Not enough attention has been provided to the issue of assigning monetary values to the benefits derived from training. This book presents ten strategies for converting data to monetary values.

This book was developed at the request of many clients and colleagues who have asked for a simplified, concise description of the ROI process, presented in a step-by-step approach. An earlier contribution to measurement and evaluation is our successful book, *Handbook of Training Evaluation and Measurement Methods*, now entering its 3rd edition. While the handbook covers ROI, it also provides coverage of many other topics and issues important to the overall evaluation and measurement process. It has become a standard reference in the HRD field and a widely used textbook for college courses. What is needed, according to practitioners, is a book that carves out the ROI process and presents a model that is rationale, feasible, and understandable to the typical practitioner. This book should meet this need.

Target Audience

The primary audience for this book is the professionals involved in training, development, and performance improvement. Whether an individual is involved in needs assessment, instructional design, delivery, or evaluation, this book will be an indispensable reference. Individuals in training and HRD leadership positions (i.e., managers, supervisors, team leaders, directors, and vice presidents) will find it to be a helpful guide to ROI. With its step-by-step approach and case presentations, it will also be useful as a self-study guide.

A second audience is those individuals involved in the design and implementation of other types of change programs, other than training, development, and performance improvement. Because the ROI process is appropriate for all change efforts, this book should be a useful reference for HR managers, change agents, quality managers, re-engineering coordinators, and information technology specialists. The ROI process described in this book has been used to measure the impact of a variety of human resources programs, re-engineering initiatives, and technology implementation situations, as well as in changes of procedures, practices, and policies. Any time change is realized, this process will capture the return on investment.

A third audience is the management group. Because of the tremendous interest among the management team and clients involved in ROI studies, this book should be a very useful reference for them. In a simple, easy to recreate process, it shows how the ROI is developed, in language that managers understand.

The fourth target audience is consultants, researchers, and seminar presenters who find this process to be an effective way to measure the impact of their programs. It provides a workable model for consultants to evaluate change initiatives or consulting interventions. The book provides researchers with a sound tool for evaluating a variety of programs. Seminar presenters will find this book to be a helpful tool to measure the success of their workshops. The ROI process has been applied effectively in measuring the impact of public seminars.

Finally, professors and educators will find this book extremely useful for evaluating education and training. Its content should stimulate thought and debate on how the ROI is developed for the educational field. The book should be a useful textbook or supplemental book for a course on evaluation.

Structure of the Book

This book has two unique features that make it a very useful guide. First, it presents the ROI model in a step-by-step process. A chapter is devoted to each major part of the model as the pieces of the ROI puzzle are methodically put together. At the conclusion, the reader has a clear understanding of the overall ROI process.

The second unique feature is an application of the model in a detailed case, based on an actual situation. The case is divided into nine parts. One part is included at the end of each chapter, beginning with Chapter 2. Readers can work through the case, step-by-step, exploring the issues uncovered in the chapter and learn how to apply them to their own organizations. The actual results are presented in the next chapter where the new issue is addressed. This case presentation is a proven learning tool to understanding the ROI process.

Chapter Descriptions

Chapter One, **Measuring the Return on Investment: A Search for Best Practices**, describes how the ROI process has evolved in recent years and describes how organizations are tackling this important issue. Best practices, which form the basis for the book, are briefly described. Various ROI criteria and requirements are presented to build a foundation for the remainder of the book.

Chapter Two presents the **ROI Model**. Initially conceived in the late 1970s, the model has been developed, changed, and refined in the past 20 years to arrive at what users characterize as the most logical, rational, and credible approach to the ROI process. This chapter presents a brief summary of the model for those who are being introduced to the process for the first time.

Chapter Three, **Collecting Post Program Data**, presents a variety of approaches to one of the most fundamental issues. Ranging from conducting surveys to monitoring performance data, the ten most common ways to collect data after a program has been implemented are described in this chapter. Useful tips and techniques to help select the appropriate method for a specific situation are presented.

Chapter Four, **Isolating the Effects of Training**, presents what is perhaps the most important aspect of the ROI process. Ranging from the use of a control group arrangement to obtaining estimates directly from participants, ten strategies are presented which can determine the amount of improvement that is directly linked to the training program. The premise of this chapter is that there are many influences on business performance measures with training being only one of them.

Chapter Five, **Converting Data to Monetary Benefits**, presents an essential step for developing an economic benefit from training. Ranging from determining the profit contribution of an increased output to using expert opinion to assign a value to data, ten strategies to convert both hard and soft data to monetary values are presented along, with many examples.

Chapter Six, **Tabulating Program Costs**, details specifically what types of costs should be included in the ROI formula. Different categories and classifications of costs are explored in this chapter with the goal for developing a fully loaded cost profile for each ROI calculation.

Chapter Seven, **Calculating the Return**, describes the actual ROI calculation and presents several issues surrounding its development, calculation, and use. Examples are presented to illustrate the process.

Chapter Eight, **Identifying Intangible Measures**, is a brief chapter that focuses on non-monetary benefits from the program. Recognizing that not all of the output measures from training can or should be converted to monetary values, this chapter shows how the intangible measures should be identified, monitored, and reported. Twenty common intangible measures are examined. This chapter concludes the presentation of the basic ROI process model.

Chapter Nine, **ROI at Multiple Levels**, shows how the return on investment can be developed at different levels of evaluation, which often equates to different times in the training cycle ranging from a pre-program measure to using post-program data. Several examples are presented to highlight each concept. This chapter underscores the range of possibilities available to for calculating the ROI.

Chapter Ten, **Implementation Issues**, the concluding chapter, addresses a variety of implementation issues. To implement the ROI process effectively requires following logical steps and overcoming several hurdles. This chapter identifies the important issues that must be tackled for the ROI process to become a productive, useful, and long lasting process.

1

MEASURING THE RETURN ON INVESTMENT:
A Search for Best Practices

Basic ROI Issues and Trends

Measuring the return on investment (ROI) in training and development has consistently earned a place among the critical issues in the Human Resource Development (HRD) field. The topic appears routinely on conference agendas and at professional meetings. Journals and newsletters regularly embrace the concept with increasing print space. At least a dozen books provide significant coverage of the topic. Even top executives have stepped up their appetite for ROI information.

Although the interest in the topic has heightened and much progress has been made, it is still an issue that challenges even the most sophisticated and progressive HRD departments. Some professionals argue that it is not possible to calculate the ROI in HRD, while others quietly and deliberately proceed to develop measures and ROI calculations. Regardless of the position taken on the issue, the reasons for measuring the return are still there. Almost all HRD professionals share a concern that they must eventually show a return on their training investment. Otherwise, training funds may be reduced or the HRD department may not be able to maintain or enhance its present status and influence in the organization.

The dilemma surrounding the ROI process is a source of frustration with many senior executives and even within the HRD field itself. Most executives realize that training is a basic necessity when organizations are experiencing significant growth or increased competition. In those cases, training can prepare employees for the required skills while fine tuning skills needed to meet competitive challenges. Training is also important during business restructuring and rapid change where employees must learn new skills and often find themselves doing much more work in a dramatically downsized workforce.

While most executives see the need for training, these same executives intuitively feel that there is value in training. They can logically conclude that training can payoff in important bottom-line measures such as productivity improvements, quality enhancements, cost reductions, and time savings. Also, they believe that training can enhance customer satisfaction, improve morale, and build teamwork. Yet the frustration comes from the lack of evidence to show that the process is really working. While the payoffs are assumed to be there and training appears to be needed, more evidence is needed or training funds may not be allocated in the future. The ROI process represents the most promising way to show this accountability in a logical, rational approach, fully described in this book.

The Progress

The status of the ROI process among practitioners in the field is difficult, if not impossible, to pinpoint. Senior HRD managers are reluctant to disclose internal practices and, even in the most progressive organizations, they confess that too little progress has been made. It is difficult to find cases in the literature which show how an organization has attempted to measure the return on investment in HRD. Recognizing this void, the American Society for Training and Development (ASTD) undertook an ambitious project to develop a collection of cases which represent real life examples of measuring the return on investment. To find cases, more than 2,000 individuals were contacted for the initial volume, including practitioners, authors, researchers, consultants, and conference presenters. In addition, organizations perceived to be respected and admired were contacted.

The response was very encouraging. More than 150 individuals requested specific guidelines as they explored the possibility of developing a case. To meet the requirements, the organization had to be willing to detail specific steps, issues, and concerns involved as the ROI was developed. In the final analysis,

40 individuals were willing to submit cases, and the acquisition process was halted when 30 cases had been delivered. Ultimately, 18 of those were selected for publication in 1994 in the casebook, *In Action: Measuring Return on Investment.*[1] It became the ASTD's best seller in 1995, from over 250 of the Society's titles sold through catalogs, bookstores, and conferences. Because of the reaction and response, Volume 2 was published in 1997.

One of the most interesting signs of progress with training evaluation and measurement comes from the annual Industry Report compiled by *Training* magazine. In 1996, *Training* surveyed over 40,000 training managers and specialists to determine the status of evaluation at different levels. Table 1-1 shows the results.

Table 1-1
Status of Training Evaluation

Level	As a Percent of Organizations Measuring at this Level	Percent of Courses Measured at this Level
Level 1: Training Reaction	86%	83%
Level 2: Learning	71%	51%
Level 3: Behavior	65%	50%
Level 4: Business Results	49%	44%

Source: *Training Magazine*, October 1996, p. 63.

The results, which mirrored the 1995 results, showed some interesting statistics in terms of the use of evaluation, particularly at Level 4 (the levels of evaluation will be explained later). After the 1995 issues were released, *Training* editors admitted that perhaps the respondents were stating how they think evaluation ought to be. The editors concluded, however, that since the data was the same in the third year of this effort, the results were reflective of current practices. The editors believe that many organizations are finding innovative ways to measure training, particularly with the use of the computer. This data does contain some surprises. First, the use of Level 1 data is generally perceived to be higher than the values contained in survey results, which reveals that only 86% of organizations are measuring at Level 1. Other studies have shown higher use of Level 1 evaluation, usually over 95%. The second surprise is perhaps the overstatement of Level 4 use, which usually reflects ROI. Most studies place the value in the 5% - 20% range. Regardless of the discrepancies, there is a distinct trend toward more accountability of training, particularly at higher levels of evaluation where training is connected to business results.

ROI is now taking on increased interest in the executive suite. Top executives who watched their training budgets continue to grow without the appropriate accountability measures have become frustrated and, in an attempt to respond to the situation, have demanded a return on the training investment. The payoff of training is becoming a conversation topic in top executive circles. An illustration of this trend occurred in 1995 when the *William and Mary Business Review* selected the topic, "Corporate Training: Does It Pay Off?," as the theme of its summer issue. [2] Each year the *William and Mary Business Review* focuses on an important issue facing corporate executives to stimulate intellectual and practical debate of prevailing management issues (the 1994 topic was re-engineering). The special issue was distributed to top corporate leaders and executives. To develop this special issue, the *Business Review* provided a critical examination of the topic by assembling diverse points of view from members of academic and professional communities. Of the ten articles in the special issue, "Measuring Training's ROI: It Can Be Done!," was the lead article. [3]

Measuring the return on investment is becoming a truly global issue. Organizations from all over the world are concerned about the accountability of training and are exploring ways and techniques to measure the results of training. In a survey of 35 members of the International Federation of Training and Development Organizations, measuring return on investment was consistently rated the hottest topic among members of those organizations[4]. Whether the economy is mature or developing, the accountability of training is still a critical issue.

Finally, ROI applications have increased because of the growing interest in a variety of organizational improvement and change programs, which have dominated in organizations, particularly in North America. Organizations have embraced almost any trend or fad that has appeared on the horizon. Unfortunately, many of these change efforts have not worked and have turned out to be passing fads embraced in attempts to improve the organizations. The training and development function is often caught in the middle of this activity, either by supporting the process with programs or actually coordinating the new process in these organizations. While the ROI process is an effective way to measure the accountability of training, it has rarely been used in the past. A complete implementation of the process requires a thorough needs assessment and significant planning before an ROI program is implemented. If these two elements are in place, unnecessary passing fads, doomed for failure, can be avoided. With the ROI process in place, a new change program that does not produce results will be exposed. Management will be aware of it early so that adjustments can be made.

Examples of the progress of ROI are virtually everywhere, elevating it to a critical topic that is constantly haunting the human resource development field. The interest in ROI will be persistent as long as budgets continue to increase and the process has the potential for helping organizations improve.

The progress with ROI underscores the need for human resource development functions to have a paradigm shift in the approach to measurement and evaluation. As depicted in Table 1-2, a significant paradigm shift has occurred in recent years that will have a dramatic effect on the accountability of training, education, and development programs. Organizations have moved from training for activity to training with a focus on bottom-line results, and this shift is evident from the beginning to the end of the process. The shift has often occurred because of these forces. In some cases, the shift has occurred because progressive HRD departments have recognized the need for ROI and have been persistent in making progress on this issue.

The Concerns with ROI

Although much progress has been made, the ROI process is not without its share of problems and drawbacks. The mere presence of the process creates a dilemma for many organizations. When an organization embraces the concept and implements the process, the management team is usually anxiously waiting for results, only to be disappointed when they are not quantifiable. For an ROI process to be useful, it must balance many issues such as feasibility, simplicity, credibility, and soundness. More specifically, three major audiences must be pleased with the ROI process to accept and use it.

HRD Practitioners. For years, HRD Practitioners have assumed that ROI could not be measured. When they examined a typical process, they found long formulas, complicated equations, and complex models that made the ROI process appear to be too confusing. With this perceived complexity, HRD managers could visualize the tremendous efforts required for data collection and analysis, and more importantly, the increased cost necessary to make the process

Table 1-2
Paradigm Shift in Training Evaluation

Training for Activity	**Training for Results**
Characterized by:	**Characterized by:**
☐ no business need for the program	☐ program linked to specific business needs
☐ no assessment of performance issues	☐ assessment of performance effectiveness
☐ no specific measurable objectives for behavior and business impact	☐ specific objectives for behavior and business impact
☐ no effort to prepare program participants to achieve results	☐ results expectations communicated to participants
☐ no effort to prepare the work environment to support transfer	☐ environment prepared to support transfer
☐ no efforts to build partnerships with key managers	☐ partnerships established with key managers and clients
☐ no measurement of results or cost benefit analysis	☐ measurement of results and cost benefit analysis
☐ planning and reporting on training is input focused	☐ planning and reporting on training is output focused

work. Because of these concerns, HRD practitioners are seeking an ROI process that is simple and easy to understand so that they can easily implement the steps and strategies. Also, they need a process that will not take an excessive time frame to implement and will not consume too much precious staff time. Finally, practitioners need a process that is not too expensive. With competition for financial resources, they need a process that will not command a significant portion of the HRD budget. In summary, the ROI process, from the perspective of the HRD practitioner, must be user friendly, save time, and be cost efficient.

Senior Managers/Sponsors/Clients.   Managers who must approve HRD budgets, request HRD programs, or live with the results of programs have a strong interest in developing the ROI in training. They want a process that provides quantifiable results, using a method similar to the ROI formula applied to other types of investments. Senior managers have a never-ending desire to have it all come down to an ROI calculation, reflected as a percentage. And, as do HRD practitioners, they also want a process that is simple and easy to understand. The assumptions made in the calculations and the methodology used in the process should reflect their point of reference, background, and level of understanding. They do not want, or need, a string of formulas, charts, and complicated models. Instead, they need a process that they can explain to others, if necessary. More importantly, they need a process with which they can identify, one that is sound and realistic enough to earn their confidence.

Researchers. Finally, researchers will only support a process that measures up to their scrutiny and close examination. Researchers usually insist that models, formulas, assumptions, and theories are sound and based on commonly accepted practices. Also, they want a process that produces accurate values and consistent outcomes. If estimates are necessary, researchers want a process that provides the most accuracy within the constraints of the situation, recognizing that adjustments need to be made when there is uncertainty in the process. The challenge is to develop acceptable requirements for an ROI process that will satisfy researchers and, at the same time, please practitioners and senior managers. Sound impossible? Maybe not.

Criteria for an Effective ROI Process

To satisfy the needs of the three critical groups previously described, the ROI process must meet several requirements. Ten essential criteria for an effective ROI process follow.

1. The ROI process must be **simple**, void of complex formulas, lengthy equations, and complicated methodologies. Most ROI attempts have failed with this requirement. In an attempt to obtain statistical perfection and use too many theories, several ROI models and processes have become too complex to understand and use. Consequently, they have not been implemented.

2. The ROI process must be **economical** with the ability to be implemented easily. The process should have the capability to become a routine part of training and development without requiring significant additional resources. Sampling for ROI calculations and early planning for ROI are often necessary to make progress without adding new staff.

3. The assumptions, methodology, and techniques must be **credible**. Logical, methodical steps are needed to earn the respect of practitioners, senior managers, and researchers. This requires a very practical approach for the process.

4. From a research perspective, the ROI process must be **theoretically sound** and based on generally accepted practices. Unfortunately, this requirement can lead to an extensive, complicated process. Ideally, the process must strike a balance between maintaining a practical and sensible approach <u>and</u> a sound and theoretical basis for the process. This is perhaps one of the greatest challenges to those who have developed models for the ROI process.

5. The ROI process must **account for other factors** which have influenced output variables. One of the most often overlooked issues, isolating the influence of the HRD program, is necessary to build credibility and accuracy within the process. The ROI process should pinpoint the contribution of the training program when compared to the other influences.

6. The ROI process must be appropriate with a **variety of HRD programs**. Some models apply to only a small number of programs such as sales or productivity training. Ideally, the process must be applicable to all types of training and other HRD programs such as career development, organization development, and major change initiatives.

7. The ROI process must have the **flexibility** to be applied on a pre-program basis as well as a post-program basis. In some situations, an estimate of the ROI is required before the actual program is developed. Ideally, the process should be able to adjust to a range of potential time frames.

8. The ROI process must be **applicable with all types of data**, including hard data, which is typically represented as output, quality, costs, and time; <u>and</u> soft data, which includes job satisfaction, customer satisfaction, absenteeism, turnover, grievances, and complaints.

9. The ROI process must **include the costs of the program**. The ultimate level of evaluation is to compare the benefits with costs. Although the term ROI has been loosely used to express any benefit of training, an acceptable ROI formula must include costs. Omitting or underestimating costs will only destroy the credibility of the ROI values.

10. Finally, the ROI process must have a successful **track record** in a variety of applications. In far too many situations, models are created but never successfully applied. An effective ROI process should withstand the wear and tear of implementation and should get the results expected.

Because these criteria are considered essential, an ROI process should meet the vast majority, if not all criteria. The bad news is that most ROI processes do not meet these criteria. The good news is that the ROI process presented in this book meets all of the criteria.

The Ultimate Level of Evaluation: ROI

The ROI process adds a fifth level to the four levels of evaluation, which were developed almost 40 years ago by Kirkpatrick.[5] The concept of different levels of evaluation is both helpful and instructive in understanding how the return on investment is calculated. Table 1-3 shows the five level framework used in this book. At Level 1, *Reaction and Planned Action*, satisfaction from program participants is measured, along with a listing of how they planned to apply what they have learned. Almost all organizations evaluate at Level 1, usually with a generic, end of program questionnaire. While this level of evaluation is important as a customer satisfaction measure, a favorable reaction does not ensure that participants have learned new skills or knowledge.[6] At Level 2, *Learning*, measurements focus on what participants learned during the program using tests, skill practices, role plays, simulations, group evaluations, and other assessment tools. A learning check is helpful to ensure that participants have absorbed the material and know how to use it. However, a positive measure at this level is no guarantee that the material will be used on-the-job. The literature is laced with studies that show the failure of learning to be transferred to the job.[7] At Level 3, *Job Applications*, a variety of follow-up methods are used to determine if participants applied on-the-job what they learned. The frequency and use of skills are important measures at Level 3. While Level 3 evaluation is important to gauge the success of the program's application, it still does not guarantee that there will be a positive impact in the organization. At Level 4, *Business Results*, the measurement focuses on the actual results achieved by program participants as they successfully apply the program material. Typical Level 4 measures include output, quality, costs, time, and customer satisfaction. Although the program may produce a measurable business impact, there is still a concern that the program may have cost too much. At Level 5, the ultimate level of evaluation, *Return on Investment*, the measurement compares the program's monetary benefits with the program costs. Although the ROI can be expressed in several ways, it is usually presented as a percent or cost benefit ratio. The evaluation cycle is not complete until the Level 5 evaluation is conducted.

While almost all HRD organizations conduct evaluations to measure satisfaction, very few actually conduct evaluations at the ROI level. Perhaps the best explanation for this situation is that ROI evaluation is often characterized as a difficult and expensive process. Although business results and ROI are desired, it is very important to evaluate the other levels. A chain of impact should occur through the levels as the skills and knowledge learned (Level 2) are applied on-the-job (Level 3) to produce business results (Level 4). If

Table 1-3
Characteristics of Evaluation Levels

Level	Brief Description
1. Reaction & Planned Action	Measures participant's reaction to the program and outlines specific plans for implementation.
2. Learning	Measures skills, knowledge, or attitude changes.
3. Job Applications	Measures changes in behavior on-the-job and specific applications of the training material.
4. Business Results	Measures business impact of the program.
5. Return on Investment	Compares the monetary value of the results with the costs for the program, usually expressed as a percentage.

measurements are not taken at each level, it is difficult to conclude that the results achieved were actually caused by the HRD program.[8] Because of this, it is recommended that evaluation be conducted at all levels when a level five evaluation is planned. This practice is consistent with the practices of ASTD's benchmarking forum members.[9]

Definitions and Formulas

Although definitions and formulas are presented throughout this book, several issues need defining early in the process. The term human resource development is used throughout the book to refer to training, education, and development. This has become accepted terminology throughout the USA and reflects the pioneering work of Nadler.[10] In this context, training focuses directly on job related skills and has a short time frame for payback. Consequently, it represents a low risk investment. Education, on the other hand, focuses primarily on preparation for the next job. It has a medium time frame for payback and represents a moderate risk for payback. Development represents more of a cultural change and has a long time frame for payback. Consequently, the risks for payback are quite high. This definition, illustrated in Table 1-4, shows why many organizations place emphasis directly on training where the risk is low and the payback is soon. This definition also explains some of the difficulties of applying the ROI process. The return on investment for short term training programs is easier to capture with the ROI process. It is more difficult to attain the ROI in educational programs because of the extended time for payback and because other intervening variables may enter the process. Developmental programs are the most difficult for ROI application because of the long term focus and the full range of variables that may enter the process and complicate the linkage with the performance change.

The term "learning solution" is sometimes used in lieu of "training" to underscore the point that there are many solutions to performance problems or performance opportunities. This term is becoming more prevalent among organizations that have characterized themselves as learning organizations.

The term "program" is used to reflect learning solution, seminar, workshop, on-the-job training, or other interventions in which learning takes place. In reality, training is a process and not a one time event or program. However, because of the common use of the term, "program" will be used throughout the book to reflect the specific intervention, whether it is off the job or on the job.

The term "participant" is used to refer to the individual involved in the training program or learning solution. It replaces the term trainee or student. And, finally, the term "CEO" is used to refer to the top executive at a specific organizational entity. The CEO could be chief administrator, managing director, division president, major operations executive, or other top official, and often reflects the most senior management in the organizational entity where the program takes place.

Table 1-4
Human Resource Development Definition

	Focus	Time for Payback	Risk for Payback
Training	Job Related Skills	Short	Low
Education	Preparation for Next Job	Medium	Moderate
Development	Cultural Change	Long	High

A final definition offered in this chapter is the basic definition of return on investment. Two common formulas are offered: Benefits/Costs Ratio (BCR) and ROI:

$$BCR = \frac{Program\ Benefits}{Program\ Costs}$$

$$\text{ROI (\%)} = \frac{\text{Net Program Benefits}}{\text{Program Costs}} \times 100$$

The BCR utilizes the total benefits and costs. In the ROI formula, the costs are subtracted from the total benefits to produce net benefits which are then divided by the costs. For example, a literary skills program at Magnavox produced benefits of $321,600 with a cost of $38,233.[11]   Therefore, the benefits/costs ratio is:

$$\text{BCR} = \frac{\$321,600}{\$38,233} = 8.4 \ (\text{or } 8.4{:}1)$$

As this calculation shows, for every $1 invested, $8.4 in benefits are returned. In this example, net benefits are $321,600 - $38,233 = $283,367. Thus, the ROI is:

$$\text{ROI (\%)} = \frac{\$283,367}{\$38,233} \times 100 = 741\%$$

This means that for each $1 invested in the program, there is a return of $7.4 in *net* benefits, after costs are covered. The benefits are usually expressed as annual benefits, representing the amount saved or gained for a complete year after program completion. While the benefits may continue after the first year if the program has long term effects, the impact usually diminishes and is omitted from calculations.   This conservative approach is used throughout the application of the ROI process in this book. The values for return on investment are usually quite large, in the range of 25% to 500%, which illustrates the potential impact of successful programs.

The Evidence: ROI Cases

The cases from Volume 1 of *Measuring the Return on Investment*, ASTD's initial ROI casebook, represent a wide range of settings, methodologies, strategies, and approaches in manufacturing, service, and government organizations.   Target audiences vary from all employees to managers and specialists. Although most programs focus on training and development, others include broader development areas such as organization development, total quality, performance management, and employee selection. As a group, these cases represent a rich source of information on the thought processes and strategies of some of the best practitioners, consultants, and researchers in the field. Figure 1-1 presents a brief description of 14 of the 18 cases, showing the target groups, a brief description of the program, the evaluation process, and a quick summary of the results. It is presented here to illustrate the variety of the cases and to highlight the impressive results that have been achieved in these organizations. Since positive role models are needed for this process, only cases with excellent results were published, with returns ranging from 150% to 2000%.

Barriers to ROI Implementation

Although progress has been made in the implementation of ROI, significant barriers inhibit the implementation of the concept. Some of these barriers are realistic while others are actually myths based on false perceptions. Each barrier is briefly described in the following section.

Costs and Time. The ROI process will add some additional costs and time to the evaluation process of programs, although the added amount will not be excessive. As will be described throughout this book, a comprehensive ROI process will probably not add more than 3% - 5% to the overall training budget. The additional investment in ROI would perhaps be offset by the additional results achieved from these programs and the elimination of unproductive or unprofitable programs. This barrier alone stops many ROI implementations early in the process.

Lack of Skills and Orientation for HRD Staff. Many training staff members do not understand ROI nor do they have the basic skills necessary to apply the process within their scope of responsibilities. Also, the typical training program does not focus on results, but more on learning outcomes. Consequently, a tremendous barrier to implementation is the change needed for the overall orientation, attitude, and skills of the HRD staff. As Pogo, the cartoon character, once said, "We have met the enemy and he is us." This certainly applies to the ROI implementation.

Faulty Needs Assessment. Many of the current HRD programs do not have an adequate needs assessment. Some of these programs have been implemented for the wrong reasons based on management requests or efforts to chase a popular fad or trend in the industry. If the program is not needed, there will probably not be any benefits from the program. An ROI calculation for an unnecessary program will likely yield a negative value. This is a realistic barrier for many programs.

Setting	Target Group	Program Description	Evaluation Process	Results
Bottling Company (Coca Cola)	First Level Supervisors	Eight half-day workshops covering supervisory roles, setting goals, developing the team, etc.	• Action Planning • Follow-up Session • Performance Monitoring	• 1447% ROI • Benefit/Cost Ratio 15:1 • Variety of Measures
Paper Products Company	Managers, Supervisors, Hourly Employees	Organization Development Program (Workshops, Action Study Teams, Skill Building Programs)	• Follow-up with Interviews • Survey • Performance Monitoring	• Variance from Standard +$106,000 • Efficiencies 4% Improvement • Waste 36% Improvement • Absenteeism 35% Improvement • Safety 29% Improvement • Housekeeping 29% Improvement
Health Maintenance Organization (HMO)	All Managers, and All Employees	Organization Development Program (Team Building, Group Meetings, Customer Service Training)	• Performance Monitoring • Management Estimation	• 20,700 New HMO Members • 1270% ROI • Benefit/Cost Ratio 13.7:1

Figure 1-1. *Actual business results from training and development*

Setting	Target Group	Program Description	Evaluation Process	Results
Large Commercial Bank	Consumer Loan Officers	Two-Day Sales Training Program - Focus on Increase in Consumer Loans	• Follow-up • Performance Monitoring	• 30% Increase in Consumer Loans • 1988% ROI • Benefit/Cost Ratio 20:1
Information Services Company	Supervisors	Twelve 2 1/2 hour sessions on behavioral modeling	• Follow-up with Surveys	• 336% ROI
Electric & Gas Utility	Managers & Supervisors	Applied Behavior Management which focused on achieving employee involvement to increase quality, productivity, and profits	• Action Planning (Variety of Projects) • Performance Monitoring	• 400% ROI • Benefit/Cost Ratio 5:1
Oil Company	Dispatchers	Skills Training Program including customer interaction skills, problem solving, and teamwork	• Follow-up • Observations • Performance Monitoring	• Customer complaints reduced by 85% • Absenteeism reduced by 77% • Reduction in pull-outs saved $354,750 • 383% ROI • Benefit/Cost Ratio 4.8:1

Figure 1-1. *Cont'd.*

Setting	Target Group	Program Description	Evaluation Process	Results
Bakery (Multi-Marques, Inc.)	Supervisors/ Administration Services	15 hour Supervisory Skills Training including the role of training	• Action planning (Work Process Analyses) • Performance Monitoring	• 215% ROI • Benefit/Cost Ratio 3.2:1
Avionics (Litton Industries)	All Employees	Self Directed Work Teams	• Action Planning • Performance Monitoring	• Productivity Increased 45% • Scrap Rate Reduction 50% • 650 % ROI
Truck Leasing (Penske Truck Leasing)	All Supervisors	20 hour program on supervisory skills utilizing behavioral modeling	• Performance Monitoring	• Turnover reduction of 6% • Absenteeism reduction of 16.7%
Direct Sales	All employees in the Financial Services Division	20 hour program spread over 60 days, focusing on total quality management	• Action Planning	• Payback of program investment in one year

Figure 1-1. *Cont'd.*

Setting	Target Group	Program Description	Evaluation Process	Results
Trucking (Yellow Freight System)	Managers	Redesigned performance appraisal with training on interpersonal skills, communication, coaching	• Follow-up Interviews • Performance Monitoring	• 1115% ROI • Benefit/Cost Ratio 12:1
Federal Government	New Supervisors	5 day introduction to supervision course covering eight key competencies	• Follow-up Questionnaire	• 150% ROI • Benefit/Cost Ratio 2.5:1
Electronics (Magnavox)	Entry level electrical and mechanical assemblers	18 week literacy training program divided into 3 six week terms reading and match skills	• Performance Monitoring	• 741% ROI (on productivity and scrap) • Benefit/Cost Ratio 8.4:1

Figure 1-1. *Cont'd.*

Fear. Some HRD departments do not pursue ROI because of fear of failure or fear of the unknown. Fear of failure appears in many ways. There may be a concern about the consequence of negative ROI. Also, the ROI process will stir up the traditional fear of change. This fear, often based on unrealistic assumptions and a lack of knowledge of the process, is so strong that it becomes a realistic barrier to many ROI implementations.

Discipline and Planning. A successful ROI implementation requires much planning and a disciplined approach to keep the process on track. Implementation schedules, evaluation targets, ROI analysis plans, measurement and evaluation policies, and follow-up schedules are required. The HRD staff may not have enough discipline and determination to stay on course. This becomes a barrier, particularly when there are no immediate pressures to measure the return. If the current senior management group is not requiring ROI, the HRD staff may not allocate time for planning and coordination. Also, other pressures and priorities will often eat into the time necessary for ROI implementation. Only carefully planned implementation will be successful.

False Assumptions. Many HRD staff members have false assumptions about the ROI process, which keep them from attempting ROI. Typical of these assumptions are the following:

- Managers do not want to see the results of training and development expressed in monetary values.
- If the CEO does not ask for the ROI, then he or she is not expecting it.
- I have a professional, competent staff. Therefore, I do not have to justify the effectiveness of our programs.
- The training process is a complex, but necessary activity. Therefore, it should not be subjected to an accountability process.

These false assumptions form realistic barriers that impede the progress of ROI implementation.

Benefits of ROI

Although the benefits of adopting the ROI process may appear to be obvious, four distinct and important benefits can be derived from the implementation of ROI in an organization.

Measure Contribution. The HRD staff will know the specific contribution from a select number of programs. The ROI will determine if the benefits of the program, expressed in monetary values, have outweighed the costs. It will determine if the program made a contribution to the organization and if it was indeed a good investment.

Set Priorities. Calculating ROIs in different areas will determine which programs contribute the most to the organization, allowing priorities to be established for high impact training.

Focus on Results. The ROI process is a results-based process which brings a focus on results with all programs, even for those not targeted for an ROI calculation. The process requires instructional designers, facilitators, participants, and support groups to concentrate on measurable objectives: what the program is attempting to accomplish. Thus, this process has the added benefit of improving the effectiveness of all training programs.

Alter Management Perceptions of Training. The ROI process, when applied consistently and comprehensively, can convince the management group that training is an investment and not an expense. Managers will see training as making a viable contribution to their objectives, thus increasing the respect for the function. This is an important step in building a partnership with management.

These four key benefits, inherent with almost any type of impact evaluation process, make the ROI process an attractive challenge for the human resource development function.

ROI Strategy

One of the objectives of the research project for Volumes 1 and 2 of *Measuring Return on Investment* was to determine if there were specific strategies that appeared to be common among organizations pursuing the ROI process. Although this project did not use a carefully controlled sample, it represented a review of the efforts of many organizations. Several common strategies emerged that are considered to be the best practices for measurement and evaluation. Whether they meet the test to be labeled "best practice" will never be known, since it is risky to label any practice as a best practice. Although the following strategies are presented as a comprehensive framework, few organizations have adopted all of them. However, parts of the strategy exist in one way or another in each of the several hundred organizations studied for this comprehensive project.

Evaluation Targets

Recognizing the complexity of moving up the chain of evaluation levels, as described in Table 1-3, some organizations attempt to manage the process by setting targets for each level. A target for an evaluation level is the percentage of HRD programs measured at that level. Repeat sessions of the same program are counted in the total. For example, at Level 1, where it is easy to measure reaction, organizations achieve a high level of activity, with many organizations requiring 100% evaluation. In these situations, a generic questionnaire is administered at the end of each program. Level 2, Learning, is another relatively easy area to measure and the target is high, usually in the 40 - 70% range. This target depends on the organization, based on the nature and type of programs. At Level 3, On-the-Job Application, the percentage drops because of the time and expense of conducting follow-up evaluations. Targets in the range of 30 - 50% are common. Targets for Level 4, Business Results, and Level 5, ROI, are relatively small, reflecting the challenge of comprehending any new process. Common targets are 10% for Level 4 and 5% for Level 5. An example of evaluation targets established for a large telecommunications company is shown in Table 1-5. In this example, half of the Level 4 evaluations are taken to Level 5, the ROI.

Establishing evaluation targets has two major advantages. First, the process provides objectives for the HRD staff to clearly measure accountability progress for all programs or any segment of the HRD process. Second, adopting targets also focuses more attention on the accountability process, communicating a strong message about the extent of commitment to measurement and evaluation.

Table 1-5
Evaluation Targets for a Large Telecommunications Company

Level		Percent of Courses
Level 1	Participant Satisfaction	100%
Level 2	Learning	50%
Level 3	On-the-Job Applications (Behavior)	30%
Level 4	Results	20%
Level 5	Return on Investment	10%

Micro Level Evaluation

It is difficult to evaluate an entire HRD function such as management development, career development, executive education, or technical training. The ROI process is more effective when applied to one program that can be linked to a direct payoff. In situations where a series of courses with common objectives must be completed before the objectives can be met, an evaluation of the series of courses may be appropriate. For this reason, ROI evaluation must be a micro level activity that will usually focus on a single program or a few tightly integrated programs. This decision to evaluate several programs or just one program should include consideration of objectives of the program, timing of the programs, and cohesiveness of the series. Attempting to evaluate a group of programs conducted over a long period becomes quite difficult. The cause and effect relationship becomes more confusing and complex.

Post Program Evaluation Methods

Best practice companies use a variety of approaches to collect evaluation data. They do not become aligned with one or two practices that dominate data collection, regardless of the situation. They recognize that each program, setting, and situation is different and consequently, different techniques are needed to collect the data. In some situations, interviews, focus groups, and questionnaires work quite well. While in others, action plans, performance contracts, and performance monitoring are needed to determine the specific impact of the program. These organizations deliberately match the data collection method with the program, following a set of criteria developed internally.

Isolating the Effects of Training

One of the most critical elements of the ROI process is attempting to isolate the impact of the training program from other influences that may have occurred during the same time period. Best practice organizations recognize that many influences affect business results measures. Consequently, after a program is conducted, training must share only a part of the credit for improved performance. When an ROI calculation is planned, these organizations attempt to use one or more methods to isolate the effects of training. They go beyond the typical use of a control group arrangement, which has set the standard for this process for many years. They explore the use of a variety of other techniques to arrive at a realistic estimate of training's impact on output measures.

Sampling for ROI Calculations

Because of the resources required for the process, most training programs do not include ROI calculations. Therefore, organizations must determine the appropriate level of ROI evaluation. There is no prescribed formula, and the number of ROI impact studies depends on many variables, including:

- staff expertise on evaluation,
- the nature and type of HRD programs,
- resources that can be allocated to the process,
- the support from management for training and development,
- the organization's commitment to measurement and evaluation, and
- pressure from others to show ROI calculations.

Other variables specific to the organization may enter the process. It is rare for organizations to use statistical sampling when selecting sample programs that target ROI calculations. For most, this approach represents far too many calculations and too much analysis.   Using a practical approach, most organizations settle on evaluating one or two sessions of their most popular programs. For example, the Office of Personnel Management of the United States Government developed an ROI calculation for one of their most popular courses, Introduction to Supervision.[12] Still others select a program from each of its major training segments. For example, in a large bank, with six academies, a program is selected from each academy, each year, for an ROI calculation. For organizations implementing the ROI concept for the first time, it is recommended that only one or two courses be selected for an initial calculation, as a learning process.

While it is important to be statistically sound in the approach to sampling, it is more important to consider a tradeoff between resources available and the level of activity management is willing to accept for ROI calculations.   The primary objective of an ROI calculation is not only to convince the HRD staff that the process works, but to show others, usually senior management, that HRD does make a difference. Therefore, it is important that the sampling plan be developed with the input and approval of senior management. In the final analysis, the selection process should yield a level of sampling in which senior management is comfortable in its accountability assessment of the HRD function.

Converting Program Results to Monetary Values

Because the specific return on investment is needed, business results data must be converted to monetary benefits. Best practice organizations are not content to show that a program improved productivity, enhanced quality, reduced employee turnover, decreased absenteeism, or increased customer satisfaction. They convert these data items to monetary units so that the benefits can be compared to costs which in turn leads to an ROI calculation. These organizations take an extra step to develop a realistic value for these data items. For hard data items such as productivity, quality, and time, the process is relatively easy. However, for soft data items such as customer satisfaction, employee turnover, employee absenteeism, and job satisfaction, the process is more difficult. Yet, techniques are available that make these conversions reasonably accurate.

Versatile Applications for the ROI Process

The ROI process described in the remaining chapters of this book is a very flexible and adaptive process. Although it was initially designed for training and development programs, it has been applied successfully to performance improvement and change programs. For example, the process has been used to calculate the return on investment in:

- organization development programs,
- total quality management programs,
- re-engineering projects,
- employee selection programs,
- performance appraisal programs,
- gainsharing programs,
- safety and health programs,
- labor management cooperation programs,
- wellness/fitness centers, and
- new technology applications.

The scope of the potential applications of the model and process are almost limitless. In any situation where there is interaction of employees with new technology, procedures, or systems and the focus is on change or improvement, this process will capture the return on investment.

Conclusion

While there is almost universal agreement that more attention is needed on ROI, it is promising to note that the number of successful examples of ROI calculation is increasing. The process is not difficult. The approaches, strategies, and techniques are not overly complex and can be useful in a variety of settings. The combined and persistent efforts of practitioners and researchers will continue to refine the techniques and create successful applications.

References

[1] Phillips, J. J. (Ed.), *In Action: Measuring Return on Investment*, Alexandria, VA: American Society for Training and Development, 1994.

[2] Phillips, J. J., "Measuring Training's ROI: It Can Be Done!" *William and Mary Business Review*, Summer 1995, pp. 6-10.

[3] Phillips, J. J. "Measuring Training's ROI: It Can Be Done!" *William and Mary Business Review*, Summer 1995, pp. 6-10.

[4] Phillips, J.J., *25 Global Training Trends*, Houston, TX: Gulf Publishing, 1996.

[5] Kirkpatrick, D.L., "Techniques for Evaluating Training Programs," *Evaluating Training Programs*, Alexandria, VA: 1975, ASTD, pp. 1-17.

[6] Dixon, N.M., "Evaluation: A Tool for Improving HRD Quality," San Diego, CA: University Associates, Inc., 1990.

[7] Broad, M.L., and Newstrom, J.W., "Transfer of Training," Reading, MA: Addison-Wesley, 1992.

[8] Alliger, G.M., and Janak, E.A., "Kirkpatrick's levels of Training Criteria: Thirty Years Later," *Personnel Psychology*, 1989, 42, pp. 331-342.

[9] Kimmerling, G., "Gathering Best Practices," *Training and Development*, Vol. 47, No. 3, September 1993, pp. 28-36.

[10] Nadler, L., and Wiggs, G.D., *Managing Human Resource Development*, San Francisco, CA: Jossey-Bass, Inc., 1986.

[11] Ford, D., "Three Rs in the Workplace," *In Action: Measuring Return on Investment, Vol. 1.* J. Phillips (Ed.), Alexandria, Virginia: American Society for Training and Development, 1994, pp. 85-104.

[12] Broad, M., "Built-in Evaluation, *In Action: Measuring Return on Investment, Vol. 1.* J. Phillips (Ed.), Alexandria, Virginia: American Society for Training and Development, 1994, pp. 55-70.

2

ROI MODEL

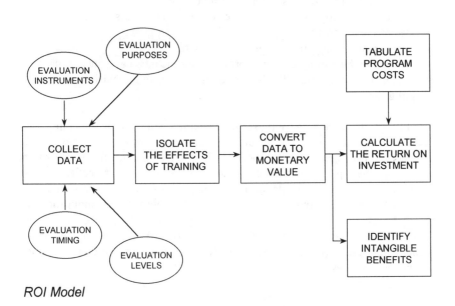

ROI Model

The calculation of the return on investment in HRD begins with the basic model illustrated above, where a potentially complicated process can be simplified with sequential steps. The ROI process model provides a systematic approach to ROI calculations. A step-by-step approach keeps the process manageable so that users can tackle one issue at a time. The model also emphasizes that this is a logical, systematic process which flows from one step to another.   Applying the model provides consistency from one ROI calculation to another.   Each step of the model is briefly described in this chapter.

Preliminary Evaluation Information

Several pieces of the evaluation puzzle must be explained when developing the evaluation plan for an ROI calculation.   Four specific elements are important to evaluation success and are outlined in the next section.

Evaluation Purposes

Although evaluation is usually undertaken to improve the HRD process, several distinct purposes can be identified.   Evaluation is planned to:

- determine if a program is accomplishing its objectives,
- identify the strengths and weaknesses in the HRD process,
- determine the cost/benefit analysis of an HRD program,
- assist in marketing HRD programs in the future,
- determine if the program was appropriate for the target audience, and
- establish a database, which can assist in making decisions about the programs.

Although there are other purposes of evaluation, these are the most important ones.[1]   Evaluation purposes should be considered prior to developing the evaluation plan because the purposes will often determine the scope of the evaluation, the types of instruments used, and the type of data collected.   For example, when an ROI calculation is planned, one of the purposes would be to compare the cost and benefits of the program.   This purpose has implications for the type of data collected (hard data), type of data collection method (Performance Monitoring), type of analysis (thorough), and the communication medium for results (Formal Evaluation Report).   For most programs, multiple evaluation purposes are pursued.

Evaluation Instruments

A variety of instruments are used to collect data. The appropriate instruments should be considered in the early stages of ROI development. The seven most common instruments used to collect data in evaluation are:

1. surveys
2. questionnaires
3. interviews
4. focus groups
5. tests
6. observation
7. performance records

The instruments most familiar to the culture of the organization and appropriate for the setting and evaluation requirements should be used in the data collection process. Additional information on how instruments are utilized in a data collection scheme will be covered later.

Evaluation Levels

Training programs are evaluated at different levels as briefly described in Chapter 1.

- **Level 1**: Measuring Reaction and Identifying Planned Actions
- **Level 2**: Measuring Learning
- **Level 3**: Assessing Application of the Program on the Job
- **Level 4**: Identifying Business Results from the Program
- **Level 5**: Calculating Return on Investment

As was emphasized in Chapter 1, data should be collected at Levels 1, 2, 3, and 4 if an ROI analysis is planned. This ensures that the chain of impact occurs as participants learn the skills, apply them on-the-job, and obtain business results.

Evaluation Timing

Another important aspect of the evaluation plan is the timing of the data collection. In some cases, pre-program measurements are taken to compare with post-program measures and, in some cases, multiple measures are taken. In other situations, pre-program measurements are not available and specific follow-ups are still taken after the program. The important issue in this part of the process is to determine the timing for the follow-up evaluation. For example, data collection for an evaluation was as early as three weeks after a customer service skills training program for a major airline. Five years was required for an Indonesian Company to measure the payback for employees attending an MBA program. For most professional and supervisory training, a follow-up is usually conducted in the range of three to six months.

These four elements: evaluation purposes, instruments, levels, and timing are all considerations in selecting the data collection methods and developing the data collection plan.

Collecting Post-Program Data

Data collection is central to the ROI process. In some situations, post-program data are collected and compared to pre-program situations, control group differences, and expectations. Both hard data, representing output, quality, cost, and time; and soft data, including work habits, work climate, and attitudes are collected. Data are collected using a variety of methods including the following:

- Follow-up **surveys** are taken to determine the degree to which participants have utilized various aspects of the program. Survey responses are often developed on a sliding scale and usually represent attitudinal data. Surveys are useful for Level 3 data.
- Follow-up **questionnaires** are administered to uncover specific applications of training. Participants provide responses to a variety of types of open-ended and forced response questions. Questionnaires can be used to capture both Level 3 and 4 data.
- On-the-job **observation** captures actual skill application and use. Observations are particularly useful in customer service training and are

more effective when the observer is either invisible or transparent. Observations are appropriate for Level 3 data.

■ Post program **interviews** are conducted with participants to determine the extent to which learning has been utilized on-the-job. Interviews allow for probing to uncover specific applications and are appropriate with Level 3 data.

■ **Focus groups** are conducted to determine the degree to which a group of participants has applied the training to job situations. Focus groups are appropriate with Level 3 data.

■ **Program assignments** are useful for simple short-term projects. Participants complete the assignment, on-the-job, utilizing skills or knowledge learned in the program. Completed assignments can often contain both Level 3 and 4 data.

■ **Action plans** are developed in training programs and are implemented on the job after the program is completed. Follow-ups provide evidence of training program success. Level 3 and 4 data can be collected with action plans.

■ **Performance contracts** are developed by the participant, the participant's supervisor, and the instructor who all agree on specific outcomes from training. Performance contracts are appropriate for both Level 3 and 4 data.

■ Programs are designed with a **follow-up session,** which is utilized to capture evaluation data as well as present additional learning material. In the follow-up session, participants discuss their successes with the program. Follow up sessions are appropriate for both Level 3 and 4 data.

■ **Performance monitoring** is useful where various performance records and operational data are examined for improvement. This method is particularly useful for Level 4 data.

The important challenge in data collection is to select the method or methods appropriate for the setting and the specific program, within the time and budget constraints of the organization. Data collection methods are covered in more detail in Chapter 3.

Isolating the Effects of Training

An often overlooked issue in most evaluations is the process of isolating the effects of training. In this step of the process, specific strategies are explored, which determine the amount of output performance directly related to the program. This step is essential because there are many factors that will influence performance data after training. The specific strategies of this step will pinpoint the amount of improvement directly related to the training program. The result is increased accuracy and credibility of the ROI calculation. The following strategies have been utilized by organizations to tackle this important issue:

- A **control group** arrangement is used to isolate training impact. With this strategy, one group receives training, while another, similar group does not receive training. The difference in the performance of the two groups is attributed to the training program. When properly setup and implemented, the control group arrangement is the most effective way to isolate the effects of training.
- **Trend lines** are used to project the values of specific output variables if training had not been undertaken. The projection is compared to the actual data after training, and the difference represents the estimate of the impact of training. Under certain conditions, this strategy can accurately isolate the training impact.
- When mathematical relationships between input and output variables are known, a **forecasting model** is used to isolate the effects of training. With this approach, the output variable is predicted using the forecasting model with the assumption that no training is conducted. The actual performance of the variable after the training is then compared with the forecasted value, which results in an estimate of the training impact.
- **Participants** estimate the amount of improvement related to training. With this approach, participants are provided with the total amount of improvement, on a pre and post program basis, and are asked to indicate the percent of the improvement that is actually related to the training program.
- **Supervisors of participants** estimate the impact of training on the output variables. With this approach, supervisors of participants are presented with the total amount of improvement and are asked to indicate the percent related to training.
- **Senior management** estimates the impact of training. In these cases, managers provide an estimate or "adjustment" to reflect the portion of the improvement related to the training program. While perhaps inaccurate, there are some advantages of having senior management involved in this process.
- **Experts** provide estimates of the impact of training on the performance variable. Because the estimates are based on previous experience, the experts must be familiar with the type of training and the specific situation.
- In supervisory and management training, the **subordinates of participants** identify changes in the work climate, which could influence the output

variables. With this approach, the subordinates of the supervisors receiving training determine if other variables changed in the work climate, which could have influenced output performance.

■ When feasible, **other influencing factors** are identified and the impact estimated or calculated, leaving the remaining, unexplained improvement attributed to training. In this case, the influence of all of the other factors are developed, and training remains the one variable not accounted for in the analysis. The unexplained portion of the output is then attributed to training.

■ In some situations, **customers** provide input on the extent to which training has influenced their decision to use a product or service. Although this strategy has limited applications, it can be quite useful in customer service and sales training.

Collectively, these ten strategies provide a comprehensive set of tools to tackle the important and critical issue of isolating the effects of training. Chapter 4 is devoted to this important process.

Converting Data to Monetary Values

To calculate the return on investment, data collected in a Level 4 evaluation are converted to monetary values and are compared to program costs. This requires a value to be placed on each unit of data connected with the program. Ten strategies are available to convert data to monetary values. The specific strategy selected usually depends on the type of data and the situation:

■ **Output data** are converted to profit contribution or cost savings. In this strategy, output increases are converted to monetary value based on their unit contribution to profit or the unit of cost reduction. These values are readily available in most organizations.

■ The **cost of quality** is calculated and quality improvements are directly converted to cost savings. This value is available in many organizations.

■ For programs where employee time is saved, the **participants' wages and benefits** are used for the value for time. Because a variety of programs focus on improving the time required to complete projects, processes, or daily activities, the value of time becomes an important and necessary issue.

■ **Historical costs** are used when they are available for a specific variable. In this case, organizational cost data are utilized to establish the specific value of an improvement.

■ When available, **internal and external experts** may be used to estimate a value for an improvement. In this situation, the credibility of the estimate hinges on the expertise and reputation of the individual.

■ **External databases** are sometimes available to estimate the value or cost of data items. Research, government, and industry databases can provide important information for these values. The difficulty lies in finding a specific database related to the situation.

■ **Participants** estimate the value of the data item. For this approach to be effective, participants must be capable of providing a value for the improvement.

■ **Supervisors of participants** provide estimates when they are both willing and capable of assigning values to the improvement. This approach is especially useful when participants are not fully capable of providing this input or in situations where supervisors need to confirm or adjust the participant's estimate.

■ **Senior management** may provide estimates on the value of an improvement. This approach is particularly helpful to establish values for performance measures that are very important to senior management.

■ **HRD staff** estimates may be used to determine a value of an output data item. In these cases, it is essential for the estimates to be provided on an unbiased basis.

This step in the ROI model is very important and is absolutely necessary for determining the monetary benefits from a training program. The process is challenging, particularly with soft data, but can be methodically accomplished using one or more of these strategies. Because of its importance, Chapter 5 is devoted to this issue.

Tabulating Cost of the Program

The other part of the equation on a cost/benefit analysis is the program cost. Tabulating the costs involves monitoring or developing all of the related costs of the program targeted for the ROI calculation. Among the cost components that should be included are:

■ the cost to design and develop the program, possibly prorated over the expected life of the program;

■ the cost of all program materials provided to each participant;

■ the cost for the instructor/facilitator, including preparation time as well as delivery time;

- the cost of the facilities for the training program;
- travel, lodging, and meal costs for the participants, if applicable;
- salaries, plus employee benefits of the participants who attend the training; and
- administrative and overhead costs of the training function, allocated in some convenient way.

In addition, specific costs related to the needs assessment and evaluation should be included, if appropriate. The conservative approach is to include all of these costs so that the total is fully loaded. Chapter 6 is devoted to this issue.

Calculating the Return on Investment

The return on investment is calculated using the program benefits and costs. The benefits/cost ratio is the program benefits divided by cost. In formula form it is:

$$BCR = \frac{\text{Program Benefits}}{\text{Program Costs}}$$

Sometimes this ratio is stated as a cost/benefit ratio, although the formula is the same as BCR.

The return on investment uses the net benefits divided by program costs. The net benefits are the program benefits minus the costs. In formula form, the ROI becomes:

$$ROI\ (\%) = \frac{\text{Net Program Benefits}}{\text{Program Costs}} \times 100$$

This is the same basic formula used in evaluating other investments where the ROI is traditionally reported as earnings divided by investment. The ROI from some training programs is high. For example, in sales, supervisory, and managerial training, the ROI can be quite large, frequently over 100%, while the ROI value for technical and operator training may be lower. Chapter 7 is devoted to ROI calculations.

Identifying Intangible Benefits

In addition to tangible, monetary benefits, most training programs will have intangible, non-monetary benefits. The ROI calculation is based on converting both hard and soft data to monetary values. Intangible benefits include items such as:

- increased job satisfaction,
- increased organizational commitment,
- improved teamwork,
- improved customer service,
- reduced complaints, and
- reduced conflicts.

During data analysis, every attempt is made to convert all data to monetary values. All hard data such as output, quality, and time are converted to monetary values. The conversion of soft data is attempted for each data item. However, if the process used for conversion is too subjective or inaccurate, and the resulting values lose credibility in the process; then the data is listed as an intangible benefit with the appropriate explanation. For some programs, intangible, non-monetary benefits are extremely valuable, often carrying as much influence as the hard data items. Chapter 8 is devoted to the non-monetary benefits.

Implementation Issues

A variety of environmental issues and events will influence the successful implementation of the ROI process. These issues must be addressed early to ensure that the ROI process is successful. Specific topics or actions include:

- a policy statement concerning results-based training and development;
- procedures and guidelines for different elements and techniques of the evaluation process;
- meetings and formal sessions to develop staff skills with the ROI process;
- strategies to improve management commitment and support for the ROI process;
- mechanisms to provide technical support for questionnaire design, data analysis, and evaluation strategy; and
- specific techniques to place more attention on results.

The ROI process can fail or be successful based on these implementation issues. Chapter 10 is devoted to this important topic.

Planning for the ROI

An important ingredient to the success of the ROI process is to properly plan for the ROI early in the training and development cycle. Appropriate upfront attention will save much time later when data are actually collected and analyzed, thus improving the accuracy and reducing the cost of the ROI process. It also avoids any confusion surrounding what will be accomplished, by whom, and at what time. Two planning documents are the key to the upfront analysis and should be completed before the program is designed or developed. Each document is described in the next section.

Data Collection Plan

Figure 2-1 shows a completed data collection form planning for an interactive sales skills program. The three-day training program was designed for retail sales associates in the electronics department of a major store chain. An ROI calculation was planned for a pilot of three groups.

This document provides a place for the major elements and issues regarding collecting data for the four evaluation levels. Broad areas for objectives are appropriate for planning. Specific, detailed objectives are developed later, before the program is designed. The objectives for Level 1 usually include positive reactions to the training program of completed action plans. If it is a new program, as is the example in Figure 2-1, another category, suggested improvements, may be included.

Level 2 evaluation focuses on the measures of learning. The specific objectives include those areas where participants are expected to change knowledge, skills, or attitudes. The method is the specific way in which learning is assessed, whether as a test, simulation, skill, practice, or facilitator assessment. The timing for Level 2 evaluation is usually during or at the end of the program, and the responsibility usually rests with the instructor or facilitator.

For Level 3 evaluation, the objectives represent broad areas of program application, including significant on-the-job activities that should follow application. The evaluation method includes one of the post program methods described earlier and usually is conducted a matter of weeks or months after program completion. Because responsibilities are often shared among several groups, including the training and development staff, division trainers, or local managers, it is important to clarify this issue early in the process.

For Level 4 evaluation, objectives focus on business impact variables influenced by the program. The objectives may include the way in which each item is measured. For example, if one of the objectives is to improve quality, a specific measure would indicate how that quality is actually measured, such as defects per thousand units produced. While the preferred evaluation method is performance monitoring, other methods such as action planning may be appropriate. The timing depends on how quickly participants can generate a sustained business impact. It is usually a matter of months after training. The participants themselves, supervisors, division training coordinators or perhaps an external evaluator may be responsible for Level 4 data collection.

The data collection plan is an important part of the evaluation strategy and should be completed prior to moving forward with the training program. For existing training programs, the plan is completed before pursuing the ROI evaluation. The plan provides a clear direction of what type of data will be collected, how it will be collected, when it will be collected, and who will collect it.

ROI Analysis Plan

Figure 2-2 shows a completed ROI analysis plan for the interactive selling skills program described earlier. This planning document is the continuation of the data collection plan presented in Figure 2-1 and captures information on several key items that are necessary to develop the actual ROI calculation. In the first column, significant data items are listed, usually Level 4 data items, but in some cases could include Level 3 items. These items will be used in the ROI analysis. The method to isolate the effect of training is listed next to each data item in the second column. For most cases the method will be the same for each data item, but there could be variations. For example, if no historical data are available for one data item, then trend line analysis is not possible for that item, although it may be appropriate for other items. The method of converting data to monetary values is included in the third

Program: Interactive Selling Skills **Responsibility**: _____ **Date**: _____

Evaluation Plan: Data Collection

Level	Objective(s)	Evaluation Method	Timing	Responsibilities
I. Reaction, Satisfaction and Planned Actions	• Positive Reaction • Recommended Improvements • Action Items	• Reaction Questionnaire	• End of 2nd Day • End of 3rd Day	• Facilitator
II. Learning	• Acquisition of Skills • Selection of Skills	• Skill Practice	• During Program	• Facilitator
III. Job Application	• Use of Skills • Frequency of Skill Use • Barriers	• Questionnaire • Follow up Session	• 3 Months After Program • 3 Weeks After the First Two Days	• Training Coordinator • Facilitator
IV. Business Results	• Sales Increase	• Performance Monitoring	• 3 Months After Program	• Training Coordinator

Figure 2-1. *Data collection plan for an interactive selling skills program*

column, using one of the ten strategies outlined earlier. The costs categories that will be captured for the training program are outlined in the fourth column. Instructions about how certain costs should be prorated would be noted here. Normally the cost categories will be consistent from one program to another. However, a specific cost that is unique to the program would also be noted. The intangible benefits expected from this program are outlined in the fifth column. This list is generated from discussions about the program with sponsors and subject matter experts.

Other issues or events that might influence program implementation would be highlighted in the sixth column. Typical items include the capability of participants, the degree of access to data sources, and unique data analysis issues. Finally, communication targets are outlined in the last column. Although there could be many groups that should receive the information, four target groups are always recommended:

1.   senior management group,
2.   supervisors of participants,
3.   program participants, and
4.   training and development staff.

All four of these groups need to know about the results of ROI analysis.

The ROI analysis plan, when combined with the data collection plan, provides detailed information on calculating the ROI, illustrating how the process will develop from beginning to end. When thoroughly completed, these two plans provide the direction necessary for ROI evaluation.

Conclusion

This chapter presented the ROI process model for calculating the return on investment for a training program. The step-by-step process takes the complicated issue of calculating ROI and breaks it into simple, manageable tasks and steps. When the process is thoroughly planned, taking into consideration all potential strategies and techniques, the process becomes manageable and achievable. The remaining chapters focus on the major elements of this model.

Introduction to Case Study

One of the most effective ways to understand the ROI process is to examine an actual case study. The following is the beginning of a case that is presented in the remaining chapters of this book. Although it represents an actual setting, a few of the issues and events have been slightly modified at the request of the organization. The case reflects the issues as they are presented in each chapter. To fully understand the case and all the issues, it is recommended that each part of the case be read and the discussion questions addressed before moving to the next part of the case.

Case Study - Part A
National Auto Products Company

Background

National Auto Products Company (NAPCo) is an important supplier to the automotive industry, producing a variety of rubber and plastic parts for automobiles, trucks, tractors, engines, and drive trains. A publicly held company, NAPCo has been operating for over 20 years with manufacturing facilities scattered throughout the USA and Canada. The company has been very successful and stable.

Although NAPCo has been a very profitable company, it recently experienced competitive cost and quality pressures, which caused some deterioration in sales. Although several factors are related to the decline, senior management is concerned about the ability of the first-line management team to supervise today's workforce. The President of NAPCo asked the Human Resource Development Director, Brenda McClenney, to provide appropriate training.

For several months, NAPCo has been attempting to convert supervisors to team leaders. Several team building sessions have been conducted, and supervisors are often referred to as team leaders. The president felt that the supervisors were experiencing some difficulty in making this transition and that they needed training to develop the skills necessary to motivate team members, improve productivity, and produce high quality products with maximum productivity.

Program: <u>Interactive Selling Skills</u> **Responsibility** _____ **Date**: _____

Evaluation Strategy: ROI Analysis

Data Items	Methods of Isolating the Effects of the Program	Methods of Converting Data	Cost Categories	Intangible Benefits	Other Influences/Issues	Communication Targets
• Weekly Sales Per Employee	• Control Group Analysis	• Direct Conversion Using Profit Contribution	• Facilitation Fees • Program Materials • Meals/ Refreshments • Facilities • Participant Salaries/Benefits • Cost of Coordination/ Evaluation	• Customer Satisfaction • Employee Satisfaction	• Must Have Job Coverage During Training • No Communication With Control Group • Seasonal Fluctuations Should be Avoided	• Program Participants • Electronics Dept. Managers- Target Stores • Store Managers- Target Stores • Senior Store Executives District, Region, Headquarters • Training Staff: Instructors, Coordinators, Designers, and Managers

Figure 2-2. _ROI analysis for an interactive selling skills program_

Situation

McClenney contacted a consulting firm located near its headquarters to inquire about potential supervisory training. The principal consultant suggested that a needs assessment be conducted to determine specific training needs and also to determine if other issues need to be addressed. NAPCo officials reluctantly agreed to a needs assessment. They were convinced that training was needed and wanted the "standard supervisor training" program. After some convincing, the consultant conducted the needs assessment using four methods:

1. reviewing operational performance documents,
2. interviewing a sample of supervisors and managers,
3. observing a small sample of supervisors on the job, and
4. administering a questionnaire to all supervisors and managers.

The assessment identified a lack of skills and a need for significant supervisor training. Most of the skills focused on understanding and motivating employees, setting goals, and providing leadership skills.

The Program

A six module, 24-hour training program was proposed for one plant as a pilot group. All production supervisors and their support supervisors would be trained at the same time. The program would be conducted in six 4-hour segments scattered over a one month period. Between sessions, participants would be requested to apply the new skills so that there would be transfer of training to the job. Initially, the program was planned to focus on the following areas:

- understanding employee needs,
- motivating employees for improved performance,
- counseling employees,
- providing appropriate leadership behavior, and
- inspiring teamwork.

The program was labeled "Motivating Employees for Improved Performance" and was planned to be conducted with 16 supervisors. A follow-up was planned several months after the training was completed. If the program was effective, NAPCo would offer it throughout their organization.

Discussion Questions
1. How important is the needs assessment for this situation? Is the resistance to a needs assessment typical? At what levels should the needs assessment be conducted?
2. At what levels should this program be evaluated?
3. Should the objectives of the program be modified? If so, how?

References

[1]   Phillips, J.J., *Handbook of Training Evaluation and Measurement Methods*, 3rd Edition. Houston, TX: Gulf Publishing, 1997.

3

COLLECTING POST PROGRAM DATA

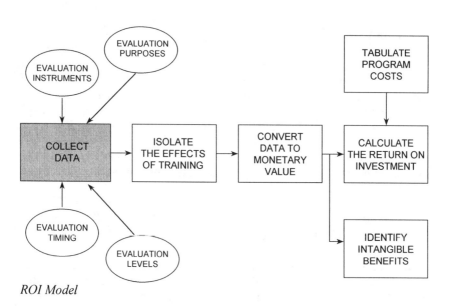

ROI Model

Collecting data after the training program has been conducted is the first operational phase of the ROI process, as depicted in the model above. This step is usually the most time consuming of all steps and is also the part of the ROI process that can be the most disruptive to the organization. Fortunately, a variety of methods are available to capture data at the appropriate time after training. This chapter outlines ten common approaches for collecting post-program data, after the sources of data are defined.

Sources of Data

When considering the possible data sources that will provide input on the success of a training program, the categories are easily defined. The six major categories are briefly described in the next section.

Organizational Performance Records

The most useful and credible data source for the ROI analysis is from the records and reports of the organization. Whether individualized or group-based, the records reflect performance in a work unit, department, division, region, or company overall. This source can include all types of measures, which are usually available in abundance throughout the organization. Collecting data from this source is preferred for Level 4 evaluation, since it usually reflects business impact data and it is relatively easy to obtain. However , sloppy record keeping by some organizations may make locating particular reports difficult.

Participants

The most widely used data source for an ROI analysis is the program participants. Participants are frequently asked how skills and knowledge, acquired in a program, have been applied on the job. Sometimes they are asked to explain the impact of those actions. Participants are a rich source of data for both Level 3 and 4 evaluations. They are very credible, since they are the individuals who have achieved the performance and are often the most knowledgeable of the processes and other influencing factors. The challenge is to find an effective and efficient way to capture data in a consistent manner between participants.

Supervisors of Participants

Another important source of data is those individuals who directly supervise or lead program participants. This group will often have a vested interest in the evaluation process, since they approved the participants to attend the program. Also, in many situations, they observe the participants as they attempt to use the knowledge and skills acquired in the program. Consequently, they can report on the successes linked to the program as well as the difficulties and problems associated with application. Although supervisor input is usually best for Level 3 data, it can be useful for Level 4 data. It is important, however, for supervisors to maintain objectivity when assessing the program participants.

Subordinates of Participants

In situations where supervisors and managers are being trained, their subordinates can provide information about the perceived changes in observable behavior that have occurred since the program was conducted. Input from subordinates is appropriate for Level 3 data but not Level 4 data. While collecting data from this source can be very helpful and instructive, it is often avoided because of the potential biases that can enter into the feedback process.

Team/Peer Group

Those individuals who serve as team members with the participant or occupy peer level positions in the organization are another source of data for a few types of programs. In these situations, peer group members provide input on perceived behavioral changes of participants. This source of data is more appropriate when all team members participate in the program, and consequently, when they report on the collective efforts of the group or behavioral changes of specific individuals. Because of the subjective nature of this process, and the lack of opportunity to fully evaluate the application of skills, this source of data is somewhat limited.

Internal/External Groups

In some situations, internal or external groups, such as the training and development staff, program facilitators, or external consultants, may provide input on the success of the individuals when they attempt to apply the skills and knowledge acquired in the program. The input from this source may be based on on-the-job observation after the training program has been completed. Collecting data from this source has limited uses. Because internal groups may have a vested interest in the outcome of evaluation, their input may lose credibility. Input from external groups are appropriate with certain types of observations of on-the-job performance.

Using Follow-Up Questionnaires and Surveys

Probably the most common form of data collection method is the follow-up questionnaire. Ranging from short reaction forms to detailed follow-up tools, questionnaires can be used to obtain subjective information about participants, as well as to objectively document measurable business results for an ROI analysis. With this versatility and popularity, the questionnaire is the preferred method for capturing Level 3 and 4 data in some organizations.

Surveys represent a specific type of questionnaire with several applications for measuring the success of training and development programs. Surveys are used in situations where attitudes, beliefs, and opinions are captured only; whereas, a questionnaire has much more flexibility and captures data ranging from attitude data to specific improvement statistics. The principles of survey construction and design are similar to questionnaire design. The development of both types of instruments are covered in this section.

Types of Questions

In addition to the types of data sought, the types of questions distinguish surveys from questionnaires. Surveys can have yes or no responses when an absolute agreement or disagreement is required, or a range of responses may be used from strongly disagree to strongly agree. A five point scale is very common.

A questionnaire may contain any or all of these types of questions:

- *Open-ended question:* has an unlimited answer. The question is followed by an ample blank space for the response.
- *Checklist:* a list of items where a participant is asked to check those that apply to the situation.
- *Two-way question:* has alternate responses, a yes/no or other possibilities.
- *Multiple-choice question:* has several choices, and the participant is asked to select the most correct one.
- *Ranking scale:* requires the participant to rank a list of items.

Questionnaire Design Steps

Questionnaire design is a simple and logical process. There is nothing more confusing, frustrating, and potentially embarrassing than a poorly designed or an improperly worded questionnaire. The following steps can ensure that a valid, reliable, and effective instrument is developed.

Determine the exact information needed. As a first step in questionnaire design, the topics, skills, or attitudes presented in the program are reviewed for potential items for the questionnaire. It is sometimes helpful to develop this information in outline form so that related questions or items can be grouped.

Other issues related to the application of the program are explored for inclusion in the questionnaire.

Involve management in the process. To the extent possible, management should be involved in this process, either as a client, sponsor, supporter, or interested party. If possible, managers most familiar with the program or process should provide information on specific issues and concerns that often frame the actual questions planned for the questionnaire. In some cases, managers want to provide input on specific issues or items. Not only is manager input helpful and useful in the questionnaire design, but it also builds ownership in the measurement and evaluation process.

Select the type(s) of questions. Using the previous five types of questions, the first step in questionnaire design is to select the type(s) that will best result in the specific data needed. The planned data analysis and variety of data to be collected should be considered when deciding which questions to use.

Develop the questions. The next step is to develop the questions based on the type of questions planned and the information needed. Questions should be simple and straightforward to avoid confusion or lead the participant to a desired response. A single question should only address one issue. If multiple issues need to be addressed, separate the question into multiple parts, or simply, develop a separate question for each issue. Terms or expressions unfamiliar to the participant should be avoided.

Check the reading level. To ensure that the questionnaire can be easily understood by the target audience, it is helpful to assess the reading level. Most word processing programs have features that will evaluate the reading difficulty according to grade level. This provides an important check to ensure the perceived reading level of the target audience matches with questionnaire design.

Test the questions. Proposed questions should be tested for understanding. Ideally, the questions should be tested on a sample group of participants. If this is not feasible, the sample group of employees should be at approximately the same job level as participants. From this sample group, feedback, critiques, and suggestions are sought to improve questionnaire design.

Address the anonymity issue. Participants should feel free to respond openly to questions without fear of reprisal. The confidentiality of their responses is of utmost importance, since there is usually a link between survey anonymity and accuracy. Therefore, surveys should be anonymous unless there are specific reasons why individuals have to be identified. In situations where participants must complete the questionnaire in a captive audience, or submit a completed questionnaire directly to an individual, a neutral third party should collect and process the data, ensuring that the identity is not revealed. In cases where the actual identity must be known (e.g., to compare output data with the previous data or to verify the data), every effort should be made to protect the respondent's identity to those who may be biased in their actions.

Design for ease of tabulation and analysis. Each potential question should be viewed in terms of data tabulation, data summary, and analysis. If possible, the data analysis process should be outlined and reviewed in mock-up form. This step avoids the problems of inadequate, cumbersome, and lengthy data analysis caused by improper wording or design.

Develop the completed questionnaire and prepare a data summary. The questions should be integrated to develop an attractive questionnaire with proper instructions so that it can be administered effectively. In addition, a summary sheet should be developed so that the data can be tabulated quickly for analysis.

Questionnaire Content Issues

One of the most difficult tasks is to determine the specific issues to address on the questionnaire. The following items represent a comprehensive list of questionnaire content possibilities for capturing both Level 3 and 4 data. Figure 3-1 presents a questionnaire used in a follow-up evaluation of a two-day program on effective meetings. The evaluation was designed to capture the ROI, and the primary method of data collection was this follow-up questionnaire. This example will be used to illustrate many of the issues involving potential content items for questionnaire design.

Progress with Objectives. Sometimes it is helpful to assess progress with the objectives in the follow-up evaluation as is illustrated in question 1 in Figure 3-1. While this issue is usually assessed during the program, because it is Level 1 data, it is sometimes helpful to revisit the objectives after the participants have had an opportunity to apply what has been learned.

Action Plan Implementation. If an action plan is required in the program, the questionnaire should reference the plan and determine the extent to which it has been implemented. If the action plan requirement is very low key, perhaps only one question would be devoted to the follow-up on the action plan, as illustrated in question 2 in Figure 3-1. If the action plan is very comprehensive and contains an abundance of Level 3 and 4 data, then the questionnaire takes a secondary role and most of the data collection process will focus directly on the status of the completed action plan.

Relevance of Program. Although the relevance of the program is often assessed during the program, as Level 1 data, it is sometimes helpful to assess the relevance of various aspects of the program after the skills and knowledge have been applied (or attempted) on the job. This feedback helps program designers know which parts of the program were actually useful on the job, providing lasting value. Question 3 in Figure 3-1 shows the approach to this issue.

Use of program materials. If participants are provided with materials to use on the job, then it may be helpful to determine the extent to which these materials have been used. This is particularly helpful when operating manuals, reference books, and job aids have been distributed and explained in the program and are expected to be used on the job. Question 4 in Figure 3-1 focuses on this issue.

Knowledge/skill enhancement. Perhaps one of the most important questions focuses on the Level 3 data, job applications. As shown in question 5 in Figure 3-1, the specific skills and knowledge areas are listed with the question framed around the amount of change since the program was conducted. This is the recommended approach when there is no pre-program data. If pre-data has been collected, it is more appropriate to compare post program assessments with pre-program assessments using the same type of question.

Skills used. As shown in question 6 in Figure 3-1, it is sometimes helpful to determine the most frequently used skills that are directly linked to the program. A more detailed variation of this question is to list each skill and indicate the frequency of use. For many skills, it is important to experience frequent use quickly after the skills are acquired so that the skills become internalized.

Changes with work. Sometimes it is helpful to determine what specific activities or processes have changed about participants' work as a result of the program. As question 7 in Figure 3-1 illustrates, the participant explores how the skill applications (listed previously) have actually changed work habits, processes, and output. Question 8 is a continuation of 7, where specific numbers or values are provided to reflect how their behavior has changed (in this case, meeting behavior is the issue). Question 9 is an opportunity for the participant to indicate the level of confidence in the information provided in question 8. Questions 8 and 9 are unique to this type of situation.

Effective Meetings
Follow-Up Impact Questionnaire

Are you currently in a people management role/capacity? Yes ☐   No ☐

1. Listed below are the objectives of the Effective Meetings program. After
    reflecting on this program, please indicate the degree of success in meeting
    the objectives:

As a result of this program, participants will have:	Failed	Limited Success	Generally Successful	Completely Successful
a. the tools and techniques to prepare for, conduct and follow up on meetings,	☐	☐	☐	☐
b. the ability to facilitate the human dynamics of meetings,	☐	☐	☐	☐
c. the strategies to participate in, and chair meetings more effectively.	☐	☐	☐	☐

2. Did you develop and implement an on-the-job action plan for Effective
    Meetings?

    Yes ☐   No ☐

    If yes, please describe the nature and outcome of the plan. If not, explain
    why. _____

    _____

    _____

3. Please rate, on a scale of 1-5, the relevance of each of the program elements
    to your job, with (1) indicating no relevance, and (5) indicating very
    relevant.

	1	2	3	4	5
Interactive Activities	☐	☐	☐	☐	☐
Groups Discussions	☐	☐	☐	☐	☐
Networking Opportunities	☐	☐	☐	☐	☐
Reading Materials/Video	☐	☐	☐	☐	☐
Program Content	☐	☐	☐	☐	☐

Figure 3-1. *Efective Meetings follow-up impact questionnaire.*

4. Have you used the materials since you participated in the program?

    Yes ☐   No ☐

5. Please explain. _____

    _____

    _____

    _____

Please indicate the degree to which your knowledge of, or skills with, the following items were enhanced as a result of your participation in Effective Meetings:

	No Change	Little Change	Some Change	Significant Change	Very Much Change	No Opportunity To Use Skill
a. Participating Effectively in Meetings	☐	☐	☐	☐	☐	☐
b. Avoiding Meetings Unless they are Necessary	☐	☐	☐	☐	☐	☐
c. Minimizing the Number of Participants Attending Meetings	☐	☐	☐	☐	☐	☐
d. Setting Objectives for Meetings	☐	☐	☐	☐	☐	☐
e. Developing an Agenda for Each Meeting	☐	☐	☐	☐	☐	☐
f. Controlling Time of Meetings	☐	☐	☐	☐	☐	☐
g. Enhancing Participant Satisfaction in Meetings	☐	☐	☐	☐	☐	☐
h. Arranging the Meeting Site for Maximum Effectiveness	☐	☐	☐	☐	☐	☐
i. Scheduling the Optimum Time for Meetings	☐	☐	☐	☐	☐	☐
j. Communicating the Ground Rules for Meetings	☐	☐	☐	☐	☐	☐

Figure 3-1. *Cont'd.*

	No Change	Little Change	Some Change	Significant Change	Very Much Change	No Opportunity To Use Skill
k. Assigning Appropriate Roles for Meeting Participants	☐	☐	☐	☐	☐	☐
l. Reaching Consensus in Meetings When Appropriate	☐	☐	☐	☐	☐	☐
m. Listening Actively to Meeting Participants	☐	☐	☐	☐	☐	☐
n. Encouraging Participation in Meetings	☐	☐	☐	☐	☐	☐
o. Using Brainstorming in Meetings When Appropriate	☐	☐	☐	☐	☐	☐
p. Dealing with Difficult Meeting Participants	☐	☐	☐	☐	☐	☐
q. Providing Feedback to Meeting Participants	☐	☐	☐	☐	☐	☐
r. Handling Conflict in Meeting	☐	☐	☐	☐	☐	☐
s. Keeping the Meeting on Focus	☐	☐	☐	☐	☐	☐
t. Accomplishing Meeting Objectives	☐	☐	☐	☐	☐	☐
u. Evaluating the Meeting Process	☐	☐	☐	☐	☐	☐
v. Implementing Action Plans	☐	☐	☐	☐	☐	☐
w. Planning a Follow-up Activity	☐	☐	☐	☐	☐	☐

Figure 3-1. *Cont'd.*

6. List the three Effective Meeting behaviors you have used most often as a result of the program.

    _____

    _____

7. What has changed about your meeting activity profile as a result of this program? (Fewer meetings, fewer participants, shorter meetings, etc.)

    _____

    _____

8. Please estimate the following monthly time saving measures. Use the most recent month compared to the month before attending this program. Provide only improvements directly related to this program and only when the time saved is used productively.

    ☐ Number of meetings avoided each month with improved planning and analysis

    _____

    ☐ Average time saved per meeting per month (in hours)

    _____

    ☐ Number of participants reduced per meeting per month

    _____

9. What level of confidence do you place on the above estimations? (0% - No Confidence, 100% = Certainty) _____ %

10. Please identify any specific accomplishments/improvements that you can link to this program (on time schedules, project completion, response times, etc.)

    _____

    _____

11. What specific value in US Dollars can be attributed to the above accomplishments/ improvements (use first year values only)? While this is a difficult question, try to think of specific ways in which the above improvements can be converted to monetary units. Use first year values along with the monetary value; please indicate the basis of your calculation.
    $_____

    Basis _____

    _____

Figure 3-1. *Cont'd.*

12. What level of confidence do you place on the above estimations? (0% - No Confidence, 100% = Certainty) _____ %

13. Other factors often influence improvements in performance. Please indicate the percent of the above improvement that is related directly to this program. _____%

    Please explain. _____
    _____

14. Do you think the Effective Meetings program represented a good investment for High Tech, Inc.?   Yes ☐   No ☐

    Please explain. _____
    _____

15. Indicate the extent to which you think this Effective Meetings program has influenced each of these measures in your work unit, department, or business unit:

	No Influence	Some Influence	Moderate Influence	Significant Influence	Very Much Influence
a. Productivity	☐	☐	☐	☐	☐
b. Customer Response Time	☐	☐	☐	☐	☐
c. Cost Control	☐	☐	☐	☐	☐
d. Employee Satisfaction	☐	☐	☐	☐	☐
e. Customer Satisfaction	☐	☐	☐	☐	☐
f. Quality	☐	☐	☐	☐	☐
g. Other	☐	☐	☐	☐	☐

16. What barriers, if any, have you encountered that have prevented you from using skills or knowledge gained in this program. Please explain, if possible.
    _____
    _____

17. What specific suggestions do you have for improving this program?
    _____

18. Other Comments:
    _____
    _____

Figure 3-1. *Cont'd.*

Improvements/accomplishments. Question 10 in Figure 3-1 begins a series of four impact questions that are appropriate for most follow-up questionnaires. The first question in the series, question 10, seeks specific accomplishments and improvements that are directly linked to the program. This question focuses on specific measurable successes that can be easily identified by the participants. Since this question is an open-ended question, it can be helpful to provide examples that indicate the nature and range of responses requested. However, examples can also be constraining in nature and may actually limit the responses.

Monetary impact. Perhaps the most difficult question, number 11 in Figure 3-1, asks participants to provide monetary values for the improvements identified in question 10. Only the first year improvement is sought. Participants are asked to specify net improvements so that the actual monetary values will represent gains from the program. An important part of the question is the basis for the calculation, where participants specify the steps taken to develop the annual net value and the assumptions made in the analysis. It is very important for the basis to be completed with enough detail to understand the process.

Confidence level. To adjust for the uncertainty of the data provided in question 11, participants were asked to offer a level of confidence for the estimation, expressed as a percentage with a range of 0% - 100%, as shown in question 12 in Figure 3-1. This input allows participants to reflect their level of uncertainty with this process.

Improvements linked with program. The final question in the impact series, question 13 in Figure 3-1, isolates the effects of the training. Participants indicate the percent of the improvement that is directly related to the program. As an alternative, participants may be provided with the various factors that have influenced the results and are asked to allocate the percentages to each factor. Still another variation is for participants to provide a confidence estimate for this particular value as was the case for the estimate in question 11.

Investment perception. The value of the program, from the viewpoint of the participant, can be useful information. As illustrated in question 14 in Figure 3-1, participants are asked if they perceive this program to be a good investment. Another option for this question is to present the actual cost of the program so that participants can respond more accurately from the investment perspective. It may be useful to express the cost as a per participant cost. Also, the question can be divided into two parts; one reflecting the investment of money by the company and the other an investment in the participants time in the program.

Linkage with output measures. Sometimes it is helpful to determine the degree to which the program has influenced certain output measures, as shown in question 15 in Figure 3-1. In some situations a detailed analysis may reveal specifically which measures have been influenced by this program. However, when this issue is uncertain, it may be helpful to list the potential business performance measures influenced by the program and seek input from the participants. The question should be worded so that the frame of reference is for the time period after the program was conducted.

Barriers. A variety of barriers can influence the successful application of the skills and knowledge learned in the training program. Question 16 in Figure 3-1 identifies the barriers. As an alternative, the perceived barriers are listed, and participants check all that apply. Still another variation is to list the barriers with a range of responses, indicating the extent to which the barrier inhibited results.

Enablers. Just as important as barriers, are the enablers; those issues, events, or situations which have enabled the process to be applied successfully on the job. The same options are available with this question as in the question on barriers.

Management support. For most programs, management support is critical to the successful application of newly acquired skills. At least one question should be included on the degree of management support. Sometimes this question is structured so that various descriptions of management support are detailed, and participants check the one that applies to their situation. This information is very helpful to help remove or minimize barriers.

Other solutions. A training program is only one of many potential solutions to a performance problem. If the needs assessment is faulty or if there are alternative approaches to developing the desired skills or knowledge, other potential solutions could be more effective and achieve the same success. The participant is asked to identify other solutions that could have been effective in obtaining the same or similar results. This information can be particularly helpful as the training and development function continues to shift to a performance improvement function.

Target audience recommendations. Sometimes it is helpful to solicit input about the most appropriate target audience for this program. In this question, the participants are asked to indicate which groups of employees would benefit the most from attending this program.

Suggestions for improvement. As a final wrap-up question, participants are asked to provide suggestions for improving any part of the program or process.

As illustrated in question 17 in Figure 3-1, the open-ended structure is intended to solicit qualitative responses to be used to make improvements.

ROI Analysis

While there are several approaches to data analysis, the recommended steps to calculate the ROI are briefly described here. The calculations are based on the responses from the series of impact questions. Five adjustments are made to the data to ensure that it is credible and accurate:

1. The participants who do not complete the questionnaire or provide usable data on the impact questions are assumed to have no improvement.
2. Extreme and unrealistic data items are omitted.
3. Only annualized values are used as requested in the responses.
4. The values are adjusted to reflect the confidence level of participants.
5. The values are adjusted for the amount of the improvement related directly to the program.

These five adjustments create a very credible value that is usually considered to be an understatement of the benefits.

Improving the Response Rate for Questionnaires and Surveys

The content items previously listed represent a wide range of potential issues to explore in a follow-up questionnaire or survey. Obviously, asking all of the questions could cause the response rate to be reduced considerably. The challenge, therefore, is to tackle questionnaire design and administration for maximum response rate. This is a critical issue when the questionnaire is the primary data collection activity and most of the evaluation hinges on the questionnaire results. The following actions can be taken to increase response rate.

Provide advance communication. If appropriate and feasible, participants should receive advance communications about the requirement for a follow-up questionnaire. This minimizes some of the resistance to the process, provides an opportunity to explain in more detail the circumstances surrounding the evaluation, and positions the follow-up evaluation as an integral part of the program; not an add-on activity that someone initiated three months after the program.

Communicate the purpose. Participants should understand the reason for the follow-up questionnaire, including who or what has initiated this specific evaluation. Participants should know if the evaluation is part of a systematic process or a special request for this program.

Explain who will see the data. It is important for participants to know who will see the data and the results of the questionnaire. If the questionnaire is anonymous, it should clearly be communicated to participants what steps will be taken to ensure anonymity. If senior executives will see the combined results of the study, participants should know it.

Describe the data integration process. Participants should understand how the questionnaire results will be combined with other data, if available. Often the questionnaire is only one of the data collection methods utilized. Participants should know how the data is weighted and integrated in the final report.

Keep the questionnaire as simple as possible. A simple questionnaire does not always provide the full scope of data necessary for an ROI analysis. However, the simplified approach should always be kept in mind when questions are developed and the total scope of the questionnaire is finalized. Every effort should be made to keep it as simple and brief as possible.

Simplify the response process. To the extent possible, it should be easy to respond to the questionnaire. If appropriate, a self-addressed stamped envelope should be included. Perhaps the e-mail system could be used for response, if it is easier. In still other situations, a response box is provided near the work station.

Utilize local manager support. Management involvement at the local level is critical to response rate success. Managers can distribute the questionnaires themselves, make reference to the questionnaire in staff meetings, follow-up to see if questionnaires have been completed, and generally show the support for completing the questionnaire. This direct supervisor support will cause some participants to respond with usable data.

Let the participants know they are part of the sample. If appropriate, participants should know that they are part of a carefully selected sample and that their input will be used to make decisions regarding a much larger target audience. This action often appeals to a sense of responsibility for participants to provide usable, accurate data for the questionnaire.

Consider incentives. A variety of different types of incentives can be offered and they usually fall into three categories. First, an incentive is provided in exchange for the completed questionnaire. For example, if participants return the questionnaire personally or through the mail, they will receive a small gift, such as a T-shirt or mug. If identity is an issue, a neutral third party can provide the incentive. In the second category, the incentive is provided to make participants feel guilty about not responding. Examples are a dollar bill clipped to the questionnaire or a pen enclosed in the envelope. Participants are asked to "take the dollar, buy a cup of coffee, and fill out the questionnaire," or "please use this pen to complete the questionnaire." A third group of incentives is designed to obtain a quick response. This approach is based on the assumption that a quick response will ensure a greater response rate. If an individual puts off completing the questionnaire, the odds of completing it diminish considerably. The initial group of participants may receive a more expensive gift or they may be part of a drawing for an incentive. For example, in one study, the first 25 returned questionnaires were placed in a drawing for a $400 gift certificate. The next 25 were added to the first 25 in the next drawing. The longer a participant waits, the lower the odds for winning.

Have an executive sign the introductory letter. Participants are always interested in who sent the letter with the questionnaire. For maximum effectiveness, the letter should be signed by a senior executive who is responsible for a major area where the participants work. Employees may be more willing to respond to a senior executive when compared to situations where a letter is signed by a member of the training and development staff.

Use follow-up reminders. A follow-up reminder should be sent a week after the questionnaire is received and another sent two weeks after it is received. Depending on the questionnaire and the situation, these times could be adjusted. In some situations, a third follow-up is recommended. Sometimes the follow-up should be sent in different media. For example, a questionnaire may be sent through regular mail, whereas, the first follow-up reminder is from the immediate supervisor and a second follow-up reminder is sent through e-mail.

Send a copy of the results to the participants. Even if it is an abbreviated form, participants should see the results of the study. More importantly, participants should understand that they will receive a copy of the study when they are asked to provide the data. This promise will often increase the response rate, as some individuals want to see the results of the entire group along with their particular input.

Collectively, these items help boost response rates of follow-up questionnaires. Using all of these strategies can result in a 50% - 60% response rate, even with lengthy questionnaires that might take 30 minutes to complete.

Follow-Up Interviews

Another helpful collection method is the interview, although it is not used as frequently as questionnaires. Interviews can be conducted by the HRD staff, the participant's supervisor, or an outside third party. Interviews can secure data not available in performance records, or data difficult to obtain through written responses or observations. Also, interviews can uncover success stories that can be useful in communicating evaluation results. Participants may be reluctant to describe their results in a questionnaire but will volunteer the information to a skillful interviewer who uses probing techniques. While the interview process uncovers changes in behavior, reaction, and results, it is primarily used with Level 3 data. A major disadvantage of the interview is that it is time consuming. It also requires training or preparing interviewers to ensure that the process is consistent.

Types of Interviews

Interviews usually fall into two basic types: (1) structured and (2) unstructured. A structured interview is much like a questionnaire. Specific questions are asked with little room to deviate from the desired responses. The primary advantages of the structured interview over the questionnaire are that the interview process can ensure that the questionnaire is completed and the interviewer understands the responses supplied by the participant.

The unstructured interview allows for probing for additional information. This type of interview uses a few general questions, which can lead into more detailed information as important data are uncovered. The interviewer must be skilled in the probing process.

Typical Probing Questions
Can you explain that in more detail?
Can you give me an example of what you are saying?
Can you explain the difficulty that you say you encountered?

Interview Guidelines

The design steps for interviews are similar to those of the questionnaire. A brief summary of key issues with interviews are outlined here.

Develop questions to be asked. Once a decision has been made about the type of interview, specific questions need to be developed. Questions should be brief, precise, and designed for easy response.

Try out the interview. The interview should be tested on a small number of participants. If possible, the interviews should be conducted as part of the trial run of the HRD program. The responses should be analyzed and the interview revised, if necessary.

Train the interviewers. The interviewer should have appropriate skills, including active listening, asking probing questions, and collecting and summarizing information into a meaningful form.

Give clear instructions to the participant.. The participant should understand the purpose of the interview and know what will be done with the information. Expectations, conditions, and rules of the interview should be thoroughly discussed. For example, the participant should know if statements will be kept confidential. If the participant is nervous during an interview and develops signs of anxiety, he or she should be made to feel at ease.

Administer the interviews according to a scheduled plan. As with the other evaluation instruments, interviews need to be conducted according to a predetermined plan. The timing of the interview, the person who conducts the interview, and the place of the interview are all issues that become relevant when developing an interview plan. For a large number of participants, a sampling plan may be necessary to save time and reduce the evaluation cost.

Follow-Up Focus Groups

An extension of the interview, focus groups are particularly helpful when in-depth feedback is needed for a Level 3 evaluation. The focus group involves a small group discussion conducted by an experienced facilitator. It is designed to solicit qualitative judgments on a planned topic or issue. Group members are all required to provide their input, as individual input builds on group input.

When compared with questionnaires, surveys, tests, or interviews, the focus group strategy has several advantages. The basic premise of using focus groups is that when quality judgments are subjective, several individual judgments are better than one. The group process, where participants often motivate one another, is an effective method for generating new ideas and hypotheses. It is inexpensive and can be quickly planned and conducted. Its flexibility makes it possible to explore a training program's unexpected outcomes or applications.

Applications for Evaluation

The focus group is particularly helpful when qualitative information is needed about the success of a training program. For example, the focus group can be used in the following situations:

- to evaluate the reactions to specific exercises, cases, simulations, or other components of a training program,
- to assess the overall effectiveness of the program as perceived by the participants immediately following a program, and
- to assess the impact of the program in a follow-up evaluation after the program is completed.

Essentially, focus groups are helpful when evaluation information is needed but cannot be collected adequately with simple, quantitative methods.

Guidelines

While there are no set rules on how to use focus groups for evaluation, the following guidelines should be helpful:

Ensure that management buys into the focus group process. Because this is a relatively new process for evaluation, it might be unknown to some management groups. Managers need to understand focus groups and their advantages. This should raise their level of confidence in the information obtained from group sessions.

Plan topics, questions, and strategy carefully. As with any evaluation instrument, planning is the key. The specific topics, questions, and issues to be discussed must be carefully planned and sequenced. This enhances the comparison of results from one group to another and ensures that the group process is effective and stays on track.

Keep the group size small. While there is no magic group size, a range of 6 to 12 seems to be appropriate for most focus group applications. A group has to be large enough to ensure different points of view, but small enough to give every participant a chance to talk freely and exchange comments.

Ensure that there is a representative sample of the target population. It is important for groups to be stratified appropriately so that participants represent the target population. The group should be homogeneous in experience, rank, and influence in the organization.

Insist on facilitators who have appropriate expertise.. The success of a focus group rests with the facilitator who must be skilled in the focus group process. Facilitators must know how to control aggressive members of the group and diffuse the input from those who want to dominate the group. Also, facilitators must be able to create an environment in which participants feel comfortable in offering comments freely and openly. Because of this, some organizations use external facilitators.

In summary, the focus group is an inexpensive and quick way to determine the strengths and weaknesses of training programs, particularly with management and supervisory training. However, for complete evaluation, focus group information should be combined with data from other instruments.

Observing Participants On the Job

Another potentially useful data collection method is observing participants and recording any changes in their behavior. The observer may be a member of the HRD staff, the participant's supervisor, a member of a peer group, or an outside party. The most common observer, and probably the most practical, is a member of the HRD staff.

Guidelines for Effective Observation

Observation is often misused or misapplied to evaluation situations, leaving some to abandon the process. The effectiveness of observation can be improved with the following guidelines.

Observers must be fully prepared. Observers must fully understand what information is needed and what skills are covered in the program. They must be trained for the assignment and provided a chance to practice observation skills.

The observations should be systematic. The observation process must be planned so that it is executed effectively without any surprises. The persons observed should know in advance about the observation and why they are being observed unless the observation is planned to be invisible. The timing of observations should be a part of the plan. There are right times to observe a participant, and there are wrong times. If a participant is observed when times are not normal (i.e., in a crisis), the data collected may be useless.

Planning a systematic observation is important. Several steps are necessary to accomplish a successful observation:

- Determine what behavior will be observed.
- Prepare the forms for the observers to use.
- Select the observers.
- Prepare a schedule of observations.
- Train observers in what to observe and what not to observe.
- Inform participants of the planned observations with explanations.
- Conduct observations.
- Summarize the observation data.

The observer's should know how to interpret and report what they see. Observations involve judgment decisions. The observer must analyze which behaviors are being displayed and what actions are being taken by the participants. Observers should know how to summarize behavior and report results in a meaningful manner.

The observer's influence should be minimized. Except for mystery observers and electronic observations, it is impossible to completely isolate the overall effect of an observer. Participants may display the behavior they think is appropriate, and they will usually be at their best. The presence of the observer must be minimized. To the extent possible, the observer should blend into the work environment.

Select observers carefully. Observers are usually independent of the participants, typically a member of the HRD staff. The independent observer is usually more skilled at recording behavior and making interpretations of behavior. They are usually unbiased in these interpretations. Using them enables the HRD department to bypass training observers and relieves the line organization of that responsibility. On the other hand, the independent observer has the appearance of an outsider checking the work of others. There may be a tendency for participants to overreact and possibly resent this kind of observer. Sometimes it might be more feasible to recruit observers from outside the organization. This approach has an advantage of neutralizing the prejudicial feelings entering the decisions.

Observation Methods

Five methods of observation are utilized, depending on the circumstances surrounding the type of information needed. Each method is described briefly.

Behavior Checklist and Codes. A behavior checklist can be useful for recording the presence, absence, frequency, or duration of a participant's behavior as it occurs. A checklist will not usually provide information on the quality, intensity, or possibly the circumstances surrounding the behavior observed. The checklist is useful, since an observer can identify exactly which behaviors should or should not occur. Measuring the duration of a behavior may be more difficult and requires a stopwatch and a place on the form to record the time interval. This factor is usually not as important when compared to whether or not a particular behavior was observed and how often. The number of behaviors listed in the checklist should be small and listed in a logical sequence, if they normally occur in a sequence. A variation of this approach involves a coding of behaviors on a form. This method is more time consuming because the code is entered that identifies a specific behavior.

Delayed Report Method. With a delayed report method, the observer does not use any forms or written materials during the observation. The information is either recorded after the observation is completed or at particular time intervals during an observation. The observer tries to reconstruct what has been observed during the observation period. The advantage of this approach is that the observer is not as noticeable, and there are no forms being completed or notes being taken during the observation. The observer can be more a part of the situation and less distracting. An obvious disadvantage is that the information written may not be as accurate and reliable as the information collected at the time it occurred. A variation of this approach is the 360° feedback process in which surveys are completed on other individuals based on observations within a specific time frame.

Video Recording. A video camera records behavior in every detail, an obvious advantage. However, this intrusion may be awkward and cumbersome, and the participants may be unnecessarily nervous or self conscious when they are being videotaped. If the camera is concealed, the privacy of the participant may be invaded. Because of this, video recording of on-the-job behavior is not frequently used.

Audio Monitoring. Monitoring conversations of participants who are using the skills taught in the training program is an effective observation technique. For example, in a large communication company's telemarketing department, sales representatives are trained to sell equipment by telephone. To determine if employees are using the skills properly, telephone conversations are monitored on a selected and sometimes random basis. While this approach may stir some controversy, it is an effective way to determine if skills are being applied consistently and effectively. For it to work smoothly, it must be fully explained and the rules clearly communicated.

Computer Monitoring. For employees who work regularly with a keyboard, computer monitoring is becoming an effective way to "observe" participants as they perform job tasks. The computer monitors times, sequence of steps, and other activities to determine if the participant is performing the work according to what was learned in the training program. As technology continues to be a significant part of jobs, computer monitoring holds promise of monitoring actual applications on the job. This is particularly helpful for Level 3 data.

Monitoring Performance Data

Data are available in every organization to measure performance. Monitoring performance data enables management to measure performance in terms of output, quality, costs, and time. In determining the use of data in the evaluation, the first consideration should be existing databases and reports. In most organizations, performance data suitable for measuring the improvement resulting from an HRD program are available. If not, additional record-keeping systems will have to be developed for measurement and analysis. At this point, as with many other points in the process, the question of economics enters. Is it economical to develop the record-keeping system necessary to evaluate an HRD program? If the costs are greater than the expected return for the entire program, then it is meaningless to develop them.

Using Current Measures

If existing performance measures are available, specific guidelines are recommended to ensure that the measurement system is easily developed.

Identify appropriate measures. Performance measures should be thoroughly researched to identify those that are related to the proposed objectives of the program. Frequently, an organization will have several performance measures related to the same item. For example, the efficiency of a production unit can be measured in a variety of ways:

- the number of units produced per hour,
- the number of on-schedule production units,
- the percent utilization of the equipment,
- the percent of equipment downtime,
- the labor cost per unit of production,
- the overtime required per piece of production, and
- total unit cost.

Each of these, in its own way, measures the efficiency of the production unit. All related measures should be reviewed to determine those most relevant to the HRD program.

Convert current measures to usable ones. Occasionally, existing performance measures are integrated with other data, and it may be difficult to keep them isolated from unrelated data. In this situation, all existing related measures should be extracted and retabulated to be more appropriate for comparison in the evaluation. At times, conversion factors may be necessary. For example, the average number of new sales orders per month may be presented regularly in the performance measures for the sales department. In addition, the sales costs per sales representative are also presented. However, in the evaluation of an HRD program, the average cost per new sale is needed. The two existing performance records are required to develop the data necessary for comparison.

Develop a collection plan. A data collection plan defines when data are collected, who will collect it, and where it will be collected. This plan should contain provisions for the evaluator to secure copies of performance reports in a timely manner so that the items can be recorded and are available for analysis.

Developing New Measures

In some cases, data are not available for the information needed to measure the effectiveness of an HRD program. The HRD staff must work with the participating organization to develop record-keeping systems, if this is economically feasible. In one organization, a new employee orientation system was implemented on a company-wide basis. Several measures were planned, including early turnover representing the percentage of employees who left the company in the first six months of their employment. An effective employee orientation program should influence this variable. At the time of the program's inception, this measure was not available. When the program was implemented, the organization began collecting early turnover figures for comparison.

Typical Questions When Creating New Measures
Which department will develop the measurement system?
Who will record and monitor the data?
Where will it be recorded?
Will forms be used?

These questions will usually involve other departments or a management decision that extends beyond the scope of the HRD department. Possibly the administration division, the HR department, or information technology section will be instrumental in helping determine if new measures are needed and, if so, how they will be collected.

Action Planning and Follow-Up Assignments

In some cases, follow-up assignments can develop Level 3 and Level 4 data. In a typical follow-up assignment, the participant is instructed to meet a goal or complete a particular task or project by the determined follow-up date. A summary of the results of these completed assignments provides further evidence of the impact of the program.

The action plan is the most common type of follow-up assignment and is fully described in this section. With this approach, participants are required to develop action plans as part of the program. Action plans contain detailed steps to accomplish specific objectives related to the program. The plan is typically prepared on a printed form such as the one shown in Figure 3-2. The action plan shows what is to be done, by whom, and the date by which the objectives should be accomplished. The action plan approach is a straightforward, easy-to-use method for determining how participants will change their behavior on the job and achieve success with training. The approach produces data answers such questions as:

Typical Questions The Action Plan Answers
What on-the-job improvements have been realized since the program was conducted?
Are the improvements linked to the program?
What may have prevented participants from accomplishing specific action items?

With this information, HRD professionals can decide if a program should be modified and in what ways, while managers can assess the findings to evaluate the worth of the program.

Developing the Action Plan

The development of the action plan requires two tasks: (1) determining the areas for action and (2) writing the action items. Both tasks should be completed during the program. The areas for action should originate from the content of the program and, at the same time, be related to on-the-job activities.

A list of potential areas for action can be developed independently by participants or a list may be generated in group discussions. The list may include an area needing improvement or represent an opportunity for increased performance.

Typical Questions When Developing Action Steps
How much time will this action take?
Are the skills for accomplishing this action item available?
Who has the authority to implement the action plan?
Will this action have an effect on other individuals?
Are there any organizational constraints for accomplishing this action item?

The specific action items are usually more difficult to write than the identification of the action areas. The most important characteristic of an action item is that it is written so that everyone involved will know when it occurs. One way to help achieve this goal is to use specific action verbs. Some examples of action items are:

- *Learn* how to operate the new RC-105 drill press machine in the adjacent department, by *(date)*.
- *Identify* and *secure* a new customer account, by *(date)*.
- *Handle* every piece of paper only once to improve my personal time management, by *(date)*.
- *Learn* to talk with my employers directly about a problem which arises rather than avoiding a confrontation, by *(date)*.

If appropriate, each action item should have a date for completion and indicate other individuals or resources required for completion. Also, planned behavior changes should be observable. It should be obvious to the participant and others when it happens. Action plans, as used in this context, do not require the prior approval or input from the participant's supervisor, although it may be helpful.

Using Action Plans Successfully

The action plan process should be an integral part of the program and not an add-on or optional activity. To gain maximum effectiveness from action plans and to collect data for ROI calculations, the following steps should be implemented.

Name: _____ Instructor Signature _____ Follow-Up Date: _____
Objective: _____ Evaluation Period _____ to _____
Improvement Measure: _____ Current Performance _____ Target Performance _____

Action Steps	Analysis
1. _____	A. What is the unit of measure? _____
2. _____	B. What is the value (cost) of one unit? $ _____
3. _____	C. How did you arrive at this value? _____
4. _____	_____
5. _____	_____
6. _____	D. How much did the measure change during the evaluation period? (monthly value) _____
7. _____	E. What percent of this change was actually caused by this program? _____ %
Intangible Benefits: _____	F. What level of confidence do you place on the above information? (100%=Certainty and 0%=No Confidence) _____ %

Comments: _____

Figure 3-2. *Action plan*

Communicate the action plan requirement early. One of the most negative reactions to action plans is the surprise factor often inherent in the way in which the process is introduced. When program participants realize that they must develop a detailed action plan, there is often immediate, built-in resistance. Communicating to participants in advance, where the process is shown to be an integral part of the program, will often minimize resistance to developing action plans. When participants fully realize the benefits before they attend the first session, they take the process more seriously and usually perform the extra steps to make it more successful.

Describe the action planning process at the beginning of the program. At the first session, action plan requirements are discussed, including an outline of the purpose of the process, why it is necessary, and the basic requirements during and after the program. Some facilitators furnish a separate notepad for participants to collect ideas and useful techniques for their action plan. This is a productive way to focus more attention and effort on the process.

Teach the action planning process. An important prerequisite for action plan success is an understanding of how it works and how specific action plans are developed. A portion of the program's agenda is allocated to teaching participants how to develop plans. In this session, the requirements are outlined, special forms and procedures are discussed, and a positive example is distributed and reviewed. Sometimes an entire program module is allocated to this process so that participants will fully understand it and use it. Any available support tools, such as key measures, charts, graphs, suggested topics, and sample calculations should be used in this session to help facilitate the plan's development.

Allow time to develop the plan. When action plans are used to collect data for an ROI calculation, it is important to allow participants to develop plans during the program. Sometimes it is helpful to have participants work in teams so they can share ideas as they develop specific plans. In these sessions, facilitators often monitor the progress of individuals or teams to keep the process on track and to answer questions. In some management and executive development programs, action plans are developed in an evening session, as a scheduled part of the program.

Have the facilitator approve the action plans. It is essential for the action plan to be related to program objectives and, at the same time, represent an important accomplishment for the organization when it is completed. It is easy for participants to stray from the intent and purposes of action planing and not give it the attention that it deserves. Consequently, it is helpful to have the facilitator actually sign off on the action plan, ensuring that the plan reflects all of the requirements and is appropriate for the program. In some cases, a space is provided for the facilitator's signature on the action plan document.

Require participants to assign a monetary value for each improvement. Participants are asked to determine, calculate, or estimate the monetary value for each   improvement outlined in the plan. When the actual improvement has occurred, participants will use these values to capture the annual monetary benefits of the plan. For this step to be effective, it may be helpful to provide examples of typical ways in which values can be assigned to the actual data.[1]

Ask participants to isolate the effects of the program. Although the action plan is initiated because of the training program, the actual improvements reported on the action plan may be influenced by other factors. Thus, the action planning process should not take full credit for the improvement. For example, an action plan to reduce employee turnover in a division could take only partial credit for an improvement, because of the other variables that will affect the turnover rate. While there are at least ten ways to isolate the effects of training, participant estimation is usually more appropriate in the action planning process.[2] Consequently, the participants are asked to estimate the percent of the improvement actually related to this particular program. This question can be asked on the action plan form or on a follow-up questionnaire.

Ask participants to provide a confidence level for estimates. Since the process to convert data to monetary values may not be exact and the amount of the improvement actually related to the program may not be precise, participants are asked to indicate their level of confidence in those two values, collectively. On a scale of 0% to 100%, where 0% means the values are completely false and 100% means the estimates represent certainty, this value provides participants a mechanism to express their uneasiness with their ability to be exact with the process.

Require action plans to be presented to the group, if possible. There is no better way to secure commitment and ownership of the action planning process than to have a participant describe his or her action plan in front of fellow participants.   Presenting the action plan helps to ensure that the process is thoroughly developed and will be implemented on the job. If the number of participants is too large for individual presentations, perhaps one participant can be selected from the team, if the plans are developed in teams. Under these circumstances, the team will usually select the best action plan for presentation to the group.

Explain the follow-up mechanism. Participants must leave the session with a clear understanding of the timing of the action plan implementation and the planned follow-up. The method in which the data will be collected, analyzed, and reported should be openly discussed. Five options are common:

1. The group is reconvened to discuss the progress on the plans.
2. Participants meet with their immediate manager and discuss the success of the plan. A copy is forwarded to the HRD department.
3. A meeting is held with the program evaluator, the participant, and the participant's manager to discuss the plan and the information contained in it.
4. Participants send the plan to the evaluator and it is discussed in a conference call.
5. Participants send the plan directly to the education and training department with no meetings or discussions. This is the most common option.

While there are other ways to collect the data, it is important to select a mechanism that fits the culture and constraints of the organization.

Collect action plans at the predetermined follow-up time. Because it is critical to have an excellent response rate, several steps may be necessary to ensure that the action plans are completed and the data are returned to the appropriate individual or group for analysis. Some organizations use follow-up reminders by mail or e-mail. Others call participants to check progress. Still others offer assistance in developing the final plan. These steps may require additional resources, which have to be weighed against the importance of having more data. When the action plan process is implemented as outlined in this chapter, the response rates will normally be very high in the 50% - 70% range. Usually participants will see the importance of the process and will develop their plans in detail before leaving the program.

Summarize the data and calculate the ROI. If developed properly, each action plan should have annualized monetary values associated with improvements. Also, each individual has indicated the percent of the improvement that is directly related to the program. Finally, each participant has provided a confidence percentage to reflect their uncertainty with the process and the subjective nature of some of the data that may be provided.

Because this process involves some estimates, it may not appear to be accurate. Several adjustments during the analysis make the process very credible and more accurate. The following adjustments are made:

Step 1: For those participants who do not provide data, it is assumed that they had no improvement to report. This is a very conservative assumption.

Step 2: Each value is checked for realism, usability, and feasibility. Extreme values are discarded and omitted from the analysis.

Step 3: Because the improvement is annualized, it is assumed the program had no improvement after the first year. Some programs should add value at year two and three.

Step 4: The improvement from step 3 is then adjusted by the confidence level, multiplying it by the confidence percent. The confidence level is actually an error suggested by the participants. For example, a participant indicating 80% confidence with the process, is reflecting a 20% error possibility. In a $10,000 estimate with an 80% confidence factor, the participant is suggesting that the value could be in the range of $8,000 to $12,000. To be conservative, the lower number is used. Thus, the confidence factor is multiplied times the amount of improvement.

Step 5: The new values are then adjusted by the percent of the improvement related directly to the program using straight multiplication. This isolates the effects of training.

The monetary values determined in these five steps are totaled to arrive at a total program benefit. Since these values are already annualized, the total of these benefits becomes the annual benefits for the program. This value is placed in the numerator of the ROI formula to calculate the ROI.

Case Application

The impact of the action plan process is impressive. In a medium-size manufacturing facility, a training program was developed for first-level supervisors that focused on improving interpersonal skills with employees. Several of the areas tackled were productivity improvement, scrap reduction, absenteeism, turnover, grievances, and safety. These areas were discussed thoroughly and supervisors improved skills to make improvements in each area. Supervisors were required to develop action plans for improvement and report the results in a follow-up six months after the program. In this situation, the improvement measures were pre-determined from the needs assessment. The following results were documented from a pilot group:

- The department unit hour was increased from 65 to 75. This is a basic measure of productivity, where a unit hour of 60 is considered to be average and acceptable work.
- Scrap was reduced from 11% to 7.4%.
- Absenteeism was reduced from 7% to 3.25%.
- The annual turnover rate was drastically reduced from 30% to 5%.
- Grievances were reduced 80%.
- Lost time accidents were reduced 95%.

These results were achieved by supervisors practicing what they had learned and reporting results of action plans. Although these results are impressive, three additional steps are needed to develop the ultimate evaluation, the return on investment. First, the amount of the improvement that is actually linked to the program must be determined. In this situation, supervisors estimated the percent of the improvement directly linked to the program. While the absenteeism improvement showed an overall decrease of 3.75, the supervisors collectively estimated that only 46% of the absenteeism reduction was actually linked to the program. Thus, a 3.75% absenteeism reduction actually becomes 1.725%. This figure can be further adjusted by factoring in a confidence level (provided by supervisors when they supplied the estimate). In this example, supervisors were 84% confident of their allocation of the absenteeism improvement. This adjustment means that 1.725% then becomes 1.45% when adjusted for the 84% confidence level. These two adjustments isolate the effects of the training program on the output variable and are fully described in the next chapter.

The second step to develop the ROI is to convert the data to monetary value. A value for a single absence must be determined and used to calculate the annual benefit of the improvement. There are at least ten ways to place values on data, and they are fully described in Chapter 5. For this example, supervisors had developed an estimated value of one absence, which was used previously in several applications where the cost of absenteeism was needed. Thus, the total number of absences avoided was calculated and multiplied by the value of one absence to obtain the training program's annual impact on absenteeism reduction. This process shows clearly the economic value of the program on that specific output variable. These two steps, isolating the effects of training and converting data to monetary values are performed for each of the six improvement variables, and the total value represents the annual economic benefit of the program.

The third step necessary to move to an ROI is to develop the fully loaded costs of the program. In this step, the costs related to the needs assessment and program development are prorated. In addition, all direct training costs are captured, along with the cost of the participants' salaries and benefits while they were actually attending training. The fully loaded cost for all participants reflects the total investment in this program for this group. This process is fully explained in Chapter 6. With these three additional steps, the ROI can be calculated using the formulas described in Chapter 2 (net benefits divided by costs). In this example, total annual benefits directly attributed to the program after converting all six improvement items to monetary units are $775,000. The fully loaded costs for the program, where needs assessment, program development, and the cost for the evaluation were prorated, resulted in a value of $65,000. Thus, the ROI becomes as follows:

$$\text{ROI} = \frac{\text{Net Program Benefits}}{\text{Program Costs}} \quad \frac{\$775,000 - \$65,000}{\$65,000} \quad \text{x } 100 \quad = 1092\%$$

This impressive ROI has credibility because of the conservative nature of the adjustments made to the data. Without these three additional steps, the target audience may be left wondering how much of the results were actually linked to the training program and how the benefits exceeded the costs.

Advantages/Disadvantages

Although there are many advantages, there are at least two concerns with action plans:

1. The process relies on direct input from the participant usually with no assurance of anonymity. As such, the information can sometimes be biased and unreliable.

2. Action plans can be time consuming for the participant and, if the participant's supervisor is not involved in the process, there may be a tendency for the participant not to complete the assignment.

As this section has illustrated, the action plan approach has many inherent advantages. Action Plans are simple and easy to administer; are easily understood by participants; are used with a wide variety of programs; are appropriate for all types of data; are able to measure reaction, learning, behavior changes, and results; and may be used with or without other evaluation methods.

Because of the tremendous flexibility and versatility of the process, and the conservative adjustments that can be made in analysis, action plans have become an important data collection tool for the ROI analysis.

Performance Contracts

The performance contract is essentially a slight variation of the action planning process. Based on the principle of mutual goal setting, a performance contract is a written agreement between a participant and the participant's supervisor. The participant agrees to improve performance in an area of mutual concern related to the subject material in the HRD program. The agreement is in the form of a project to be completed or a goal to be accomplished soon after the program is over. The agreement spells out what is to be accomplished, at what time, and with what results.

Although the steps can vary according to the specific kind of contract and the organization, a common sequence of events is as follows:

- With supervisor approval, the employee (participant) decides to attend an HRD program.
- The participant and supervisor mutually agree on a subject for improvement.
- Specific, measurable goals are set.
- The participant attends the program where the contract is discussed, and plans are developed to accomplish the goals.
- After the program, the participant works on the contract against a specific deadline.
- The participant reports the results of the effort to his supervisor.
- The supervisor and participant document the results and forward a copy to the HRD department along with appropriate comments.

The individuals mutually select the subject or action to be performed or improved prior to program inception. The process of selecting the area for improvement is similar to the process used in the action planning process. The topic can cover one or more of the following areas:

- *Routine performance* - includes specific improvements in routine performance measures such as production targets, efficiency, and error rates.
- *Problem solving* - focuses on specific problems such as an unexpected increase in accidents, a decrease in efficiency, or a loss of morale.
- *Innovative or creative applications* - includes initiating changes or improvements in work practices, methods, procedures, techniques, and processes.
- *Personal development* - involves learning new information or acquiring new skills to increase individual effectiveness.

The topic selected should be stated in terms of one or more objectives. The objectives should state what is to be accomplished when the contract is complete. These objectives should be:

- written,
- understandable (by all involved),
- challenging (requiring an unusual effort to achieve),
- achievable (something that can be accomplished),
- largely under the control of the participant,
- measurable and dated.

The details required to accomplish the contract objectives are developed following the guidelines under the action plans presented earlier. Also, the methods for analyzing data and reporting progress are essentially the same, as with the action planning process.

Program Follow-Up Session

For some situations, the program is redesigned to allow for a follow-up session where evaluation is addressed along with additional education and training. For example, an interactive selling skills program (a consecutive three day program) was redesigned as a two-day workshop to build skills, followed by a one-day session three weeks earlier. Thus, the follow-up session provided an opportunity for additional training and evaluation. During the first part of the day Level 3 evaluation data was collected using a focus group process. Also, specific barriers and problems encountered in applying the skills were discussed. The second half of the day was devoted to additional skill building and refinement along with techniques to overcome the particular barriers to using the skills. Thus, in effect, the redesigned program provided a mechanism for follow-up.

Selecting the Appropriate Method

This chapter has presented ten methods to capture post program data for an ROI analysis. Collectively, they offer a wide range of opportunities to collect data in a variety of situations. Eight specific issues should be considered when deciding which method is appropriate for a situation.

Type of Data

Perhaps one of the most important issues to consider when selecting the method is the type of data to be collected. Some methods are more appropriate for Level 4, while others are best for Level 3. Table 3-1 shows the most appropriate type of data for a specific method. Follow-up surveys, observations, interviews, and focus groups are best suited for Level 3 data, sometimes exclusively. Performance monitoring, action planning, and questionnaires can easily capture Level 4 data.

Participants' Time for Data Input

Another important factor in selecting the data collection method is the amount of time that participants must spend with the data collection and evaluation systems. Time requirements should always be minimized, and the method should be positioned so that it is value-added activity (i.e., the participants understand that this activity is something they perceive as valuable so they will not resist). This requirement often means that sampling is used to keep the total participant time to a reasonable amount. Some methods, such as performance monitoring, require no participant time, while others such as interviews and focus groups, require a significant investment in time.

Supervisory Time for Data Input

The time that a participant's direct supervisor must allocate to data collection is another important issue in the method selection. This time

Table 3-1
Collecting Post Program Data: The Methods

	Level 3	Level 4
❑ Follow-Up Surveys	✓	
❑ Follow-Up Questionnaires	✓	✓
❑ Observation On the Job	✓	
❑ Interviews with Participants	✓	
❑ Follow-Up Focus Groups	✓	
❑ Program Assignments	✓	✓
❑ Action Planning	✓	✓
❑ Performance Contracting	✓	✓
❑ Program Follow-Up Session	✓	✓
❑ Performance Monitoring		✓

requirement should always be minimized. Some methods, such as performance contracting, may require much involvement from the supervisor prior to and after the program. Other methods, such as questionnaires administered directly to participants, may not require any supervisor time.

Cost of Method

Cost is always a consideration when selecting the method. Some data collection methods are more expensive than others. For example, interviews and observations are very expensive. Surveys, questionnaires, and performance monitoring are usually inexpensive.

Disruption of Normal Work Activities

Another key issue in selecting the appropriate method, and perhaps the one that generates the most concern with managers, is the amount of disruption the data collection will create. Routine work processes should be disrupted as little as possible. Some data collection techniques, such as performance monitoring, require very little time and distraction from normal activities. Questionnaires generally do not disrupt the work environment, and can often be completed in only a few minutes, or even after normal work hours. On the other extreme, some items such as observations and interviews may be too disruptive for the work unit.

Accuracy of Method

The accuracy of the technique is another factor when selecting the method. Some data collection methods are more accurate than others. For example, performance monitoring is usually very accurate; whereas, questionnaires can be distorted and unreliable. If actual on-the-job behavior must be captured, observation is clearly one of the most accurate processes.

Utility of an Additional Method

Because there are many different methods to collect data, it is tempting to use too many data collection methods. Multiple data collection methods add to the time and costs of the evaluation and may result in very little additional value. Utility refers to the added value of the use of an additional data collection method. As more than one method is used, this question should always be addressed. Does the value obtained from the additional data warrant the extra time and expense of the method? If the answer is no, the additional method should not be implemented.

Cultural Bias for Data Collection Method

The culture or philosophy of the organization can dictate which data collection methods are used. For example, some organizations are accustomed to using questionnaires and find the process to fit well within their culture. Some organizations will not use observation because their culture does not support the potential "invasion of privacy" associated with it.

Summary

This chapter has provided an overview of ten data collection approaches that can be used in the ROI analysis. A variety of options are available, which can usually match any budget or situation. Some methods are gaining more acceptance for ROI calculations. In addition to performance monitoring, follow-up questionnaires and action plans, as described in this chapter, are regularly used to collect data for an ROI analysis. Other methods can be helpful to develop a complete picture of on-the-job application of the training and subsequent business impact.

Case Study - Part B
National Auto Products Company

Needs Assessment

An improper or inadequate needs assessment may result in a program designed around unnecessary skills. This specific needs assessment was conducted at Level 4 (organization needs), Level 3 (on-the-job behavior deficiencies), and Level 2 (skill and knowledge deficiencies). Without a multiple level needs assessment, it would be more difficult to evaluate the program for on-the-job behavior changes (Level 3) and business impact (Level 4). Thus, the needs assessment became a very critical issue for identifying performance deficiencies at all three levels and was an important component in NAPCo's plan to train supervisors.

Performance Measures

The needs assessment identified several performance areas where improvement was needed, all related to inadequate skills. These included the following data items:

- productivity of the work units, measured by the percentage of shipments met;
- quality, measured by the number of rejects per million units of production;
- employee turnover; and
- absenteeism.

There was some skepticism among management that productivity could be enhanced significantly by the training, although most of the supervisors agreed that they could boost productivity with applications of the proper skills. Quality could be improved by keeping employees more focused on quality standards and processes. Employee turnover was very high and, although there were many factors that influenced turnover, most supervisors felt that turnover was a variable under their control. Finally, absenteeism was extremely high, particularly on second shifts and on Mondays and Fridays.

NAPCo had developed an adequate measurement system, which monitored, among other variables, productivity, quality, turnover, and absenteeism measures by the production unit. Each supervisor received absenteeism and turnover data monthly, and productivity and quality measures were available weekly for the production departments. Support departments can significantly influence the measures by providing excellent support and assistance.

Top management approved the program proposal including the structure and timing.

Evaluation Levels

Because NAPCo management was interested in the accountability of training, and the consulting firm was eager to show results of training, both parties were anxious to conduct an ROI evaluation for this project. ROI data can be very convincing for marketing a program to other groups. With this approach, Level 4 data would be collected, converted to monetary values, and compared to the program cost to develop the ROI (Level 5). When Level 4 data was collected, data would also be collected at Levels 2 and 3 to assess learning and on-the-job applications. Also, since this was a new program, a Level 1 evaluation was necessary. Thus, all five levels of evaluation were pursued.

There was another important reason for evaluating this program at all five levels. Because this program is linked to key organizational measures, a success would show a direct linkage to the company's bottom-line. A significant payoff to the company would clearly show management that training is a high impact process and that it can make a difference by improving important business performance measures.

Objectives

Because Level 3 and 4 data must be collected, it is essential that specific objectives be measurable and directly related to the Level 3 and 4 data obtained from the needs assessment. Therefore, program objectives were revised to include the following. After attending this program, participants should be able to:

- Describe and identify applications for two motivational models.
- Describe and identify applications for two leadership models.
- Set measurable performance goals each month for each employee.
- Apply performance feedback skills each day with each employee.
- Reduce employee turnover from an average annual rate of 29% to 25% in four months.
- Reduce absenteeism from a weekly average of 5% to 3% in four months.
- Improve quality by 2 parts per million in four months.
- Increase productivity by 2 percentage points in four months.

The specific targets were difficult to develop and required the complete cooperation of the plant manager and the department heads. The principal consultant admitted that it was rare for the client to be willing to suggest specific targets for improvements within a specific time frame.

Discussion Questions

1. What is your reaction to these measures? Do you think each measure could be influenced by this program?
2. What are the recommended post-program data collection methods?
3. Complete the data collection plan for evaluation (see Figure 3-3.)

References

[1] Phillips, J. J., How Much is the Training Worth? *Training and Development*, Vol. 50, No. 4, 1996, pp. 20-24.

[2] Phillips, J. J., Was it the Training? *Training and Development*, Vol. 50, No. 3, March 1996, pp. 28-32.

Program: _____   Responsibility: _____   Date: _____

Evaluation Plan: Data Collection

Level	Objective(s)	Evaluation Method	Timing	Responsibilities
I Reaction, Satisfaction and Planned Actions				
II Learning				
III Job Application				
IV Business Results				

Figure 3-3. *Evaluation plan: data collection*

4

ISOLATING THE EFFECTS OF TRAINING

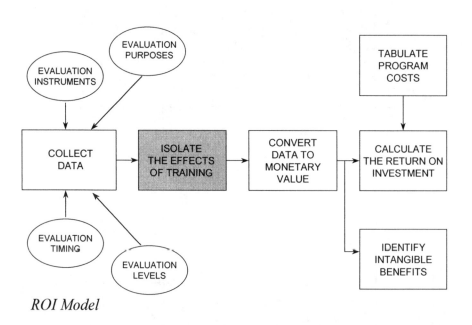

ROI Model

The following situation is repeated often. A significant increase in performance is noted after a major training program was conducted and the two events appear to be linked. A key manager asks, "How much of this improvement was caused by the training program?" When this potentially embarrassing question is asked, it is rarely answered with any degree of accuracy and credibility. While the change in performance may be linked to the training program, other non-training factors usually have contributed to the improvement. As depicted in the model above, this chapter explores ten useful strategies to isolate the effects of training. These strategies are utilized in some of the best organizations as they attempt to measure the return on investment in training and development. Portions of this chapter were first published in one of the HRD field's leading publications.[1]

The cause and effect relationship between training and performance can be very confusing and difficult to prove, but can be accomplished with an acceptable degree of accuracy. The challenge is to develop one or more specific strategies to isolate the effects of training early in the process, usually as part of an evaluation plan. Upfront attention ensures that appropriate strategies will be utilized with minimum costs and time commitments.

Preliminary Issues

Chain of Impact

Before presenting the strategies, it is helpful to examine the chain of impact implied in the different levels of evaluation. Measurable results achieved from a training program should be derived from the application of skills/knowledge on the job over a specified period of time after a program has been conducted. This on-the-job application of training is referred to as Level 3 in the five evaluation levels described in Chapter 2 and reported elsewhere.[2] Continuing with this logic, successful application of program material on-the-job should stem from participants learning new skills or acquiring new knowledge in the training program, which is measured as a Level 2 evaluation. Therefore, for a business results improvement (Level 4 evaluation), this chain of impact implies that measurable on-the-job applications are realized (Level 3 evaluation) and new knowledge and skills are learned (Level 2 evaluation). Without this preliminary evidence, it is difficult to isolate the effects of training. In other words, if there is no learning or application of the material on-the-job, it is virtually impossible to conclude that any performance improvements were caused by the training program. This chain of impact requirement with the different levels of evaluation is supported in the literature.[3] From a practical standpoint, this issue requires data collection at four levels for an ROI calculation. If data is collected on business results, it should also be collected for other levels of evaluation to ensure that the training program helped to produce the business results. This approach is consistent with the practice in leading organizations' participation in ASTD's benchmarking project, where it was reported that most organizations collecting Level 4 data on business results also collected data at the previous three levels.[4] While this requirement is a prerequisite to isolating the effects of training, it does not prove that there was a direct connection nor does it pinpoint how much of the improvement was caused by training. It merely shows that without improvements at previous levels, it is difficult to make a connection between the ultimate outcome and the training program.

Identifying Other Factors: A First Step

As a first step in isolating training's impact on performance, all of the key factors which may have contributed to the performance improvement should be identified. This step communicates to interested parties that other factors may have influenced the results, underscoring that the training program is not the sole source of improvement. Consequently, the credit for improvement is shared with several possible variables and sources, an approach that is likely to gain the respect of management.

Several potential sources identify major influencing variables. If the program is designed on request, the client may be able to identify factors that will influence the output variable. The client will usually be aware of other initiatives or programs that may impact the output.

Program participants are usually aware of other influences which may have caused performance improvement. After all, it is the impact of their collective efforts that is being monitored and measured. In many situations, they witness previous movements in the performance measures and pinpoint the reasons for changes.

Program analysts and developers are another source for identifying variables that have an impact on results. The needs analysis will usually uncover these influencing variables. Program designers usually analyze these variables while addressing the training transfer issue.

In some situations, participants' supervisors may be able to identify variables that influence the performance improvement. This is particularly useful when training program participants are non-exempt employees (operatives) who may not be fully aware of the variables that can influence performance.

Finally, middle and top management may be able to identify other influences based on their experience and knowledge of the situation. Perhaps they have monitored, examined, and analyzed the variables previously. The authority positions of these individuals often increase the credibility of the data.

Taking time to focus attention on variables that may have influenced performance brings additional accuracy and credibility to the process. It moves beyond the scenario where results are presented with no mention of other influences, a situation which often destroys the credibility of a training impact report. It also provides a foundation for some of the strategies described in this book by identifying the variables that must be isolated to show the effects of training. A word of caution is appropriate here. Halting the process after this step would leave many unknowns about actual training impact and might leave a negative impression with management, since it may have identified variables that management did not previously consider. Therefore, it is recommended that the HRD staff go beyond this initial step and utilize one or more of the ten strategies that isolate the impact of training - the focus of this chapter.

Use of Control Groups

The most accurate approach to isolate the impact of training is the use of control groups in an experimental design process.[5] This approach involves the use of an experimental group that attends training and a control group that does not. The composition of both groups should be as identical as possible and, if feasible, the selection of participants for each group should be on a random basis. When this is possible and both groups are subjected to the same environmental influences, the difference in the performance of the two groups can be attributed to the training program.

As illustrated in Figure 4-1, the control group and experimental group do not necessarily have pre-program measurements. Measurements are taken after the program and the difference in the performance of the two groups shows the amount of improvement that is directly related to the training program.

Control group arrangements appear in many settings. A recent review cited a Federal Express company's ROI analysis which used control groups, as a good example of the state of the art in measuring ROI.[6] The study focused on 20 employees who went through an intense, redesigned two-week training program soon after being hired to drive company vans. Their performance was compared

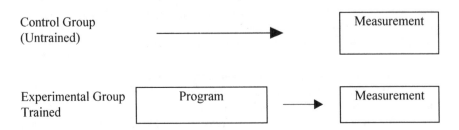

Figure 4-1. *Post-test only, control group design*

with a control group of 20 other new hires whose managers were told to do no more or less on-the-job training than they normally would do. Performance was tracked for the two groups for 90 days in categories such as accidents, injuries, time-card errors, and domestic air-bill errors. The ten performance categories were assigned dollar values by experts from engineering, finance, and other groups. The program demonstrated that the performance of the highly trained employees was superior (resulting in a 24% return on investment) to that of the group which did not receive the upgraded training.

One caution to keep in mind is that the use of control groups may create an image that the HRD staff is creating a laboratory setting, which can cause a problem for some executives. To avoid this stigma, some organizations run a pilot program using pilot participants as the experimental group and not informing the non-participating control group. Another example will illustrate this approach. An international specialty manufacturing company developed a program for its customer service representatives who sell directly to the public.[7] The program was designed to improve selling skills and to produce higher levels of sales. Previously, sales skills acquisition was informal, on-the-job, by trial and error. The HRD manager was convinced that formal training would significantly increase sales. Management was skeptical and wanted proof, a familiar scenario. The program was pilot-tested by teaching the art of selling to 16 customer service representatives randomly selected from the 32 most recently hired. The remaining 16 served as a control group and did not receive training. Prior to training, performance was measured using average daily sales (sales divided by number of days) for 30 days (or length of service, if shorter) for each of the two groups. After training, the average daily sales were recorded for another 30 days. A significant difference in the sales of the two groups emerged, and because the groups were almost identical and were subjected to the same environmental influences, it was concluded that the sales differences were a result of training and not other factors. In this setting, pilot testing allowed the use of a control group without the publicity and potential criticism that is typical using control groups.

The control group process does have some inherent problems that may make it difficult to apply in practice. The first major problem is the selection of the groups. From a practical perspective it is virtually impossible to have identical control and experimental groups. Dozens of factors can affect employee performance, some of them individual and others contextual. To tackle the issue on a practical basis, it is best to select two or three variables that will have the greatest influence on performance. For example, in an interactive selling skills program in a retail store chain, three groups were trained and their performances were compared to three similar groups, which were the control groups. The selection of the particular groups was based on three variables store executives thought would influence performance most from one store to another: actual market area, store size, and customer traffic. Although there are other factors which could influence performance, these three variables were used to make the selection.

Another problem is contamination, which can develop when participants in the training program actually teach others who are in the control group. Sometimes the reverse situation occurs when members of the control group model the behavior from the trained group. In either case, the experiment becomes contaminated as the influence of training is passed on to the control group. This can be minimized by ensuring that control groups and experimental groups are at different locations, have different shifts, or are on different floors in the same building. When this is not possible, sometimes it is helpful to explain to both groups that one group will receive training now and another will receive training at a later date. Also, it may be helpful to appeal to the sense of responsibility of those being trained and ask them not to share the information with others.

A third problem occurs when the different groups function under different environmental influences. Because they may be in different locations, the groups may have different environmental influences. Sometimes the selection of the groups can help prevent this problem from occurring. Also, using more groups than necessary and discarding those with some environmental differences is another tactic.

A fourth problem with using control groups is that it may appear to be too research oriented for most business organizations. For example, management may not want to take the time to experiment before proceeding with a program or they may not want to withhold training from any group just to measure the impact of an experimental program. Because of this concern, some HRD practitioners do not entertain the idea of using control groups. When the process is used, however, some organizations conduct it with pilot participants as the experimental group and non-participants as the control group. Under this arrangement, the control group is not informed of their control group status.

Because this is an effective approach for isolating the impact of training, it should be considered as a strategy when a major ROI impact study is planned. In these situations it is important for the program impact to be isolated to a high level of accuracy; the primary advantage of the control group process is accuracy.

Trend Line Analysis

Another useful technique for approximating the impact of training is trend line analysis. With this approach, a trend line is drawn, using previous performance as a base, and extending the trend into the future. When training is conducted, actual performance is compared to the trend line. Any improvement of performance over what the trend line predicted can then be reasonably attributed to training. While this is not an exact process, it provides a reasonable estimation of the impact of training.

Figure 4-2 shows an example of this trend line analysis taken from a shipping department of a large distribution company. The percent reflects the level of actual shipments compared to scheduled shipments. Data is presented before and after a team training program which was conducted in July. As shown in the figure, there was an upward trend on the data prior to conducting the training program. Although the program apparently had a dramatic effect on shipment productivity, the trend line shows that improvement would have continued anyway, based on the trend that had been previously established. It is tempting to measure the improvement by comparing the average six-months shipments prior to the program (87.3%) to the average of six months after the program (94.4%) yielding a 6.9% difference However, a more accurate comparison is the six month average after the program compared to the trend line (92.3%). In this example, the difference is 2.1%. Using this more modest measure increases the accuracy and credibility of the process to isolate the impact of the program.

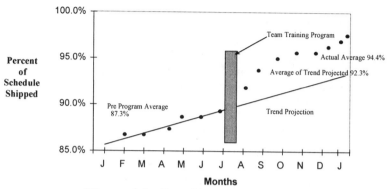

Figure 4-2. *Trend line analysis example*

The trend line, projected directly from the historical data using a straightedge, may be acceptable. If additional accuracy is needed, the trend line can be projected with a simple computer program, available in many calculators and software packages.

A primary disadvantage of this trend-line approach is that it is not always accurate. The use of this approach assumes that the events which influenced the performance variable prior to the program are still in place after the program, except for the implementation of the training program (i.e., the trends that were established prior to training will continue in the same relative direction.) Also, it assumes that no new influences entered the situation at the time training was conducted. This may not always be the case.

The primary advantage of this approach is that it is simple and inexpensive. If historical data are available, a trend line can quickly be drawn and differences estimated. While not exact, it does provide a very quick assessment of training's impact.

Forecasting Methods

A more analytical approach to trend line analysis is forecasting methods which predict a change in performance variables. This approach represents a mathematical interpretation of the trend line analysis discussed above when other variables entered the situation at the time of training. A linear model, in the form of $y = ax + b$, is appropriate when only one other variable influences the output performance and that relationship is characterized by a straight line.

Instead of drawing the straight line, a linear equation is developed, which calculates a value of the anticipated performance improvement.

An example will help explain the application of this process. A large retail store chain implemented a sales training program for sales associates.[8] The three-day program was designed to enhance sales skills and prospecting techniques. The application of the skills should increase the sales volume for each sales associate. An important measure of the program's success is the sales per employee six months after the program compared to the same measure prior to the program. The average daily sales per employee prior to training, using a one month average, was $1,100 (rounded to the nearest $100). Six months after the program, the average daily sales per employee was $1,500. Two related questions must be answered: Is the difference in these two values attributable to the training program? Did other factors influence the actual sales level?

After reviewing potential influencing factors with several store executives only one factor, the level of advertising, appeared to have changed significantly during the period under consideration. When reviewing the previous sales per employee data and the level of advertising, a direct relationship appeared to exist. As expected, when advertising expenditures were increased, the sales per employee increased proportionately.

Using the historical values to develop a simple linear model yielded the following relationship between advertising and sales: $y = 140 + 40x$, where y is the daily sales per employee and x is the level of advertising expenditures per week (divided by 1,000). This equation was developed by the marketing department using the method of least squares to derive a mathematical relationship between two variables. This is a routine option on some calculators and is included in many software packages.

The level of weekly advertising expenditures in the month preceding training was $24,000 and the level of expenditures in the sixth month after training was $30,000. Assuming that the other factors possibly influencing sales were insignificant, the store executives determined the impact of the advertising by plugging in the new advertising expenditure amount, 30, for x and calculating the daily sales, which yields $1,340.

Thus, the new sales level caused by the increase in advertising is $1,340, as shown in Figure 4-3. Since the new actual value is $1500, then $160 (i.e., 1500-1340) must be attributed to the training program. Figure 4-4 shows graphically the effect of both the training and advertising.

A major disadvantage with this approach occurs when many variables enter the process. The complexity multiplies and the use of sophisticated statistical

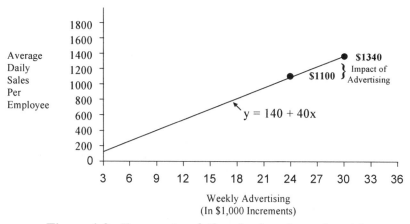

Figure 4-3. *Forecasting daily sales based on advertising*

packages for multiple variable analysis is necessary. Even then, a good fit of the data to the model may not be possible. Unfortunately, some organizations have not developed mathematical relationships for output variables as a function of one or more inputs. Without them, the forecasting method is difficult to utilize.

The primary advantage of this process is that it can accurately predict business performance measures without training, if appropriate data and models are available. The presentation of specific methods is beyond the scope of this book and is contained in other works.[9]

Participant Estimate of Training's Impact

An easily implemented method to isolate the impact of training is to obtain information directly from program participants. The effectiveness of this approach rests on the assumption that participants are capable of determining or estimating how much of a performance improvement is related to the training program. Because their actions have produced the improvement, participants may have very accurate input on the issue. They should know how much of the change was caused by applying what they have learned in the program. Although an estimate, this value will usually have considerable credibility with management because participants are at the center of the change or improvement. Participant estimation is obtained by asking the following series of questions after describing the improvement.

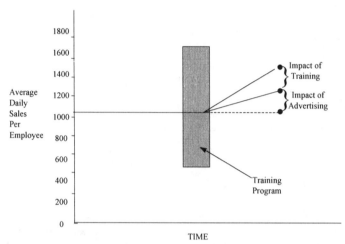

Figure 4-4. *Isolating the impact of training*

Typical Questions to Determine
What percent of this improvement can be attributed to the application of skills/techniques/knowledge gained in the training program?
What is the basis for this estimation?
What confidence do you have in this estimate, expressed as a percent?
What other factors contributed to this improvement in performance?
What other individuals or groups could estimate this percentage or determine the amount?

Table 4-1 illustrates this approach with an example of one participant's estimations.

Participants who do not provide information on these questions are excluded from the analysis. Also, erroneous, incomplete, and extreme information should be discarded before analysis. To be conservative, the confidence percentage can be factored into the values. The confidence percentage is actually a reflection of the error in the estimate. Thus, an 80% confidence level equates to a potential

Table 4-1
Example of a Participant's Estimation

Factor Which Influenced Improvement	Percent of Improvement Caused By	Confidence Expressed as a Percent
1. Training Program	50%	70%
2. Change in Procedures	10%	80%
3. Adjustment in Standards	10%	50%
4. Revision to Incentive Plan	20%	90%
5. Increased Management Attention	10%	50%
6. Other _____	___%	___%
Total	100%	

error range of ± 20%. With this approach, the level of confidence is multiplied by the estimate using the lower side of the range. In the example, the participant allocates 50% of the improvement to the training program, but is only 70% confident about this estimate. The confidence percentage is multiplied by the estimate to develop a usable training factor value of 35%. This adjusted percentage is then multiplied by the actual amount of the improvement (post-program minus pre-program value) to isolate the portion attributed to training. The adjusted improvement is now ready for conversion to monetary values and, ultimately, used in the return on investment.

Perhaps an illustration of this process can reveal its effectiveness and acceptability. In a large global organization, the impact of a leadership program for new managers was being assessed. Because the decision to calculate the impact of training was made after the program had been conducted, the control group arrangement was not feasible as a method to isolate the effects of training. Also, before the program was implemented, no specified Level 4 (business results) data were identified that were linked to the program. Consequently, it was difficult to use trend line analysis. Participants' estimates proved to be the most useful way to estimate the impact. In a detailed follow-up questionnaire, participants were asked a variety of questions regarding the job applications of what was learned from the program. As part of the program, the individuals were asked to develop action plans and implement them, although there was no specific follow-up plan needed. The following series of impact questions provided participants with estimations of the impact:

Impact Questions
How have you and your job changed as the result of attending this program? (Skills and Knowledge Application)
What is the impact of these changes in your work unit? (Specific Measures)
What is the annual value of this change or improvement in your work unit? (Although this is difficult, please make every effort to estimate this value.)
What is the basis for the estimate provided above? (Please indicate the assumptions you made and the specific calculations you performed to arrive at the value.)
What confidence do you place in the estimate above? (100% = Certainty, 0% = No Confidence)
Recognizing that many factors influence output results in addition to training, please estimate the percent of the improvement that is directly related to this program. (It may be helpful to first identify all the other factors first and then provide an estimate of this factor.)

Although this series of questions is challenging, when set up properly and presented to participants in an appropriate way, they can be very effective for collecting impact data. Table 4-2 shows a sample of the calculations from these questions for this particular program.

Although this is an estimate, this approach does have considerable accuracy and credibility. Five adjustments are effectively utilized with this approach to reflect a conservative approach:

1. The individuals who do not respond to the questionnaire or provide usable data on the questionnaire are assumed to have no improvements. This is probably an overstatement since some individuals will have improvements, but not report them on the questionnaire.
2. Extreme data and incomplete, unrealistic, and unsupported claims are omitted from the analysis, although they maybe included in the intangible benefits.
3. Since only annualized values are used, it is assumed that there are no benefits from the program after the first year of implementation. In reality, leadership training should be expected to add value perhaps for several years after training has been conducted.
4. The confidence level, expressed as a percent, is multiplied by the improvement value to reduce the amount of the improvement by the potential error.
5. The improvement amount is adjusted by the amount directly related to training, expressed as a percent.

When presented to senior management, the results of this impact study were perceived to be an understatement of the program's success. The data and the process were considered to be credible and accurate.

As an added enhancement to this method, management may be asked to review and approve the estimates from participants. For example, in an HRD program involving the performance management skills program for Yellow Freight Systems, a large trucking company, participants estimated the amount of savings that should be attributed to the program.[10] A sample of these estimates is shown in Table 4-3. Managers at the next two levels above participants reviewed and approved the estimates. Thus, the managers actually confirmed participants' estimates.

This process has some disadvantages. It is an estimate and, consequently, it does not have the accuracy desired by some HRD managers. Also, the input data may be unreliable since some participants are incapable of providing these types of estimates. They might not be aware of exactly which factors contributed to the results.

Several advantages make this strategy attractive. It is a simple process, easily understood by most participants and by others who review evaluation data. It is inexpensive, takes very little time and analysis, thus results in an efficient addition to the evaluation process. Estimates originate from a credible source; the individuals who actually produced the improvement.

The advantages seem to offset the disadvantages. Isolating the effects of training will never be precise. and this estimate may be accurate enough for most clients and management groups. The process is appropriate when the participants are managers, supervisors, team leaders, sales associates, engineers, and other professional and technical employees.

Supervisor Estimate of Training's Impact

In lieu of, or in addition to, participant estimates, the participants' supervisor may be asked to provide the extent of training's role in producing a performance improvement. In some settings, participants' supervisors may be more familiar with the other factors influencing performance. Consequently, they may be better equipped to provide estimates of impact. The recommended questions to ask supervisors, after describing the improvement caused by the participants, are:

Table 4-2

Sample of Input from Participants in a Leadership Program for New Managers

Participant	Annual Improvement Value	Basis for Value	Confidence	Isolation Factor	Adjusted Value
11	$36,000	Improvement in efficiency of group. $3,000 month x 12 (Group Estimate)	85%	50%	$15,300
42	90,000	Turnover Reduction. Two turnover statistics per year. Base salary x 1.5 = 45,000	90%	40%	32,400
74	24,000	Improvement in customer response time. (8 hours to 6 hours). Estimated value: $2,000/month	60%	55%	7,920
55	$2,000	5% improvement in my effectiveness ($40,500 x 5%)	75%	50%	750
96	$10,000	Absenteeism Reduction (50 absences per year x $200)	85%	75%	6,375
117	$8,090	Team project completed 10 days ahead of schedule. Annual salaries $210,500 = $809 per day x 10 days	90%	45%	3,279
118	159,000	Under budget for the year by this amount	100%	30%	47,700

Typical Questions to Ask Supervisors
What percent of the improvement in performance measures of the participant resulted from the training program?
What is the basis for this estimate?
What is your confidence in this estimate, expressed as a percentage?
What other factors could have contributed to this success?
Please list the factors with the estimates in the table provided.
What other individuals or groups would know about this improvement and could estimate this percentage?

These questions are essentially the same ones described in the participant's questionnaire. Supervisor estimates should be analyzed in the same manner as participant estimates. To be more conservative, actual estimates may be adjusted by the confidence percentage. When participants' estimates have also been collected, the decision of which estimate to use becomes an issue. If there is some compelling reason to think that one estimate is more credible than the other, then it should be used. The most conservative approach is to use the lowest value and include an appropriate explanation. Another potential option is to recognize that each source has its own unique perspective and that an average of the two is appropriate, placing an equal weight on each input. If feasible, it is recommended that inputs be obtained from both participants and supervisors.

An example will illustrate the process for both participant estimates and supervisor estimates. A restaurant chain implemented a training program on performance management for manager trainees. The program teaches participants how to establish measurable goals for employees, provide performance feedback, measure progress toward goals, and how to take action to ensure that goals are met. During the program, each manager trainee developed an action plan for improvement, utilizing the skills taught in the program. As part of the program, managers learned how to convert measurable improvements into an economic value for the restaurant. The action plan could focus on any improvement area as long as it was accompanied with skills acquired in the program and was converted to either cost savings or restaurant profits. Some of the improvement areas were inventory, food spoilage, cash shortages, employee turnover, absenteeism, and productivity.

Table 4-3
Sample of Results from Performance Management Skills

Terminal in Division I	Improvement	Percentage of improvement attributed to performance management skills	Dollar Value*
A	To reduce high cost per bill due to poor planning on pickup and delivery and low sales, manager installed job models and feedback systems, coached supervisors and drivers, and praised all employees for improved performance. Cost per bill decreased an average of $1.30.	25%	6,928 (C)
B	In new terminal with cost per bill running high, manager installed job models and used coaching and rewards for supervisory, clerical, and sales staff. Terminal's profits increased from $43,253 to $49,024.	10%	27,680(R)
C	Terminal had low bill count and high cost per bill. Manager installed job models and feedback systems, and used interpersonal skills. Cost per bill decreased an average of $1.79, over same period before the program.	5%	800(C)
D	Terminal had low bill count, which contributed to a high cost per bill. Manager installed job models and feedback systems, and used rewards and coaching with office staff, supervisors, and sales representatives. Cost per bill decreased an average of $0.92; number of bills increased from 7,765 to 9,405 per month.	25%	9,856(C)
E	Terminal had low bill count and high cost per bill. Manager installed job models and had his sales manager and operations manager install job models, also. All managers used rewards; coaching, and interpersonal skills. Cost per bill decreased from $22.49 to $21.00; number of bills increased from 11,716 to 12,974 per month.	50%	56,060(C)
F	Terminal had rising cost per bill with a fluctuating bill count. Manager used job models and feedback reports. Cost per bill decreased from $17.13 to $15.46; number of bills rose from 6,160 to 7,357 per month.	10%	5,754(C)

(R) indicates a revenue gain; (C) indicates decreased costs.

As part of the follow-up evaluation, each action plan was thoroughly documented showing results in quantitative terms, which were converted to monetary values.   Realizing that other factors could have influenced the improvement, manager trainees were asked to estimate the percent of improvement that resulted from the application of the skills acquired in the training program.   Each manager trainee was asked to be conservative with the estimates. The annual monetary value for each improvement for each participant was calculated.   Independently, restaurant managers (immediate supervisors) were asked to estimate, for each manager trainee, the percent of improvement from the action plan, which should be attributed to the training program. The restaurant managers (who were closely involved in the action planning process for this program) usually are aware of factors that influence costs and profits and usually know how much of an improvement is traceable to the training program. Also, they. The results are shown in Table 4-4.

The estimate of training's impact can be calculated using the conservative approach of selecting the lower value. As an alternative, the average value of the two can be used. The conservative approach yields an overall improvement of $78,905, whereas, the average of the two percentages yields a value of $83,721. Participant 5 did not submit a completed action plan and is discarded from the analysis, although the costs are still included in the ROI calculation.

Another interesting observation emerges from this type of analysis. When the average of the three largest participant improvements is compared with the average of the three smallest values, important information is revealed about the potential for return on investment (in this case, $21,667 compared to $1,947, before adjustments).   If all of the participants focused on high impact improvements, a substantially higher ROI could have been achieved. This can be helpful information for the management group whose support is often critical to the success of programs. While an impressive ROI is refreshing, a potentially much greater ROI is outstanding.

This approach has the same disadvantages as participant estimates. It is subjective and, consequently, may be viewed with skepticism by senior management. Also, supervisors may be reluctant to participate, or be incapable of providing accurate impact estimates. In some cases they may not know about other factors which contributed to the improvement.

The advantages of this approach are similar to the advantages of participant estimation. It is simple and inexpensive and enjoys an acceptable degree of credibility because it comes directly from the supervisors of those individuals who received the training. When combined with participant estimation, the credibility is enhanced considerably. Also, when factored by the level of confidence, its value further increases.

Management Estimate of Training's Impact

In some cases, upper management may estimate the percent of improvement that should be attributed to the training program. For example, in Litton Guidance and Control Systems, the results from a self-directed team process were adjusted by management.[11] After considering additional factors, such as technology, procedures, and process changes, which could have contributed to the improvement, management then applied a subjective factor, in this case 60%, to represent the portion of the results that should be attributed to the training program. The 60% factor was developed in a meeting with top managers and therefore had the benefit of group ownership. While this process is very subjective, the input is received from the individuals who often provide or approve funding for the program. Sometimes their level of comfort with the process is the most important consideration.

Customer Input of Training's Impact

Another helpful approach in some narrowly focused situations is to solicit input on the impact of training directly from customers. In these situations, customers are asked why they chose a particular product or service or to explain how their reaction to the product or service has been influenced by individuals applying skills and abilities learned in a training program. This strategy focuses directly on what the training program is often designed to improve. For example, after a teller training program was conducted following a bank merger, market research data showed that the percentage of customers who were dissatisfied with teller knowledge was reduced by 5% when compared to market survey data before training.[12] Since teller knowledge was increased by training, the 5% reduction of dissatisfied customers was directly attributable to the training program.

In another example, a large real estate company provided a comprehensive training program for agents, focusing on presentation skills. As customers listed

Table 4-4
Estimates of Training Impact from Participants and Supervisors

Participant	Improvement (Dollar Value)	Basis	Percent Estimate from Manager Trainees	Percent Estimate from Store Managers	Conservative Integration	Average Value Integration
1	$5,500	Labor Savings	60%	50%	$2,750	$3,025
2	15,000	Turnover	50%	40%	6,000	6,750
3	9,300	Absenteeism	65%	75%	6,045	6,510
4	2,100	Shortages	90%	80%	1,680	1,785
5	0				----	----
6	29,000	Turnover	40%	50%	11,600	13,050
7	2,241	Inventory	70%	100%	1,569	1,905
8	3,621	Procedures	100%	90%	3,259	3,440
9	21,000	Turnover	75%	70%	14,700	15,225
10	1,500	Food Spoilage	100%	100%	1,500	1,500
11	15,000	Labor Savings	80%	70%	10,500	11,250
12	6,310	Accidents	70%	75%	4,417	4,575
13	14,500	Absenteeism	80%	75%	11,600	11,238
14	3,650	Productivity	100%	90%	3,285	3,468
Total	$128,722				$78,905	$83,721

their homes with an agent, they received a survey, exploring the reasons for deciding to list their home with the company. Among the reasons listed was the presentation skills of the agent. Responses on this question and related questions provided evidence of the percentage of new listings attributed to the training program.

Expert Estimation of Training's Impact

External or internal experts can sometimes estimate the portion of results that can be attributed to training. When using this strategy, experts must be carefully selected based on their knowledge of the process, program, and situation. For example, an expert in quality might be able to provide estimates of how much change in a quality measure can be attributed to training and how much can be attributed to other factors in the implementation of a TQM program.

An example will illustrate this process. Omega Consultants, training providers for the banking industry, implemented sales training programs in a variety of settings. Utilizing control group arrangements, Omega determined that one of their programs will generate a 30% increase in sales volume, three months after implementation. Given this value, implementation should result in a 30% improvement in another financial institution with a similar target audience. Although the situation can vary considerably, this is an approximate value to use in comparison. If more than 30% was achieved, the additional amount could be due to a factor other than training. Experts, consultants, or researchers are usually available for almost any field. They can bring their experience with similar situations into the analysis.

This approach does have disadvantages. It can be inaccurate unless the program and setting in which the estimate is made is very similar to the program in question. Also, this approach may lose credibility because the estimates come from external sources and may not necessarily involve those who are close to the process.

This process has an advantage in that its credibility often reflects the reputation of the expert or independent consultant. It is a quick source of input from a reputable expert or independent consultant. Sometimes top management will place more confidence in external experts than their own internal staff.

Subordinate's Input of Training's Impact

In some situations, the subordinates of the participants being trained can provide input concerning the extent of training's impact. Although they will not usually be able to estimate how much of an improvement can be attributed to the training, they can provide input in terms of what other factors might have contributed to the improvement. This approach is appropriate in programs where leaders, supervisors, and managers are being trained to implement work unit changes or develop new skills for use with employees. Improvements are realized through the utilization of the skills. The supervisor's employees provide input about changes that have occurred since the training was conducted. They help determine the extent to which other factors have changed in addition to supervisor behavior.

Subordinate input is usually obtained through surveys or interviews. When the survey results show significant changes in supervisor behavior after training and no significant change in the general work climate, the improvement in work performance, therefore, must be attributed to the changes in supervisor behavior since other factors remained constant.

An example illustrates this process. In a training program designed to improve performance of work units through enhancing supervisory skills, significant results were obtained at CIGNA, a large insurance company.[13] After the training program was conducted, action plans were developed and the supervisors reported significant improvements in the performance of their work units. To isolate the impact of training, pre and post survey data were taken with the employees to determine the extent of changes in supervisor behavior and the general climate. The survey consisted of 36 likert-type, five point scale items that were used to create seven different indices. Six of these indices measured the supervisor's behavior and the seventh measured general organizational climate for which the supervisor is not necessarily responsible. The survey results showed significant differences in supervisor behavior before and after training. It did not, however, show a significant change in the general climate. Therefore, the improvement in work performance must be attributed to the changes in supervisor behavior, since other factors appeared to remain constant.

This approach has some disadvantages. Data from subordinates is subjective and may be questionable because of the possibility for biased input. Also, in some cases the subordinates may have difficulty in determining changes in the work climate. This approach does offer a useful way to isolate the impact of training from other sources. In some cases, subordinates are aware of the factors that caused changes in their work unit and they can provide input about the magnitude or quantity of these changes. When combined with other methods that isolate impact, this process has increased credibility.

Calculating the Impact of Other Factors

Although not appropriate in all cases, there are some situations where it may be feasible to calculate the impact of factors (other than training) which influenced the improvement and then conclude that training is credited with the remaining portion. In this approach, training takes credit for improvement that cannot be attributed to other factors.

An example will help explain the approach.[14] In a consumer lending program for a large bank, a significant increase in consumer loan volume was generated after a training program was conducted for consumer loan officers. Part of the increase in volume was attributed to training and the remaining was due to the influence of other factors operating during the same time period. Two other factors were identified by the evaluator: A loan officer's production improved with time, and falling interest rates caused an increase in consumer volume.

In regard to the first factor, as loan officers make loans their confidence improves. They use consumer lending policy manuals and gain knowledge and expertise through trial and error. The amount of this factor was estimated by using input from several internal experts in the marketing department.

For the second factor, industry sources were utilized to estimate the relationship between increased consumer loan volume and falling interest rates. These two estimates together accounted for a certain percent of increased consumer loan volume. The remaining improvement was attributed to the training program.

This method is appropriate when the other factors are easily identified and the appropriate mechanisms are in place to calculate their impact on the improvement. In some cases it is just as difficult to estimate the impact of other factors as it is for the impact of the training program, leaving this approach less advantageous. This process can be very credible if the method used to isolate the impact of other factors is credible.

Using the Strategies

With ten strategies available that isolate the impact of training, selecting the most appropriate strategies for the specific program can be difficult. Some strategies are simple and inexpensive, while others are more time consuming and costly. When attempting to make the selection decision, several factors should be considered:

■ feasibility of the strategy,
■ accuracy provided with the strategy,
■ credibility of the strategy with the target audience,
■ specific cost to implement the strategy,
■ the amount of disruption in normal work activities as the strategy is implemented, and
■ participant, staff, and management time needed with the particular strategy.

Multiple strategies or multiple sources for data input should be considered since two sources are usually better than one. When multiple sources are utilized, a conservative method is recommended to combine the inputs. A conservative approach builds acceptance. The target audience should always be provided with explanations of the process and the various subjective factors involved. Multiple sources allow an organization to experiment with different strategies and build confidence with a particular strategy. For example, if management is concerned about the accuracy of participants' estimates, a combination of a control group arrangement and participants' estimates could be attempted to check the accuracy of the estimation process.

It is not unusual for the ROI in training and development to be extremely large. Even when a portion of the improvement is allocated to other factors, the numbers are still impressive in many situations. The audience should understand that, although every effort was made to isolate the impact, it is still a figure that is not precise and may contain error. It represents the best estimate of the impact given the constraints, conditions, and resources available. Chances are it is more accurate than other types of analyzes regularly utilized in other functions within the organization.

Conclusion

This chapter presented a variety of strategies that isolate the effects of training. The strategies represent the most effective approaches to tackle this issue and are utilized by some of the most progressive organizations. Too often results are reported and linked with training without any attempt to isolate the portion of results that can be attributed to training. If the training and development function is to continue to improve its professional image as well as to meet its responsibility for obtaining results, this issue must be addressed early in the process.

Case Study - Part C
National Auto Products Company

Data Collection Plan

The consultant and the HRD Manager decided that the action planning process would be utilized in the follow-up evaluation. Supervisors should know how to develop action plans and their managers should be able to provide assistance and support with the process. The action plan would show how the newly acquired skills are applied to improve productivity, quality, turnover, and absenteeism. A portion of session 5 was planned for a discussion of action plans, and the program facilitator was required to approve the action plan verifying that it meets basic requirements. A model action plan would be provided to help ensure that supervisors understand the process.

Because all of the action plans involve different time frames, each participant was asked to provide a progress report in four months, or in some cases, the completed project. This would provide a snapshot of the performance improvement within that time frame.

After discussions with management, it was felt that within four months supervisors should be able to implement the training program to achieve measurable results. Although a six-month time frame was recommended, senior management indicated that they might want to proceed with the program in other plants before six months and therefore preferred a three-month period. Four months was a compromise.

Although the action plan, by design, collected Level 3 and 4 data, a follow-up questionnaire was planned to gain more evidence of on-the-job behavior change (Level 3). Because Level 4 data was planned for the program, performance data was monitored for a six-month period prior to the program and for a four-month period after the program. Responsibilities for data collection at Levels 1 and 2 usually rest with the facilitator and that was the case here. The plant training coordinator was assigned the responsibility for collecting the questionnaire data (Level 3) and monitoring performance (Level 4). The data collection plan is presented as Figure 4-5.Isolating the Effects of Training.

Isolating the Effects of Training

One of the most important challenges facing program evaluators is determining the specific strategy that isolates the effects of the training program, recognizing that other factors may influence output measures at the same time the program is being conducted. This is one of the most important issues (usually raised by management) when they want to know exactly how much of the results is related specifically to the program.

Discussion Questions
1. What method(s) should be used to isolate the effects of training?
2. Should more than one strategy be used to isolate the effects of training? Please explain.

Program: _____ **Responsibility:** _____ **Date:** _____

Evaluation Plan: Data Collection

Level	Objective(s)	Evaluation Method	Timing	Responsibilities
I. Reaction, Satisfaction and Planned Actions	• Positive Reaction • Improvements • Completed Action Items	• Questionnaire	• During and at the end of program	• Facilitator
II. Learning	• Knowledge of Motivation Models • Knowledge of Leadership Models • Use of Performance Feedback Skills	• Tests • Skill Practices	• During Program	• Facilitator
III. Job Application	• Use of Skills • Monthly Goal Setting	• Questionnaire • Action Plan	• Four Months After Program	• Training Coordinator
IV. Business Results	• Improved Productivity • Improved Quality • Improved Turnover • Improved Absenteeism	• Performance Monitoring • Action Plan	• Monthly • Four Months After Program	• Routine Reports • Training Coordinator

Figure 4-5. *Data Collection Plan*

References

1. Phillips, J.J., "Was it the Training?" *Training and Development*, March 1996, pp. 28-32.

2. Phillips, J., Return on Investment -- Beyond the Four Levels, *Academy of HRD 1995 Conference Proceedings*, E. Holton (Ed.), 1995.

3. Alliger, G.M., and Janak, E.A., "Kirkpatrick's Levels of Training Criteria: Thirty Years Later." *Personnel Psychology*, Vol. 42, 1989, pp. 331-342.

4. Kimmerling, G., "Gather Best Practices", *Training and Development*, September 1993, pp. 28-36.

5. Pine, J., and Tingley, J.C., "ROI of Soft Skills Training", *Training*, February 1993, pp. 55-66.

6. Hassett, J., "Simplifying ROI", *Training*, September 1992, p. 54.

7. This brief example is taken from a case where the company preferred not to be identified.

8. This brief example is taken from a very complicated case. Some of the values have been changed and it has been simplified to enhance the understanding of this process.

9. For additional information, see Makridakis, S., *Forecasting Methods for Management* (5th Ed.). New York, NY: Wiley, 1989.

10. Zigon, J., "Performance Management Training", *In Action: Measuring Return on Investment*, Vol. 1, Phillips, J. J. (Ed.), Alexandria, VA: American Society for Training and Development, 1994, pp. 253-270.

11. Graham, M., Bishop, K., and Birdsong, R., "Self-Directed Work Teams", *In Action: Measuring Return on Investment*, Vol. 1, Phillips, J. J. (Ed.), Alexandria, VA: American Society for Training and Development, 1994, pp. 105-122.

12. Rust, R.T., Zahorik, A.J. and Keiningham, T.L., *Return on Quality: Measuring the Financial Impact of Your Company's Quest for Quality*. Chicago: Probus Publishers, 1994.

13. Kirkpatrick, D.L., "The Bottom Line: CIGNA Corporation," *Evaluating Training Programs*. San Francisco: CA Berrett Koehler, 1994, pp. 190-206.

14. Phillips, J.J., "Measuring ROI in an Established Program", *In Action: Measuring Return on Investment*, Vol. 1, Phillips, J. J. (Ed.), Alexandria, VA: American Society for Training and Development, 1994, pp. 187-197.

5

CONVERTING DATA TO MONETARY BENEFITS

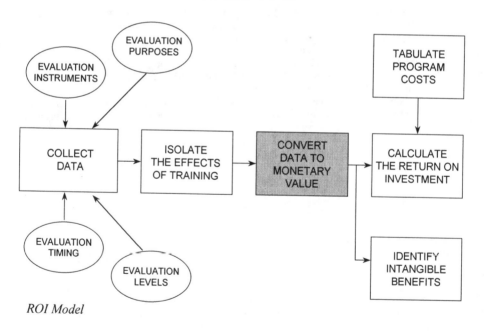

ROI Model

Traditionally, most impact evaluation studies stop with a tabulation of business results, which is a Level 4 evaluation. In those situations, the program is considered successful if it produced improvements such as quality enhancements, reduced absenteeism, or improved customer satisfaction. While these results are important, it is more insightful to compare the value of the results to the cost of the program. This evaluation is the ultimate level of the five-level evaluation framework presented in Chapter 1. This chapter shows how leading organizations are moving beyond tabulating business results (Level 4) to calculating a return on investment (Level 5).

Chapter 2 presented the process of calculating the ROI and Chapter 3 outlined the methods used to collect data. Chapter 4 described a variety of strategies that separate the effects of training from other factors. This chapter outlines techniques that convert data to monetary benefits.

Preliminary Issues

Sorting Out Hard and Soft Data

After collecting performance data, many organizations find it helpful to divide data into hard and soft categories. Hard data are the traditional measures of organizational performance, as they are objective, easy to measure, and easy to convert to monetary values. Hard data are often very common measures, achieve high credibility with management, and are available in every type of organization.

Hard data represent the output, quality, cost, and time of work-related processes. Table 5-1 shows a sampling of typical hard data under these four categories. Almost every department or unit will have hard data performance measures. For example, a government office approving applications for work visas in a foreign country will have these four measures among its overall performance measurement: the number of applications processed (Output), cost per application processed (Cost), the number of errors made processing applications (Quality), and the time it takes to process and approve an application (Time). Ideally, training programs for employees in this unit should be linked to one or more hard data measures.

Table 5-1
Examples of Hard Data

OUTPUT	TIME
Units Produced	Equipment Downtime
Tons Manufactured	Overtime
Items Assembled	On Time Shipments
Items Sold	Time to Project Completion
Forms Processed	Processing Time
Loans Approved	Supervisory Time
Inventory Turnover	Training Time
Patients Visited	Meeting Schedules
Applications Processed	Repair Time
Students Graduated	Efficiency
Productivity	Work Stoppages
Work Backlog	Order Response
Shipments	Late Reporting
New Accounts Opened	Lost Time Days

COSTS	QUALITY
Budget Variances	Scrap
Unit Costs	Waste
Cost By Account	Rejects
Variable Costs	Error Rates
Fixed Costs	Rework
Overhead Costs	Shortages
Operating Costs	Product Defects
Number of Cost Reductions	Deviation From Standard
Project Cost Savings	Product Failures
Accident Costs	Inventory Adjustments
Program Costs	Time Card Corrections
Sales Expense	Percent of Tasks Completed Properly
	Number of Accidents

Because many training programs are designed to develop soft skills, soft data are needed in evaluation. Soft data are usually subjective, sometimes difficult to measure, almost always difficult to convert to monetary values, and behaviorally oriented. When compared to hard data, soft data are usually less credible as a performance measure.

Soft data items can be grouped into several categories; Table 5-2 shows one such grouping. Measures such as employee turnover, absenteeism, and grievances appear as soft data items, not because they are difficult to measure, but because it is difficult to accurately convert them to monetary values.

Table 5-2
Examples of Soft Data

WORK HABITS	NEW SKILLS
Absenteeism	Decisions Made
Tardiness	Problems Solved
Visits to the Dispensary	Conflicts Avoided
First Aid Treatments	Grievances Resolved
Violations of Safety Rules	Counseling Success
Number of Communication Break-	Listening
downs	Reading Speed
Excessive Breaks	Intention to Use New Skills
Follow-Up	Frequency of Use of New Skills

WORK CLIMATE	DEVELOPMENT/ADVANCEMENT
Number of Grievances	Number of Promotions
Number of Discrimination Charges	Number of Pay Increases
Employee Complaints	Number of Training Programs Attended
Job Satisfaction	Requests for Transfer
Employee Turnover	Performance Appraisal Ratings
Litigation	Increases in Job Effectiveness

ATTITUDES	INITIATIVE
Favorable Reactions	Implementation of New Ideas
Attitude Changes	Successful Completion of Projects
Perceptions of Job Responsibilities	Number of Suggestions Implemented
Perceived Changes in Performance	Setting Goals and Objectives
Employee Loyalty	
Increased Confidence	

General Steps to Convert Data

Before describing the specific strategies to convert either hard or soft data to monetary values, the general steps used to convert data in each strategy are briefly summarized. These steps should be followed for each data conversion.

Focus on a unit of measure. First, identify a unit of improvement. For output data, the unit of measure is the item produced, service provided, or sale consummated. Time measures are varied and include items such as the time to complete a project, cycle time, or customer response time. The unit is usually expressed as minutes, hours, or days. Quality is a common measure, and the unit may be one error, reject, defect, or rework item. Soft data measures are varied, and the unit of improvement may include items such as a grievance, an absence, an employee turnover statistic, or a one point change in the customer satisfaction index.

Determine a value of each unit. Place a value (V) on the unit identified in the first step. For measures of production, quality, cost, and time, the process is relatively easy. Most organizations have records or reports reflecting the value of items such as one unit of production or the cost of a defect. Soft data are more difficult to convert to a value, as the cost of one absence, one grievance, or a one point change in the employee attitude survey is often difficult to pinpoint. The ten strategies in this chapter provide an array of techniques to make this conversion. When more than one value is available, either the most credible or the lowest value is used.

Calculate the change in performance data. Calculate the change in output data after the effects of training have been isolated from other influences. The change (ΔP) is the performance improvement, measured as hard or soft data, that is directly attributable to a training program. The value may represent the performance improvement for an individual, a team, a group or several groups of participants.

Determine an annual amount for the change. Annualize the ΔP value to develop a total change in the performance data for one year. This procedure has become a standard approach with many organizations that wish to capture the total benefits of a training program. Although the benefits may not be realized at the same level for an entire year, some programs will continue to produce benefits beyond one year. Therefore, using one year of benefits is considered a conservative approach.

Calculate the total value of the improvement. Develop the total value of improvement by multiplying the annual performance change (ΔP) by the unit value (V) for the complete group in question. For example, if one group of participants for a program is being evaluated, the total value will include total improvement for all participants in the group. This value for annual program benefits is then compared to the cost of the program, usually through the return on investment formula presented in Chapter 1.

Strategies for Converting Data to Monetary Values

An example taken from a team building program at a manufacturing plant describes the five-step process of converting data to monetary values. This program was developed and implemented after a needs assessment revealed that a lack of teamwork was causing an excessive number of grievances. Thus, the actual number of grievances resolved at Step two in the grievance process was selected as an output measure. Table 5-3 shows the steps taken to assign a monetary value to the data arrived at a total program impact of $546,000.

Ten strategies are available to convert data to monetary values. Some strategies are appropriate for a specific type of data or data category, while other strategies can be used with virtually any type of data. The HRD staff's challenge is to select the particular strategy that best matches the type of data and situation. Each strategy is presented next, beginning with the most credible approach.

Converting Output Data to Contribution

When a training program has produced a change in output, the value of the increased output can usually be determined from the organization's accounting or operating records. For organizations operating on a profit basis, this value is usually the marginal profit contribution of an additional unit of production or unit of service provided. For example, a production team in a major appliance manufacturer is able to boost production of small refrigerators with a series of comprehensive training programs. The unit of improvement, therefore, is the profit margin of one refrigerator. In organizations that are performance rather than profit driven, this value is usually reflected in the savings accumulated when

Table 5-3

An Example to Illustrate Steps to Convert Data to Monetary Values

Setting:	Team building Program in a Manufacturing Plant
Step 1	Focus on a Unit of Improvement. One grievance reaching Step two in the four step grievance resolution process.
Step 2	Determine a Value of Each Unit. Using internal experts, the labor relations staff, the cost of an average grievance was estimated to be $6500 when considering time and direct costs. (V = $6500)
Step 3	Calculate the Change in Performance Data Six months after the program was completed, total grievances per month reaching Step two declined by ten. Seven of the ten grievance reductions were related to the program as determined by supervisors (Isolating the Effects of Training).
Step 4	Determine an Annual Amount for the Change. Using the six month value, 7 per month, yields an annual improvement of 84 ($\Delta P=84$)
Step 5	Calculate the Annual Value of the Improvement Annual Value = ΔP times V = 84 times $6500 = $546,000

an additional unit of output is realized for the same input requirements. For example, in a visa section of a government office, an additional visa application is processed at no additional cost. Thus, an increase in output translates into a cost savings equal to the unit cost of processing a visa.

The formulas and calculations used to measure this contribution depend on the organization and its records. Most organizations have this type of data readily available for performance monitoring and goal setting. Managers often use marginal cost statements and sensitivity analyses to pinpoint the value associated with changes in output. If the data are not available, the HRD staff must initiate or coordinate the development of appropriate values.

In one case involving a commercial bank, a sales seminar for consumer loan officers was conducted that resulted in additional consumer loan volume (output).[1] To measure the return on investment in the training program, it was necessary to calculate the value (profit contribution) of one additional consumer loan. This was a relatively easy item to calculate from the bank's records. As shown in Table 5-4, several components went into this calculation.

Table 5-4
Loan Profitability Analysis

Profit Component	Unit Value
Average loan size	$15,500
Average loan yield	9.75%
Average cost of funds (including branch costs)	5.50%
Direct costs for consumer lending	0.82%
Corporate overhead	1.61%
Net Profit Per Loan	**1.82%**

The first step was to determine the yield, which was available from bank records. Next, the average spread between the cost of funds and the yield received on the loan was calculated. For example, the bank could obtain funds from depositors at 5.5% on average, including the cost of operating the branches. The direct costs of making the loan, such as salaries of employees directly involved in consumer lending and advertising costs for consumer loans, had to be subtracted from this difference. Historically, these direct costs amounted to 0.82% of the loan value. To cover overhead costs for other corporate functions, an additional 1.61% was subtracted from the value. The remaining 1.82% of the average loan value represented the bank's profit margin on a loan.

Calculating the Cost of Quality

Quality is a critical issue, and its cost is an important measure in most manufacturing and service firms. Since many training programs are designed to improve quality, the HRD staff must place a value on the improvement in certain quality measures. For some quality measures, the task is easy. For example, if quality is measured with a defect rate, the value of the improvement is the cost to repair or replace the product. The most obvious cost of poor quality is the scrap or waste generated by mistakes. Defective products, spoiled raw materials, and discarded paperwork are all the results of poor quality. This scrap and waste translates directly into a monetary value. For example, in a production environment, the cost of a defective product is the total cost incurred to the point the mistake is identified minus the salvage value.

Employee mistakes and errors can cause expensive rework. The most costly rework occurs when a product is delivered to a customer and must be returned for correction. The cost of rework includes both labor and direct costs. In some organizations, the cost of rework can be as much as 35% of operating costs.[2] In one example of a program involving customer service training for dispatchers in an oil company, a measure of rework is the number of pullouts[3]. A pullout occurs when a delivery truck cannot fill an order for fuel at a service station. The truck returns to the terminal for an adjustment to the order. The average cost of the pullout is developed by tabulating the cost of a sample of actual pullouts. The cost elements include driver time involved, the cost of the truck, the cost of terminal use, and an estimate of administrative costs.

Perhaps the costliest element of poor quality is customer and client dissatisfaction. In some cases, serious mistakes can result in lost business. Customer dissatisfaction is difficult to quantify, and attempts to arrive at a monetary value may be impossible using direct methods. Usually the judgment and expertise of sales, marketing, or quality managers are the best sources by which to try to measure the impact of dissatisfaction. A growing number of quality experts are now measuring customer and client dissatisfaction with market surveys.[4] However, other strategies discussed in this chapter may be more appropriate to measure the cost of customer dissatisfaction.

Converting Employee Time

Reduction in employee time is a common objective for training programs. In a team environment, a program could enable the team to perform tasks in a shorter time frame, or with fewer people. On an individual basis, time management workshops are designed to help professional, sales, supervisory, and managerial employees save time in performing daily tasks. The value of the time saved is an important measure of the program's success, and this conversion is a relatively easy process.

The most obvious time savings are from labor reduction costs in performing work. The monetary savings is found by multiplying the hours saved times the labor cost per hour. For example, after attending a time management training program called Priority Manager, participants estimated that each saves an average of 74 minutes per day, worth \$31.25 per day or \$7,500 per year.[5] This time savings was based on the average salary plus benefits for the typical participant.

The average wage with a percent added for employee benefits will suffice for most calculations. However, employee time may be worth more. For example, additional costs in maintaining an employee (office space, furniture, telephone, utilities, computers, secretarial support, and other overhead expenses) could be included in the average labor cost. Thus, the average wage rate may quickly escalate to a large number. However, the conservative approach is to use the salary plus employee benefits.

In addition to the labor cost per hour, other benefits can result from a time savings. These include improved service, avoidance of penalties for late projects, and the creation of additional opportunities for profit. These values can be estimated using other methods discussed in this chapter.

A word of caution is in order when the time savings are developed. Time savings is only realized when the amount of time saved translates into a cost reduction or profit contribution. If a training program results in a savings in manager time, a monetary value is realized only if the manager used the additional time in a productive way. If a team-based program generates a new process that eliminates several hours of work each day, the actual savings will be realized only if there is a cost savings from a reduction in employees or a reduction in overtime pay. Therefore, an important preliminary step in developing time savings is to determine if a "true" savings will be realized.

Using Historical Costs

Sometimes historical records contain the value of a measure in and reflect the cost (or value) of a unit of improvement. This strategy involves identifying the appropriate records and tabulating the actual cost components for the item in question. For example, a large construction firm implemented a training program to improve safety performance. The program improved several safety-related performance measures, ranging from OSHA fines to total worker compensation costs. Examining the company's records using one year of data, the HRD staff calculated the average cost for each safety measure.

Historical data are usually available for most hard data. Unfortunately, this is generally not true for soft data, and other strategies, explained in this chapter, must be employed to convert the data to monetary values.

Using Internal and External Experts' Input

When faced with converting soft data items for which historical records are not available, it might be feasible to consider input from experts on the processes. With this approach, internal experts provide the cost (or value) of one unit of improvement. Those individuals who have knowledge of the situation and the respect of the management group are often the best prospects for expert input. These experts must understand the processes and be willing to provide estimates as well as the assumptions used in arriving at the estimate. When requesting input from these individuals, it is best to explain the full scope of what is needed, providing as many specifics as possible. Most experts have their own methodology to develop this value.

An example will help clarify this approach. In one manufacturing plant, a teambuilding program was designed to reduce the number of grievances filed at Step 2 (See Table 3). This is the step in which the grievance is recorded in writing and becomes a measurable soft data item. Except for the actual cost of settlements and direct external costs, the company had no records of the total costs of grievances (i.e., there were no data for the time required to resolve a grievance). Therefore, an estimate was needed from an expert. The manager of labor relations, who had credibility with senior management and thorough knowledge of the grievance process, provided an estimate of the cost. He based his estimate on the average settlement when a grievance was lost, the direct costs related to the grievances (arbitration, legal fees, printing, research), the estimated amount of supervisory, staff, and employee time associated with the grievance, and a factor for reduced morale. This internal estimate, although not a precise figure, was appropriate for this analysis and had adequate credibility with management.

When internal experts are not available, external experts are sought. External experts must be selected based on their experience with the unit of measure. Fortunately, many experts are available who work directly with important measures such as employee attitudes, customer satisfaction, turnover, absenteeism, and grievances. They are often willing to provide estimates of the cost (or value) of these items. Because the credibility of the value is directly related to his or her reputation, the credibility and reputation of the expert are critical.

Using Values from External Databases

For some soft data items, it may be appropriate to use estimates of the cost (or value) of one unit based on the research of others. This strategy taps external databases which contain studies and research projects focusing on the cost of data items. Fortunately, many databases are available which report cost studies of a variety of data items related to training programs. Data are available on the cost of turnover, absenteeism, grievances, accidents, and even customer satisfaction. The difficulty lies in finding a database with studies or research efforts for a situation similar to the program under evaluation. Ideally, the data would come from a similar setting in the same industry, but that is not always possible. Sometimes data on all industries or organizations would be sufficient, perhaps with an adjustment to fit the industry under consideration.

An example illustrates the use of this process. An HRD program was designed to reduce turnover of branch managers in a financial services company.[6] To complete the evaluation and calculate the ROI, the cost of turnover was needed. To develop the turnover value internally, several costs would have to be identified, including the cost of recruiting, employment processing, orientation, training new managers, lost productivity while a new manager is trained, quality problems, scheduling difficulties, and customer satisfaction problems. Additional costs include regional manager time to work with the turnover issues and, in some cases, exit costs of litigation, severance, and unemployment. Obviously, these costs are significant. Most HRD managers do not have the time to calculate the cost of turnover, particularly when it is needed for a one-time event such as evaluating a training program. In this example, turnover cost studies in the same industry placed the value at about one-and-a-half times the average annual salaries of the employees. Most turnover cost studies report the cost of turnover as a multiple of annual base salaries. In this example, management decided to be conservation and adjusted the value downward to equal the average base salary of branch managers.

Using Estimates from Participants

In some situations, program participants estimate the value of a soft data improvement. This strategy is appropriate when participants are capable of providing estimates of the cost (or value) of the unit of measure improved by applying the skills learned in the program. When using this approach, participants should be provided with clear instructions, along with examples of the type of information needed. The advantage of this approach is that the individuals closest to the improvement are often capable of providing the most reliable estimates of its value.

An example illustrates this process. A group of supervisors attended an interpersonal skills training program, "Improving Work Habits," which was designed to lower the absenteeism rate of the employees in their work units. Successful application of the training program should result in a reduction in absenteeism. To calculate the ROI for the program, it was necessary to determine the average value of one absence in the company. As is the case with most organizations, historical records for the cost of absenteeism were not available. Experts were not available, and external studies were sparse for this particular industry. Consequently, supervisors (program participants) were asked to estimate the cost of an absence. In a group-interview format, each participant was asked to recall the last time an employee in his or her work group was unexpectedly absent and describe what was necessary to compensate for the absence. Because the impact of an absence will vary considerably from one employee to another within the same work unit, he group listened to all explanations. After reflecting on what must be done when an employee is absent, each supervisor was asked to provide an estimate of the average cost of an absence in the company. Although some supervisors are reluctant to provide estimates, with prodding and encouragement they will usually provide a value. The values are averaged for the group, and the result is the cost of an absence to be used in evaluating this program. Although this is an estimate, it is probably more accurate than data from external studies, calculations using internal records, or estimates from experts. And because it comes from supervisors who deal with the issue daily, it will usually have credibility with senior management.

Using Estimates from Supervisors

In some situations, participants may be incapable of placing a value on the improvement. Their work may be so far removed from the output of the process that they cannot reliably provide estimates. In these cases, the team leaders, supervisors, or managers of participants may be capable of providing estimates. Consequently, they may be asked to provide a value for a unit of improvement linked to the program. For example, a training program for customer service representatives was designed to reduce customer complaints. Applying the skills and knowledge learned from the program resulted in a reduction in complaints but the value of a single customer complaint was needed to determine the value of improvement. Although customer service representatives had knowledge of some issues surrounding customer complaints, they were not well versed in the full impact, so their supervisors were asked to provide a value.

In other situations, supervisors are asked to review and approve participants' estimates. For example, an HRD program for terminal managers with Yellow Freight Systems involved the implementation of both performance appraisal and training.[7] After the program was completed, participants estimated the value of their improvements that were directly related to their participation in the program. Their immediate managers were then asked to review the estimates and the process used by the participants to arrive at the estimates. Supervisors could either confirm, adjust, or discard the values provided by the participants.

Using Estimates from Senior Managers

In some situations senior management provides estimates of the value of data. With this approach, senior managers interested in the process or program are asked to place a value on the improvement based on their perception of its worth. This approach is used in situations in which it is very difficult to calculate the value or other sources of estimation are unavailable or unreliable. An example will illustrate this strategy. A hospital chain was attempting to improve customer satisfaction with a training program for all employees. The program was designed to improve customer service, and thus improve the external customer satisfaction index. To determine the value of the program, a value for a unit of improvement (one point on the index) was needed. Because senior management was very interested in improving the index, they were asked to provide input on the value of one unit. In a regular staff meeting, each senior manager and hospital administrator was asked to describe what it means for a hospital when the index increases. After some discussion, each individual was asked to provide an estimate of the monetary value gained when the index moves one point. Although initially reluctant to provide the information, with some encouragement, values were furnished and averaged. The result was an estimate of the worth of one unit of improvement, which was used as a basis of calculating the benefit of the program. Although this process is subjective, it does have the benefit of ownership from senior executives, the same executives who approved the program budget.

Using HRD Staff Estimates

The final strategy for converting data to monetary values is to use HRD staff estimates. Using all the available information and experience, the staff members most familiar with the situation provide estimates of the value. For example, an international oil company created a dispatcher training program designed to reduce dispatcher absenteeism along with other performance measure problems. The HRD staff estimated the cost of an absence to be $200.[8] This value was then used in calculating the savings for the reduction of absenteeism following training for the dispatchers. Although the staff may be capable of providing accurate estimates, this approach may be perceived as being biased. It should be used only when other approaches are not available.

Selecting the Appropriate Strategy

With so many strategies available, the challenge is to select one or more strategies appropriate to the situation. The following guidelines can help determine the proper selection.

Use the strategy appropriate for the type of data. Some strategies are designed specifically for hard data, while others are more appropriate for soft data. Consequently, the actual type of data will often dictate the strategy. Hard data, while always preferred, are not always available. Soft data are often required, and thus must be addressed with the strategies appropriate for soft data.

Move from most accurate to least accurate strategies. The ten strategies are presented in order of accuracy and credibility, beginning with the most credible. Working down the list, each strategy should be considered for its feasibility in the situation. The strategy with the most accuracy is recommended, if it is feasible in the situation.

Consider availability and convenience when selecting strategy. Sometimes the availability of a particular source of data will drive the selection. In other situations, the convenience of a technique may be an important factor in selecting the strategy.

When estimates are sought, use the source who has the broadest perspective on the issue. The person providing an estimate must be knowledgeable of the processes and the issues surrounding the value of the data.

Use multiple strategies when feasible. Sometimes it is helpful to have more than one strategy for obtaining a value for the data. When multiple sources are available more than one source should be used to serve as a comparison or to provide another perspective. When multiple sources are used, the data must be integrated using a convenient decision rule such as the lowest value. This is preferred because of the conservative nature of the lowest value.

Minimize the amount of time required to select and implement the appropriate strategy. As with other processes, it is important to keep the time invested as low as possible, so that the total time and effort for the ROI does not become excessive. Some strategies can be implemented with less time than others. Too much time at this step can dampen an otherwise enthusiastic attitude about the process.

Accuracy and Credibility of Data

The Credibility Problem

The strategies presented in this chapter assume that each data item collected and linked with training can be converted to a monetary value. Although estimates can be developed using one or more strategies, the process of converting data to monetary values may lose credibility with the target audience, who may doubt its use in analysis. Very subjective data, such as a change in employee morale or a reduction in the number of employee conflicts, are difficult to convert to monetary values. The key question for this determination is this: "Could these results be presented to senior management with confidence?" If the process does not meet this credibility test, the data should not be converted to monetary values and instead listed as an intangible benefit. Other data, particularly hard data items, could be used in the ROI calculation, leaving the very subjective data as intangible improvements.

The accuracy of data and the credibility of the conversion process are important concerns. HRD professionals sometimes avoid converting data because of these issues. They are more comfortable in reporting that a training program resulted in reducing absenteeism from 6% to 4% without attempting to place a value on the improvement. They assume that each person receiving the information will place a value on the absenteeism reduction. Unfortunately, the target audience may know little about the cost of absenteeism and will usually underestimate the actual value of the improvement. Consequently, there should be some attempt to include this conversion in the ROI analysis.

How the Credibility of Data is Influenced

When ROI data is presented to selected target audiences, its credibility will be an issue. The degree to which the target audience will believe the data will be influenced by the following factors.

Reputation of the source of data. The actual source of the data represents the first credibility issue. How credible is the individual or groups providing the data? Do they understand the issues? Are they knowledgeable of all the processes? The target audience will often place more credibility on data obtained from those who are closest to the source of the actual improvement or change.

Reputation of the source of the study. The target audience scrutinizes the reputation of the individual, group, or organization presenting the data. Do they have a history of providing accurate reports? Are they unbiased with their analyses? Are they fair in their presentation? Answers to these and other questions will form an impression about the reputation.

Motives of the evaluators. Do the individuals presenting the data have an ax to grind? Do they have a personal interest in creating a favorable or unfavorable result? These issues will cause the target audience to examine the motives of those who have conducted the study.

Methodology of the study. The audience will want to know specifically how the research was conducted. How were the calculations made? What steps were followed? What processes were used? A lack of information on the methodology will cause the audience to become wary and suspicious of the results.

Assumptions made in the analysis. In many ROI studies, assumptions are made on which calculations and conclusions are based. What are the assumptions? Are they standard? How do they compare with other assumptions in other studies? When assumptions are omitted, the audience will substitute their own often unfavorable assumptions.

Realism of the outcome data. Impressive ROI values could cause problems. When outcomes appear to be unrealistic, it may be difficult for the target audience to believe them. Huge claims often fall on deaf ears, causing reports to be thrown away before they are reviewed.

Types of data. The target audience will usually have a preference for hard data. They are seeking business performance data tied to output, quality, costs, and time. These measures are usually easily understood and closely related to organizational performance. Conversely, soft data are sometimes viewed suspiciously from the outset, as many senior executives are concerned about its soft nature and limitations on the analysis.

Scope of analysis. Is the scope of the analysis very narrow? Does it involve just one group or all of the employees in the organization? Limiting the study to a small group, or series of groups, of employees makes the process more accurate.

Collectively, these factors will influence the credibility of an ROI impact study and provide a framework from which to develop the ROI report. Thus, when considering each of the issues, the following key points are suggested for an ROI impact study:

- Use the most credible and reliable source for estimates.
- Present the material in an unbiased, objective way.
- Fully explain the methodology used throughout the process, preferably on a step-by-step basis.
- Define the assumptions made in the analysis, and compare them to assumptions made in other similar studies.
- Consider factoring or adjusting output values when they appear to be unrealistic.
- Use hard data whenever possible and combine with soft data if available.

■ Keep the scope of the analysis very narrow. Conduct the impact with one or more groups of participants in the program, instead of all participants or all employees.

Making Adjustments

Two potential adjustments should be considered before finalizing the monetary value. In some organizations where soft data are used and values are derived with imprecise methods, senior management is sometimes offered the opportunity to review and approve the data. Because of the subjective nature of this process, management may factor (reduce) the data so that the final results are more credible. In one example, senior managers at Litton Industries adjusted the value for the benefits derived from the implementation of self-directed teams.[9]

The other adjustment concerns the time value of money. Since an investment in a program is made at one time period and the return is realized in a later time period, a few organizations adjust the program benefits to reflect the time value of money, using discounted cash flow techniques. The actual monetary benefits of the program are adjusted for this time period. The amount of this adjustment, however, is usually small compared with the typical benefits realized from training and development programs.

Conclusion

In conclusion, organizations are attempting to be more aggressive when defining the monetary benefits of training and development. Progressive HRD managers are no longer satisfied with reporting business performance results from training. Instead, they are taking additional steps to convert business results data to monetary values and compare them with the program's cost thereby obtaining an ultimate level of evaluation, the return on investment. This chapter presented ten strategies to convert business results to monetary values, offering an array of techniques to fit any situation and program.

Case Study - Part D
National Auto Products Company

Isolating the Effects of Training

In discussions with plant management and participants in the training program, two factors were identified which could have an influence on each of the business performance measures, in addition to the training program. First, the implementation of the total quality management program placed emphasis on improving all four measures in this case. Quality was defined in a broad sense, including being at work (absenteeism), remaining with the company (turnover), and ensuring that customer shipments were on time (productivity).

The second factor was the various team-building activities that were initiated as NAPCo attempted to move to a team-based structure. Supervisors were encouraged to use employee input, conduct meetings with employees, and to take action to improve productivity and quality. If successful, team building should increase productivity, reduce turnover and absenteeism, and improve quality.

Because it was important to determine the precise impact of the training program, it was necessary to isolate the effects of training. One of the most effective approaches is the use of a control group arrangement in which one group receives training and another similarly situated group does not receive training. NAPCo explored the control group arrangement in this setting. Initially it appeared to be an excellent opportunity to use this plant location as a pilot group and select another similar plant as a control group. However, no other plant had the same product line, same type of machines, same work force characteristics, and same environmental conditions, all important variables to reflect performance. Thus, the control group arrangement was not considered a feasible approach.

It was decided that two other approaches would be used to isolate the effects of training. The first approach would be to use a trend-line analysis, because six months of data is available in each of the output variables. The projections would be made for the data assuming that no training is conducted. For the second approach, participants will be asked to indicate how much of their improvement is linked directly to their training. Participants provide information about the various factors that influenced their performance in a portion of the follow-up questionnaire. Each participant is presented with a six-months average of the data prior to training to compare with post-training data. After training, supervisors regularly receive reports for each of the items as part of their operating data.

Because this is not a precise process, two methods can sometimes provide supporting evidence to help pinpoint the actual amount of the improvement related to training. In addition, when some strategies are used that are unproven in the organization, another, more credible approach can help provide convincing evidence of the effectiveness of the unproven practical approach. At NAPCo, management was uncomfortable with participants training impact estimates. The trend line analysis provided more confidence in arriving at the value and also provided a basis for comparison with estimates. Thus, if both methods result in similar values, it can perhaps build confidence in the estimating process.

Converting Data to Monetary Values

The next task in setting up the ROI process is to select the techniques that convert data to monetary values. The challenge facing the evaluation team is to determine the most credible and accurate techniques for placing values on each of the Level 4 data items.

Discussion Questions
1. What is the most effective technique to place a value on productivity (expressed as a percent of shipments met)?
2. What is the most appropriate technique to assign a value to quality (expressed as rejects per million units of production)?
3. What is the most logical way to convert employee turnover to a monetary value?
4. What is the most appropriate method to place a monetary value on an absence?

References

[1] Phillips, J.J. (1994). "Measuring ROI in an Established Program", *In Action: Measuring Return on Investment*, Vol. 1. (pp. 187-198). J.J. Phillips (Ed.). Alexandria, Virginia: American Society for Training and Development.

[2] Seimke, R. "Cost of Quality: You Can Measure It", *Training*, August 1990, pp. 62-63.

[3] Payne, Rebecca. (1994). "Improving Customer Service Skills" *In Action: Measuring Return on Investment*, Vol. 1. (pp. 169-186). J.J. Phillips (Ed.) Alexandria, Virginia: American Society for Training and Development.

[4] Rust, R.T., A.J. and Keiningham, T.L. (1994). *Return on Quality: Measuring the Financial Impact of Your Company's Quest for Quality*, Chicago: Probus Publishers.

[5] Stamp, D. (1992). *The Workplace of the 21st Century.* A Publication of Priority Management Systems. Bellevue, Washington.

[6] Schoeppel, Cynthia. (1994) "Turning Down Manager Turnover" J.J. Phillips (Ed.) *In Action: Measuring Return on Investment*, Vol. 1. (pp. 213-222). Alexandria, Virginia: American Society for Training and Development.

[7] Zigon, J. (1994). "Performance Management Training:. *In Action: Measuring Return on Investment*, Vol. 1. (pp. 253-270). J.J. Phillips (Ed.), Alexandria, Virginia: American Society for Training and Development.

[8] Payne, Rebecca. (1994). "Improving Customer Service Skills", *In Action: Measuring Return on Investment*, Vol. 1. (pp. 169-186). J.J. Phillips (Ed.), Alexandria, Virginia: American Society for Training and Development.

[9] Graham, M., Bishop K., and Birdsong, R. (1994). "Self-Directed Work Teams:, *In Action: Measuring Return on Investment*, Vol. 1. (pp. 105-122), J.J. Phillips (Ed.), Alexandria, Virginia: American Society for Training and Development.

6

TABULATING PROGRAM COSTS

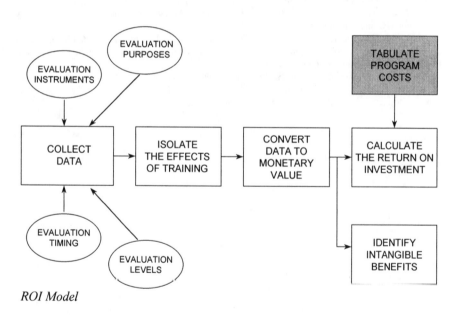

ROI Model

Tabulating program costs is an essential step in developing the ROI calculation since it represents the denominator in the ROI formula. It is just as important to pay attention to costs as it is to benefits. In practice, however, costs are often more easily captured than benefits. This chapter explores the costs accumulation and tabulation steps, outlining the specific costs that should be captured, and some economical ways in which they can be developed.

Cost Strategies

Importance of Costs

Capturing costs is challenging because the figures must be accurate, reliable, and realistic. Although most organizations develop costs with much more ease than the economic value of the benefits, the true cost of training is often an elusive figure even in some of the best organizations. While the total HRD direct budget is usually a number that is easily developed, it is more difficult to determine the specific costs of a program, including the indirect costs related to it. To develop a realistic ROI, costs must be accurate and credible. Otherwise, the painstaking difficulty and attention to the benefits will be wasted because of inadequate or inaccurate costs.

Pressure to Disclose All Costs

Today there is more pressure than ever before to report all training costs, or what is referred to as fully-loaded costs. This takes the cost profile beyond the direct cost of training and includes the time that participants are involved in training, including their benefits and other overhead. For years, management has realized that there are many indirect costs of training. Now they are asking for an accounting of these costs. Perhaps this point is best illustrated in a situation that recently developed in state government. The management controls of a large state agency were audited by the state auditor. A portion of the audit focused on training costs. The following comments are taken from the auditor's report.

Costs tracked at the program level focus on direct or "hard" costs and largely ignore the cost of time spent participating in or supporting training. The costs of participant time to prepare for and attend training are not tracked. For one series of programs, including such costs raised the total training cost dramatically. The agency stated that the total two-year costs for the specific program was about $600,000. This figure generally includes only direct costs and, as such, is substantially below the costs of the time spent by staff in preparing for and attending the program. When accounting for prework and attendance, the figure comes to a total of $1.39 million. If the statewide average of 45.5% for fringe benefits is considered, the total indirect cost of staff time to prepare for and attend the program becomes $2 million. Finally, if the agency's direct costs of

$600,000 are added to the $2 million total indirect cost just noted, the total becomes over $2.6 million. Among other factors that would drive actual total costs higher still are:

- cost of travel, meals, and lodging for training participants;
- allocated salaries and fringes of staff providing administrative and logistic support; and
- opportunity costs of productivity lost by staff in doing prework and attending training.

Failure to consider all indirect or "soft" costs may expose the agency to non-compliance with the Fair Labor Standards Act (FLSA), particularly as training spreads through rank-and-file staff. Since FLSA requires that such staff be directly compensated for overtime, it is no longer be appropriate for the agency to ask employees to complete training prework on their own time. Continuing to handle such overtime work this way may also encourage false overtime reporting, skew overtime data, and/or increase the amount of uncompensated overtime.

Numerous barriers exist to agency efforts at determining "How much does training cost?":

- Cost systems tend to hide administrative, support, internal, and other indirect or "soft" costs.
- Costs generally are monitored at the division level rather than at the level of individual programs or activities.
- Cost information required by activity-based cost systems is not being generated.

As this case vividly demonstrates, the cost of training is much more than direct expenditures, and the training and development departments are expected to report fully-loaded costs in their reports.

Fully Loaded Costs

To take the conservative approach to calculating the ROI, it is recommended that training costs be fully loaded. With this approach, all costs that can be identified and linked to a particular program are included. The philosophy is simple: When in doubt in the denominator, put it in (i.e., if it is questionable whether a cost be included, it is recommended that it be included, even if the cost guidelines for the organization do not require it). When an ROI is calculated and reported to target audiences the process should withstand even the closest scrutiny in terms of its accuracy and credibility. The only way to meet this test is to ensure that all costs are included. Of course, from a realistic viewpoint, if the controller or chief financial officer insists on not using certain costs, then it is best to leave them out.

The Danger of Costs Without Benefits

It is dangerous to communicate the costs of training without presenting benefits. Unfortunately, many organizations have fallen into this trap for years. Because costs can easily be collected, they are presented to management in all types of ingenious ways such as cost of the program, cost per employee, and cost per development hour. While these may be helpful for efficiency comparisons, it may be troublesome to present them without benefits. When most executives review training costs, a logical question comes to mind: What benefit was received from the program? This is a typical management reaction particularly when costs are perceived to be very high. For example, in one organization, all of the costs associated with its executive leadership programs were tabulated and reported to the senior management team to let them know the total investment on these programs. The total figure exceeded the perceived estimates from the executive group, and their immediate reaction was to request a summary of benefits derived from these programs. This reaction initiated a review of the programs with the conclusion that there was little, if any, economic benefits from the programs. Consequently, the programs were drastically reduced. While this may be an extreme example, it shows the danger of presenting only half of the equation. Because of this, some organizations have developed a policy of not communicating training cost data unless the benefits can be captured and presented along with the costs. Even if the benefit data is subjective and intangible, it is included with the cost data. This helps to keep balance in the two issues.

Policies and Guidelines

For organizations it may be helpful to detail the philosophy and policy on costs in guidelines for the HRD staff or others who monitor and report costs. Cost guidelines detail specifically what costs are included with training and how the data is captured, analyzed, and reported. Cost guidelines can range from a one page document to a hundred page manual in a large, complex organization.

The simpler approach is better. When fully developed, they should be reviewed by the finance and accounting staff. The final document serves as the guiding force in collecting, monitoring, and reporting costs. When an ROI is calculated and reported, costs are included in a summary form and the cost guidelines are referenced in a footnote or attached as an appendix.

Typical Cost Categories

The most important task is to define which specific costs are included in a tabulation of the program costs. This task involves decisions which will be made by the HRD staff and usually approved by management. If appropriate, the finance and accounting staff may need to approve the list. Table 6-1 shows the recommended cost categories for a fully loaded, conservative approach to estimating costs. Each category is described below.

Table 6-1
Training Program Cost Categories

Cost Item	Prorated	Expensed
Needs Assessment	✓	
Design and Development	✓	
Acquisition	✓	
Delivery		✓
• Salaries/Benefits - Facilitators		✓
• Salaries/Benefits - Coordination		✓
• Program Materials and Fees		✓
• Travel/Lodging/Meals		✓
• Facilities		✓
• Participants Salaries/Benefits		✓
• Contact Time		✓
• Travel Time		✓
• Preparation Time		✓
Evaluation	✓	
Overhead/Training and Development	✓	

Major Cost Categories

Prorated vs. Direct Costs

Usually all costs related to a program are captured and expensed to that program. However, three categories are usually prorated over several sessions of the same program. Needs assessment, design and development, and acquisition are all significant costs that should be prorated over the shelf life. With a conservative approach, the shelf life of the program should be very short. Some organizations will consider one year of operation for the program, others may consider two or three years. If there is some question about the specific time period to be used in the proration formula, the finance and accounting staff should be consulted.

A brief example will illustrate the proration for development costs. In a large telecommunications company, a computer-based training program was developed at a cost of $98,000. It was anticipated that it would have a three-year life cycle before it would have to be updated. The revision costs at the end of the three years were estimated to be about one half of the original development costs, or $49,000. The program would be conducted with 25 groups in a three-year period with an ROI calculation planned for one specific group. Since the program will have one half of its residual value at the end of three years, one half of the cost should be written off for this three-year period. Thus, the $49,000, representing half of the development costs, would be spread over the 25 groups as a prorated development cost. Thus, an ROI for one group would have a development cost of $2,000 included in the cost profile.

Benefits Factor

When presenting participant salaries and staff associated with programs, the benefits factor should be included. This number is usually well known in the organization and is used in other costing formulas. It represents the cost of all employee benefits expressed as a percent of base salaries. In some organizations this value is as high as 50% - 60%. In others, it may be as low as 25% - 30%. The average in the USA is 38%.[1]

Needs Assessment

One of the most often overlooked items is the cost of conducting a needs assessment. In some programs this cost is zero because the program is conducted without a needs assessment. However, as more organizations focus increased attention on needs assessment, this item will become a more significant cost in the future. All costs associated with the needs assessment should be captured to the fullest extent possible. These costs include the time of staff members conducting the assessment, direct fees and expenses for external consultants who conduct the needs assessment, and internal services and supplies used in the analysis. The total costs are usually prorated over the life of the program. Depending on the type and nature of the program, the shelf life should be kept to a very reasonable number in the one- to two-year timeframe. Of course the exception would be very expensive programs which are not expected to change significantly for several years.

Design and Development Costs

One of the more significant items is the cost of designing and developing the program. These costs include internal staff time in both design and development and the purchase of supplies, videos, CD ROM's, and other materials directly related to the program. It would also include the use of consultants. As with needs assessment costs, design and development costs are usually prorated, perhaps using the same timeframe. One to two years is recommended unless the program is not expected to change for many years and the costs are very significant.

Acquisition Costs

In lieu of development costs, many organizations purchase programs to use directly or in a modified format. The acquisition costs for these programs include the purchase price for the instructor materials, train-the-trainer sessions, licensing agreements, and other costs associated with the right to deliver the program. These acquisition costs should be prorated using the same rationale above; one to two years should be sufficient. If modification of the program is needed or some additional development is required, these costs should be included as development costs. In practice, many programs have both acquisition costs and development costs.

Delivery Costs

Usually the largest segment of training costs would be those associated with delivery. Five major categories are included.

Salaries of facilitators and coordinators. The salaries of facilitators or program coordinators should be included. If a coordinator is involved in more than one program, the time should be allocated to the specific program under review. If external facilitators are used, all charges should be included for the session. The important issue is to capture all of the direct time of internal employees or external consultants who work directly with the program. The benefits factor should be included each time direct labor costs are involved. This factor is a widely accepted value, usually generated by the finance and accounting staff and in the 30% - 40% range.

Program Materials and Fees. Specific program materials such as notebooks, textbooks, case studies, exercises, and participant workbooks should be included in the delivery costs, along with license fees, user fees, and royalty payments. Pens, paper, certificates, and calculators are also included in this category.

Travel, Lodging, and Meals. Direct travel for participants, facilitators, or coordinators are included. Lodging and meals are included for participants during travel, as well as meals during the stay for the program. Refreshments should also be included.

Facilities. The direct cost of the training facilities should be included. For external programs, this is the direct charge from the conference center, hotel, or motel. If the program is conducted in-house, the conference room represents a cost for the organization, and the cost should be estimated and included even if it is not the practice to include facilities' cost in other reports.

Participants' Salaries and Benefits. The salaries plus employee benefits of participants represent an expense that should be included. For situations where the program has been conducted, these costs can be estimated using average or midpoint values for salaries in typical job classifications. When a program is targeted for an ROI calculation, participants can provide their salaries directly and in a confidential manner.

Evaluation

Usually the total evaluation cost is included in the program costs to compute the fully loaded cost. ROI costs include the cost of developing the evaluation strategy, designing instruments, collecting data, data analysis, and report preparation and distribution. Cost categories include time, materials, purchased instruments, or surveys. A case can be made to prorate the evaluation costs over several programs instead of charging the total amount as an expense. For example, if 25 sessions of a program are conducted in a three-year period and one group is selected for an ROI calculation, then the ROI costs could logically be prorated over the 25 sessions, since the results of the ROI analysis should reflect the success of the other programs and will perhaps result in changes that will influence the other programs as well.

Overhead

A final charge is the cost of overhead, the additional costs in the training function not directly related to a particular program. The overhead category represents any training department cost not considered in the above calculations. Typical items include the cost of clerical support, the departmental office expenses, salaries of training managers, and other fixed costs. Some organizations obtain an estimate for allocation by dividing the total overhead by the number of program participant days for the year. This becomes a standard value to use in calculations.

Cost Accumulation and Estimation

There are two basic ways to classify HRD costs. One is by a description of the expenditure such as labor, materials, supplies, travel, etc. These are expense account classifications. The other is by categories in the HRD process or function such as program development, delivery, and evaluation. An effective system monitors costs by account categories according to the description of those accounts but also includes a method for accumulating costs by the HRD process/functional category. Many systems stop short of this second step. While the first grouping sufficiently gives the total program cost, it does not allow for a useful comparison with other programs or indicate areas where costs might be excessive by relative comparisons.

Cost Classification Matrix

Costs are accumulated under both of the above classifications. The two classifications are obviously related and the relationship depends on the organization. For instance, the specific costs that comprise the analysis part of a program may vary substantially with the organization.

An important part of the classification process is to define the kinds of costs in the account classification system which normally apply to the process/functional categories. Table 6-2 is a matrix that represents the categories for accumulating all HRD-related costs in the organization. Those costs, which normally are a part of a process/functional category, are checked in the matrix. Each member of the HRD staff should know how to charge expenses properly (e.g., equipment that is rented to use in the development and the delivery of a program). Should all or part of the cost be charged to development? Or to delivery? More than likely the cost will be allocated in proportion to the extent in which the item was used for each category.

Table 6-2
Cost Classification Matrix

	Expense Account Classification	Process / Functional Categories			
		Analysis	Development	Delivery	Evaluation
00	Salaries and Benefits - HRD Personnel	X	X	X	X
01	Salaries and Benefits - Other Company Personnel		X	X	
02	Salaries and Benefits - Participants			X	X
03	Meals, Travel, and Incidental Expenses - HRD Personnel	X	X	X	X
04	Meals, Travel, and Accommodations - Participants			X	
05	Office Supplies and Expenses	X	X		X
06	Program Materials and Supplies		X	X	
07	Printing and Reproduction	X	X	X	X
08	Outside Services	X	X	X	X
09	Equipment Expense Allocation	X	X	X	X
10	Equipment - Rental		X	X	
11	Equipment – Maintenance			X	
12	Registration Fees	X			
13	Facilities Expense Allocation			X	
14	Facilities Rental			X	
15	General Overhead Allocation	X	X	X	X
16	Other Miscellaneous Expenses	X	X	X	X

Cost Accumulation

With expense account classifications clearly defined and the process/functional categories determined, it is easy to track costs on individual programs. This is accomplished by using special account numbers and project numbers. An example illustrates the use of these numbers.

A project number is a three-digit number representing a specific HRD program. For example:

New Professional Associates' Orientation	112
New Team Leader Training	215
Statistical Quality Control	418
Valuing Diversity	791

Numbers are assigned to the process/functional breakdowns. Using the example presented earlier, the following numbers are assigned:

Analysis	1
Development	2
Delivery	3
Evaluation	4

Using the two-digit numbers assigned to account classifications in Table 6-2, an accounting system is complete. For example, if workbooks are reproduced for the valuing diversity workshop, the appropriate charge number for that reproduction is 07-3-791. The first two digits denote the account classification, the next digit the process/functional category, and the last three digits the project number. This system enables rapid accumulation and monitoring of HRD costs. Total costs can be presented:

- by HRD program (valuing diversity workshop),
- by process/functional categories (delivery), and
- by expense account classification (printing and reproduction).

Cost Estimation

The previous sections covered procedures for classifying and monitoring costs related to HRD programs. It is important to monitor and compare ongoing costs with the budget or with projected costs. However, a significant reason for tracking costs is to predict the cost of future programs. Usually this goal is accomplished through a formal cost estimation method unique to the organization.

Some organizations use cost estimating worksheets to arrive at the total cost for a proposed program. Figure 6-1 shows an example of a cost estimating worksheet which calculates analysis, development, delivery, and evaluation costs. The worksheets contain a few formulas that make it easier to estimate the cost. In addition to these worksheets, current charge rates for services, supplies, and salaries are available. These data become outdated quickly and are usually prepared periodically as a supplement.

The most appropriate basis for predicting costs is to analyze the previous costs by tracking the actual costs incurred in all phases of a program; from analysis to evaluation. This way, it is possible to see how much is spent on programs and how much is being spent in the different categories. Until adequate cost data are available, it is necessary to use the detailed analysis in the worksheets for cost estimation.

Summary

Costs are important and should be fully loaded in the ROI calculation. From a practical standpoint, including some of the costs may be optional-based on the organization's guidelines and philosophy. However, because of the scrutiny involved in ROI calculations, it is recommended that all costs be included, even if it goes beyond the requirements of the company policy.

Case Study Part E
National Auto Products Company

Converting Data to Monetary Values

As part of the next step in the ROI process, NAPCo's data are converted to monetary values. The value of improved productivity was a standard value developed by engineering and production control. Each 1% of improvement in productivity would save the plant $21,000, annually.

Analysis Costs	**Total**
Salaries & Employee Benefits--HRD Staff (No. of People x Average Salary x Employee Benefits Factor x No. of Hours on Project)	
Meals, Travel, and Incidental Expenses	_____
Office Supplies and Expenses	_____
Printing and Reproduction	_____
Outside Services	_____
Equipment Expenses	_____
Registration Fees	_____
General Overhead Allocation	_____
Other Miscellaneous Expenses	_____
Total Analysis Cost	_____

Development Costs		**Total**
Salaries & Employee Benefits (No. of People x Avg. Salary x Employee Benefits Factor x No. of Hours on Project)		
Meals, Travel, and Incidental Expenses		_____
Office Supplies and Expenses		_____
Program Materials and Supplies		_____
Film	_____	
Videotape	_____	
Audiotapes	_____	
35mm Slides	_____	
Overhead Transparencies	_____	
Artwork	_____	
Manuals and Materials	_____	
Other	_____	
Printing and Reproduction		_____
Outside Services		_____
Equipment Expense		_____
General Overhead Allocation		_____
Other Miscellaneous Expense		_____
Total Development Costs		_____

Figure 6-1. *Cost estimating worksheet*

Delivery Costs	Total
Participant Costs	
Salaries & Employee Benefits (No. of Participants x Avg. Salary x Employee Benefits Factor x Hrs. or Days of Training Time)	_____
Meals, Travel, & Accommodations (No. of Participants x Avg. Daily Expenses x Days of Training)	_____
Program Materials and Supplies	
Participant Replacement Costs (if applicable)	_____
Lost Production (Explain Basis)	
Instructor Costs	
Salaries & Benefits	_____
Meals, Travel, & Incidental Expense	_____
Outside Services	_____
Facility Costs	
Facilities Rental	_____
Facilities Expense Allocation	_____
Equipment Expense	
General Overhead Allocation	_____
Other Miscellaneous Expense	_____
Total Delivery Costs	_____

Evaluation Costs	Total
Salaries & Employee Benefits--HRD Staff (No. of People x Avg. Salary x Employee Benefits Factor x No. or Hours on Project)	_____
Meals, Travel and Incidental Expense	
Participant Costs	_____
Office Supplies and Expense	_____
Printing and Reproduction	_____
Outside Services	_____
Equipment Expense	_____
General Overhead Allocation	_____
Other Miscellaneous Expenses	_____
Total Evaluation Costs	_____
TOTAL PROGRAM COSTS	_____

Figure 6-1. *Cont'd.*

The quality engineer estimated that the value of improving quality by one unit was $3,100 annually. He based this estimate on the cost to replace the product, the time involved in working with the customer, the consequences of the defect in terms of liability and damages, and the cost of customer dissatisfaction.

The company had no detailed historical records on turnover costs, although the company expected these costs to be significant when considering the cost of employment, recruiting, training, and lost productivity. The consultant provided information from external studies, which showed that turnover can cost one times the annual wages of the employees. Annual wages of non-supervisory employees averaged $19,750. Management thought that a one-time wage figure would be too high for the cost of turnover since the training period was relatively short, recruiting costs were normally quite low, and exit costs were not very significant. After discussing this with senior management, the consultant selected a figure of $5,000 for the cost of turnover. He considered this to be a very conservative estimate. The total number of supervisors trained in this program was 16, and they supervised a total of 385 employees.

The consultant located some previous studies about the cost of absenteeism in the manufacturing sector, which showed a range of $89 - $210 per absence with an average of $180. Brief estimates taken in the training session, with input from the 16 supervisors, yielded an average cost of $98. NAPCo employees worked an average of 228 days per year.

Costs

Because the consultant firm provided standard material for the new program, development costs were insignificant. The consultant also decided to include all direct costs of participant materials as well as the participants' salaries. Although the supervisors were not replaced while they were in training, the salaries and benefits of supervisors were included for the time during the training sessions. The average salary of the supervisors was $27,500. The employee benefits factor was 39% of salaries. The total charge for the program from the consulting firm was $21,500, including development time, facilitation, and needs assessment. The course materials' charge was $85 per participant and miscellaneous refreshments and food was $95 per participant. The cost for the use of the conference room was estimated to be $100 per session, although NAPCo usually does not capture and report this as a part of training, the consultant estimated the additional cost of the evaluation to be $3,000.

Discussion Questions
1. What major cost categories should always be included in the analysis?
2. What is the total cost for the program?
3. Should any other costs be included? Please explain.

References

[1]Annual Employee Benefits Report, *Nations Business*, January 1996, p. 28.

7

CALCULATING THE RETURN

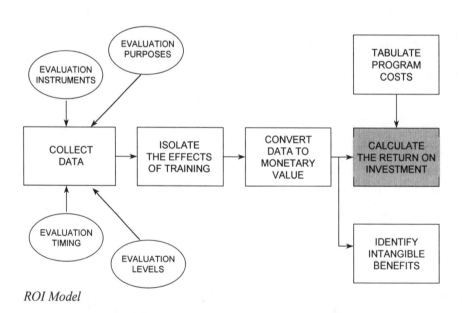

ROI Model

The monetary values for program benefits, developed in Chapter 5, are combined with program cost data, developed in Chapter 6, to calculate the return on investment. This chapter explores several approaches for developing the return on investment, describing the various techniques, processes, and issues involved. Before presenting the formulas for calculating the ROI, a few basic issues are described. An adequate understanding of these issues is necessary to complete this major step in the ROI process.

Basic Issues

Definitions

The term, "return on investment in HRD", is often misused, sometimes intentionally. In some situations, a very broad definition for ROI includes any benefit from the program. In these situations, ROI is a vague concept in which even subjective data linked to a program is included in the concept of the return. In this book, the return on investment is more precise and is meant to represent an actual value developed by comparing program costs to benefits. The two most common measures are the cost/benefit ratio and the ROI formula. Both are presented along with other approaches that calculate the return.

For many years, training and development practitioners and researchers have sought to calculate the actual return on the investment for training. If employee training is considered an investment, not an expense, then it is appropriate to place the training and development investment in the same funding mechanism as other investments, such as the investment in equipment and facilities. Although these other investments are quite different, they are often viewed by management in the same way. Thus, it is critical to the success of the training and development field to develop specific values which reflect the return on the investment.

Annualized Values

All of the formulas presented in this chapter use annualized values so that the first year impact of the program investment is developed. Using annual values is becoming a generally accepted practice for developing the ROI in many organizations. This approach is a conservative way to develop the ROI, since many short-term training programs have added value in the second or third year. For long-term training programs, annualized values are inappropriate and longer time frames need to be used. For example, in an ROI analysis of a program to send employees to the USA to obtain MBA degrees, a Singapore-based company used a seven-year timeframe. The program itself required two years and a five year impact, with post-program data used to develop the ROI. However, for most programs that last one-day to one month, first year values are appropriate.

When selecting the approach to measure ROI, it is important to communicate to the target audience the formula used and the assumptions made to arrive at the decision to use it. This action can avoid misunderstandings and confusion surrounding how the ROI value was actually developed. Although several approaches are described in this chapter, two stand out as the preferred methods: the benefit/cost ratio and the basic ROI formula. These two approaches are described next along with brief coverage of the other approaches.

Benefits/Costs Ratio

One of the earliest methods for evaluating training investments is the benefit/cost ratio. This method compares the benefits of the program to the costs in a ratio. In formula form, the ratio is:

$$BCR = \frac{\text{Program Benefits}}{\text{Program Costs}}$$

In simple terms, the BCR compares the annual economic benefits of the program to the cost of the program. A BCR of one means that the benefits equal the costs. A BCR of two, usually written as 2:1, indicates that for each dollar spent on the program, two dollars were returned as benefits.

The following example will illustrate the use of the benefit/cost ratio. An applied behavior management program, designed for managers and supervisors, was implemented at an electric and gas utility.[1] In a follow-up evaluation, action planning and business performance monitoring were used to capture benefits. The first year payoff for the program was $1,077,750. The total fully loaded implementation costs was $215,500. Thus, the ratio was:

$$BCR = \frac{\$1,077,750}{\$215,500} = 5:1$$

For every one dollar invested in this program, five dollars in benefits was returned.

The principal advantage of using this approach is that it avoids traditional financial measures so that there is no confusion when comparing training investments with other investments in the company. Investments in plants, equipment, or subsidiaries, for example, are not usually evaluated with the benefit/cost method. Some training and development executives prefer not to use the same method to compare the return on training investments with the return on other investments. Consequently, the ROI for training stand alone as a unique type of evaluation.

Unfortunately, there are no standards as to what constitutes an acceptable benefit/cost ratio. A standard should be established within an organization, perhaps even for a specific type of program. However, a 1:1 ratio is unacceptable for most programs, and in some organizations, a 1.25:1 ratio is required, where 1.25 times the cost of the program is the benefit.

ROI Formula

Perhaps the most appropriate formula for evaluating training investments is net program benefits divided by cost. The ratio is usually expressed as a percent when the fractional values are multiplied by 100. In formula form, the ROI becomes:

$$\text{ROI (\%)} \quad = \quad \frac{\text{Net Program Benefits}}{\text{Program Costs}} \quad \text{x } 100$$

Net benefits are program benefits minus program costs. The ROI value is related to the BCR by a factor of one. For example, a BCR of 2.45 is the same as an ROI value of 145%. This formula is essentially the same as ROI in other types of investments. For example, when a firm builds a new plant, the ROI is found by dividing annual earnings by the investment. The annual earnings is comparable to net benefits (annual benefits minus the cost). The investment is comparable to program costs, which represent the investment in the program.

An ROI on a training investment of 50% means that the costs are recovered and an additional 50% of the costs are reported as "earnings." A training investment of 150% indicates that the costs have been recovered and an additional 1.5 multiplied by the costs are captured as "earnings." An example illustrates the ROI calculation. Magnavox Electronics Systems Company conducted an 18-week literacy program for entry level electrical and mechanical assemblers.[2] The results of the program were impressive. Productivity and quality alone yielded an annual value of $321,600. The total fully loaded costs for the program were $38,233. Thus, the return on investment becomes:

$$ROI (\%) \quad = \quad \frac{\$321,600 - \$38,233}{\$38,233} \quad x \; 100 \quad = 741\%$$

For each dollar invested, Magnavox received $7.4 dollars in return after the cost of the program had been recovered.

Using the ROI formula essentially places training investments on a level playing field with other investments using the same formula and similar concepts. The ROI calculation is easily understood by key management and financial executives who regularly use ROI with other investments.

While there are no generally accepted standards, some organizations establish a minimum requirement or hurdle rate for an ROI in a training program. An ROI minimum of 25% is set by some organizations. This target value is usually above the percentage required for other types of investments. The rationale: The ROI process for training is still relatively new and often involves some subjective input, including estimations. Because of that, a higher standard is required or suggested, with 25% being the desired figure for these organizations.

BCR / ROI Case Application

Background Information

Retail Merchandise Company (RMC), a large national store chain located in most major USA markets, attempted to boost sales by conducting an interactive selling skills program for sales associates. The program, developed and delivered by an outside vendor, was a response to a clearly defined need to increase the level of interaction between the sales associate and the customer. The program consisted of two days of skills training followed by three weeks of on-the-job application of the skills. The third day of the program was used for follow-up and additional training. Three groups representing the electronics departments of three stores were initially trained for a pilot implementation. A total of 4 participated.

ROI Analysis

Post-program data collection was accomplished using three methods. First, the average weekly sales of each associate was monitored (business performance monitoring of output data). Second, a follow-up questionnaire was distributed three months after the training was completed to determine Level 3 success (actual application of the skills on the job). Third, Level 3 data was solicited in a follow-up session, which was conducted on the third day. In this session, participants disclosed their success (or lack of success) with the application of new skills. They also discussed techniques to overcome the barriers to program implementation.

The method used to isolate the effects of training was a control group arrangement. Three store locations were identified (control group) and compared with the three groups in the pilot training (experimental group). The variables of store size, store location, and customer traffic levels were used to match the two groups so that they could be as identical as possible. The method to convert data to monetary values is a direct profit contribution of the increased output. The actual profit obtained from an additional one dollar of sales was readily available and used in the calculation.

BCR and ROI Calculations

Although the program was evaluated at all five levels, the emphasis of this study was on the Level 5 calculation. Level 1, 2 and 3 data either met or exceeded expectations. Table 7-1 shows the Level 4 data, which is the average weekly sales of both groups after the training. For convenience and at the request of management, a three-month follow up period was used. Management wanted to make the decision to implement the program at other locations if it appeared to be successful in this first three months of operation. Three months may be premature to determine the total impact of the program, but often becomes a convenient time period for evaluation. Data for the first three weeks after training are shown in Table 7-1 along with the last three weeks of the evaluation period (weeks 13, 14, and 15). The data show what appears to be a significant difference in the two values.

Table 7-1
Level 4 Data: Average Weekly Sales

Weeks After Training	Post Training Data Trained Groups	Control Groups
1	$9,723	$9,698
2	9,978	9,720
3	10,424	9,812
13	13,690	11,572
14	11,491	9,683
15	11,044	10,092
Average for Weeks 13, 14, 15	$12,075	$10,449

Two steps are required to move from the Level 4 data to Level 5. Step 1, Level 4 data must be converted to monetary values, and Step 2, the cost of the program must be tabulated. Table 7-2 shows the annualized program benefits. The total benefit was $71,760. Only 46 participants were still in their current job after three months. To be conservative, the other two participants' potential improvements were removed from the calculation. The profit contribution at the store level, obtained directly from the accounting department, was 2%. For every one dollar of additional sales attributed to the program, only two cents would be considered to be the added value. At the corporate level, the number was even smaller, about 1.2%. First year, values are used to reflect the total impact of the program. Ideally, if new skills are acquired, as indicated in the Level 3 evaluation, there should be some value for the use of those skills in year two, or perhaps, even year three. However, for short-term training programs, only first year values are used, requiring the investment to have an acceptable return in a one year time period. The total benefit was $71,760.

Table 7-3 shows the cost summary for this program. Costs are fully loaded, including data for all 48 participants. Since the program is conducted by a vendor, there are no direct development costs. The facilitation fee actually covers the pro-rated development costs as well as the delivery costs. The participants' salaries plus a 35% factor for employee benefits were included in the costs. Facilities costs were included, although the company does not

Table 7-2
Annualized Program Benefits

46 participants were still in job after 3 months

Average Weekly Sales	
Trained Groups	$12,075
Average Weekly Sales	
Untrained Groups	10,449
Increase	1,626
Profit Contribution 2%	32.50
Total Weekly Improvement (32.50 x 46)	1,495

Total Annual Benefits ($1495 x 48 Weeks)   **$71,760**

normally capture the costs when internal facilities are used, as was the case with this program. The estimated cost for the coordination and evaluation was also included. The total cost was $32,984. Thus, the benefit/cost ratio becomes:

$$\text{BCR} \quad = \quad \frac{\$71,760}{\$32,984} \quad = 2.2:1$$

and the return on investment becomes:

$$\text{ROI (\%)} \quad = \quad \frac{\$71,760 - \$32,984}{\$32,984} \quad \text{x } 100 \quad = 118\%$$

Table 7-3
Cost Summary

48 participants in 3 courses	
Facilitation Fees: 3 courses @ $3750	$11,250
Program Materials: 48 @ $35/participant	1,680
Meals/Refreshments: 3 days @ $28/participant	4,032
Facilities: 9 days @ $120	1,080
Participant Salaries Plus Benefits (35%)	12,442
Coordination/Evaluation	2,500
Total Costs	**$32,984**

Thus, the program has an excellent return on investment in its initial trial run after three months of on-the-job applications of the skills.

Other ROI Measures

In addition to the traditional ROI formula previously described, several other measures are occasionally used under the general term of return on investment. These measures are designed primarily for evaluating other types of financial measures, but sometimes work their way into training evaluations.

Payback Period

The payback period is a common method for evaluating capital expenditures. With this approach, the annual cash proceeds (savings) produced by an investment are equated to the original cash outlay required by the investment to arrive at some multiple of cash proceeds equal to the original investment. Measurement is usually in terms of years and months. For example, if the cost savings generated from an HRD program are constant each year, the payback period is determined by dividing the total original cash investment (development costs, outside program purchases, etc.) by the amount of the expected annual or actual savings. The savings represent the net savings after the program expenses are subtracted. To illustrate this calculation, assume that an initial program cost is $100,000 with a three-year useful life. The annual net savings from the program is expected to be $40,000. Thus, the payback period becomes:

$$\text{Payback period} \quad = \quad \frac{\text{Total Investment}}{\text{Annual Savings}} \quad = \quad \frac{100,000}{40,000} \quad = \quad 2.5 \text{ years}$$

The program will "pay back" the original investment in 2.5 years.

The payback period is simple to use, but has the limitation of ignoring the time value of money. It has not enjoyed widespread use in evaluating training investments.

Discounted Cash Flow

Discounted cash flow is a method of evaluating investment opportunities in which certain values are assigned to the timing of the proceeds from the investment. The assumption, based on interest rates, is that a dollar earned today is more valuable than a dollar earned a year from now.

There are several ways of using the discounted cash flow concept to evaluate capital expenditures. The most popular one is probably the net present value of an investment. This approach compares the savings, year by year, with the outflow of cash required by the investment. The expected savings received each year is discounted by selected interest rates. The outflow of cash is also discounted by the same interest rate. If the present value of the savings should exceed the present value of the outlays after discounting at a common interest rate, the investment is usually acceptable in the eyes of management. The discounted cash flow method has the advantage of ranking investments, but it becomes difficult to calculate.

Internal Rate of Return

The internal rate of return (IRR) method determines the interest rate required to make the present value of the cash flow equal to zero. It represents the maximum rate of interest that could be paid if all project funds were borrowed and the organization had to break even on the projects. The IRR considers the time value of money and is unaffected by the scale of the project. It can be used to rank alternatives and can be used to make accept/reject decisions when a minimum rate of return is specified. A major weakness of the IRR method is that it assumes all returns are reinvested at the same internal rate of return. This can make an investment alternative with a high rate of return look even better than it really is, and a project with a low rate of return look even worse. In practice, the IRR is rarely used to evaluate training investments.

Utility Analysis

Another interesting approach for developing the training payoff is utility analysis. Utility is a function of the duration of a training program's effect on employees' performance, the number of employees trained, the validity of the training program, the value of the job for which training was provided, and the total program cost.[3]

Utility analysis measures the economic contribution of a program according to how effective the program was in identifying and modifying behavior, hence the future service contribution of employees. Schmidt, Hunter, and Pearlman derived the following formula for assessing the dollar value of a training program:[4]

$$\Delta U = T \times N \times dt \times Sdy - N \times C$$

where:

ΔU	=	Monetary value of the training program
T	=	Duration in number of years of a training program's effect on performance
N	=	Number of employees trained
dt	=	True difference in job performance between the average trained and the average untrained employees in units of standard deviation
Sdy	=	Standard deviation of job performance of the untrained group in dollars
C	=	Cost of training per employee

Of all the factors in this formula, the true difference in job performance and the value of the target job are the most difficult to develop. The validity is determined by noting the performance differences between trained and untrained employees. The simplest method for obtaining this information is to have supervisors rate the performance of each group. Supervisors and experts estimate the value of the target job, Sdy.

Utility analysis is based totally on estimations. Because of the subjective nature of this approach, it has not achieved widespread acceptance by training and development professionals as a practical tool for evaluating the return on training investments.

Consequences of Not Training

For some organizations, the consequences of not training can be very serious. A company's inability to perform adequately might mean that it is unable to take on additional business or that it may lose existing business because of an untrained work force. Also, training can help avoid serious operational problems (accidents) or non-compliance issues (EEO violations). This method of calculating the return on training has received recent attention and involves the following steps:

- Establish that there is a potential problem, loss, or opportunity.
- Isolate the problems that lack of performance may create, such as non-compliance issues, loss of business, or the inability to take on additional business.
- Develop an estimate of the potential value of the problem, loss, or opportunity.
- If other factors are involved, determine the impact of each factor on the loss of income.
- Estimate the total cost of training using the techniques outlined in Chapter 6.
- Compare benefits with costs.

This approach has some disadvantages. The potential loss of income can be highly subjective and difficult to measure. Also, it may be difficult to isolate the factors involved and to determine their weight relative to lost income. Because of these concerns, this approach to evaluating the return on training investments is limited to certain types of programs and situations.

ROI Issues

ROI Complexity

As discussed in Chapter 1, developing the return on investment in training and development is a complex issue. The approach presented in this book is to take the complex process and simplify it by breaking it into small steps so it is understandable and acceptable to a variety of audiences. Figure 7-1 illustrates the complexity of this process.

The Number of Possibilities Make the Process Complex

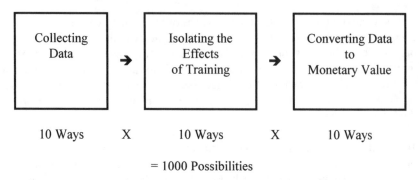

= 1000 Possibilities

Figure 7-1. *ROI complexity*

This book has presented the ten most common ways to collect post program data, ten ways to isolate the effects of training on business performance measures, and ten ways to convert data into monetary values. In essence, there are 1000 possible ways to evaluate a training program, as shown in Figure 7-1. This fact alone is often enough to cause some of the most eager individuals to avoid the ROI process. However, when each step is taken separately and issues addressed for a particular topic, the decisions are made incrementally all the way through the process. This helps to reduce a complex process to a more simplified and manageable effort. Figure 7-1 underscores an important advantage of this process. With so many different ways to tackle these three critical issues, the ROI process can be applied to almost any type of program in any setting.

Cautions When Using ROI

Because of the complexity and sensitivity of the ROI process, caution is needed when developing, calculating, and communicating the return on investment. The implementation of the ROI process is a very important issue which is a goal of many training and development departments. A few issues, described next, should be addressed to keep the process from going astray.

The ROI process should be developed for programs where a needs assessment has been conducted. Because of the evaluation problems that can develop when there is not a clear needs assessment, it is recommended that the

ROI be conducted only with programs that have had a comprehensive needs assessment, preferably with Level 3 and 4 data.   However, practical considerations and management requests may prohibit this suggested requirement.

The ROI analysis should always include one or more strategies for isolating the effects of training. Because of the importance of accounting for the influence of other factors, this step in the process must not be ignored. Too often, an excellent study, from what appears to be a very successful training effort, is perceived to be worthless because there was no attempt to account for other factors. Omission of this step seriously diminishes the credibility of the study.

When making estimates, use the most reliable and credible sources. Because estimates are critical to any type of analysis, they will usually be an important part of the ROI process.   When they are used, they should be developed properly and obtained from the most reliable and credible sources, those individuals who best understand the overall situation and can provide the most accurate estimation.

Take a conservative approach when developing both benefits and costs. Conservatism in ROI analysis builds accuracy and credibility.   What matters most is how the target audience perceives the value of the data. A conservative approach is always recommended for both the numerator of the ROI formula (benefits) and the denominator (program costs).

Use caution when comparing the ROI in training and development with other financial returns. There are many ways to calculate the return on funds invested or assets employed.   The ROI is just one of them.   Although the calculation for ROI in training and development uses the same basic formula as in other investment evaluations, it may not be fully understood by the target group.   Its calculation method and its meaning should be clearly communicated. More importantly, it should be an item accepted by management as an appropriate measure for training program evaluation.

Involve management in developing the return.   Management ultimately makes the decision if an ROI value is acceptable.   To the extent possible, management should be involved in setting the parameters for calculations and establishing targets by which programs are considered acceptable within the organization.

Approach sensitive and controversial issues with caution. Occasionally, sensitive and controversial issues will be generated when discussing an ROI value. It is best to avoid debates over what is measurable and what is not measurable unless there is clear evidence of the issue in question. Also, some programs are so fundamental to the survival of the organization that any attempt to measure it is unnecessary. For example, a program designed to improve customer service in a customer-focused company may escape the scrutiny of an ROI evaluation, on the assumption that if the program is well designed, it will improve customer service.

Teach others the methods for calculating the return. Each time an ROI is calculated, the training and development manager should use this opportunity to educate other managers and colleagues in the organization. Even if it is not in their area of responsibility, these individuals will be able to see the value of this approach to training and development evaluation. Also, when possible, each project should serve as a case study to educate the HRD staff on specific techniques and methods.

Do not boast about a high return. It is not unusual to generate what appears to be a very high return on investment for an HRD program. Several examples in this book have illustrated the possibilities. An HRD manager who boasts about a high rate of return will be open to potential criticism from others unless there are indisputable facts on which the calculation is based.

Do not try to use ROI on every program. Some programs are difficult to quantify, and an ROI calculation may not be feasible. Other methods of presenting the benefits may be more appropriate. As discussed in Chapter 1, HRD executives are encouraged to set targets for the percent of programs in which ROIs are developed. Also, specific criteria should be established that select programs for ROI analysis.

Conclusion

After the program benefits are collected and converted to monetary values and the program costs are developed in a fully loaded profile, the ROI calculation becomes a very easy step. It is just a matter of plugging the values into the appropriate formula. This chapter has presented the two basic approaches for calculating the return; the ROI formula and the cost/benefit ratio.

Each has its own advantages and disadvantages. Alternatives to ROI development were briefly discussed. Several examples were presented along with key issues that must be addressed in ROI calculations.

Case Study - Part F
National Auto Products Company

Costs

The costs to train 16 supervisors are:

Needs Assessment, Program Development, Facilitation	=	$21,500
Supplies and Materials ($85 x 16)	=	1,360
Food ($95 x 16)	=	1,520
Facilities	=	600
Evaluation	=	3,000
Salaries and Benefits ($362 x 1.39 x 16)	=	8,051
Total	=	$36,031

The facilitation charge from the vendor, which totaled $21,500, actually includes the costs for needs assessment, program development, and facilitation. If the program had been developed internally, these three charges would have to be developed separately. The daily salary was developed by dividing average salary ($27,500) by the total days worked (228). To obtain the total salaries and benefits cost, this number is multiplied by 3, adjusted upward by the benefits factor of 39%. This is equivalent to multiplying by 1.39. The total for each participant is multiplied by 16 to obtain the salaries and benefits.

Follow-Up

Because management was interested in knowing the results of the program as soon as possible, a four-month evaluation period was used. Data for six months prior to and four months after the program are presented in figure 702, which shows the productivity, quality, turnover, and absenteeism values for the plant. The training was conducted during a one-month period and no improvements were expected during that month. Consequently, the one month training period was excluded from the analysis.

As Figure 7-2 shows, productivity was enhanced after the implementation of training. According to the records of the production control department, the average percent of on-time production for six months prior to training was 92%. A value of 95% was used as post-training performance, which is the average of months three and four. Averaging the two monthly values avoids a spike in the calculations.

The reject rates, in parts per million (Quality Results), are presented in Figure 7-2 for the six months prior to training and for the four months after training. The pre-training six month average for reject rates was 110.7. Months 3 and 4 are averaged to yield a 106.5 value for the post-training value.

The plant's annual turnover rates averaged 29.5% for the six months prior to training and are presented in Figure 7-2. Turnover was calculated monthly and was reported as an annualized value for comparison, (i.e., a 2% monthly turnover was reflected as a 24% annual turnover rate on the report). The average for months 3 and 4 yields a value of 24.7%.

The absenteeism rate for the six months prior to training averaged 5.2% and was considered much too high by management. This figure includes only unexpected and unplanned absences. The average for months 3 and 4 yields a value of 2.7%. The monthly absenteeism rates are shown in Figure 7-2.

In addition to action plans, supervisors completed a brief questionnaire where they estimated how much of the improvement in performance was related to each of the three factors influencing the output variables. The results are presented in Table 7-4.

Productivity

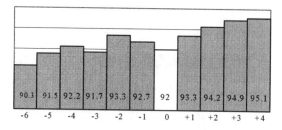

Percent of
on Time
Production

| 90.3 | 91.5 | 92.2 | 91.7 | 93.3 | 92.7 | 92 | 93.3 | 94.2 | 94.9 | 95.1 |

-6   -5   -4   -3   -2   -1   0   +1   +2   +3   +4

Months Before and After Training
Figure 7.2

Reject Rates

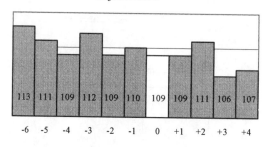

Parts
Per
Million

| 113 | 111 | 109 | 112 | 109 | 110 | 109 | 109 | 111 | 106 | 107 |

-6   -5   -4   -3   -2   -1   0   +1   +2   +3   +4

Months Before and After Training
Figure 7.2 continued

Turnover

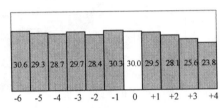

Annual
Turnover
Presented
As a Percent

Months Before and After Training
Figure 7.2 continued

Absenteeism

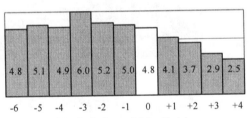

Monthly
Absenteeism
Percent

Months Before and After Training
Figure 7.2 continued

Table 7-4

	Pre-Training 6 Months Average	Post-Training, Months 3 and 4 Average	Pre-Post Differences	Participant's Estimate of Impact of Training	Annual Impact of Training (Estimates)	Trend Line Differences	Annual Impact of Training (Trend Line)
Productivity (% of Schedule)					$		$
Quality (Parts Per Million)					$		$
Turnover (Annualized)					$		$
Absenteeism (% Absence)					$		$

Table 7-5
Performance Improvement Estimates

	Training Program	TQM	Team Building	Total
Productivity (% of Schedule)	32%	49%	19%	100%
Quality (Parts Per Million)	37%	46%	17%	100%
Turnover (Annualized)	72%	7%	21%	100%
Absenteeism (% Absence)	76%	4%	20%	100%

Discussion Questions

1. Using the six months of data prior to the program, as shown in Figure 7-2, project the trend line for the data. Estimate the value for the third and fourth month average after training. Compare this value to the average of months 3 and 4 before training. The differences represent an estimate of the impact of training.
2. Using the data in the case, complete Table 7-5:
3. What are the total benefits expected from the program using both estimates from participants and estimates based on the trend line analysis?
4. What is the benefit/cost ratio and the ROI for the program using both the participant estimates of impact and the trend line estimate? How do you account for the differences?

References

[1] Wescott, R., "Applied Behavior Management Training," *In Action: Measuring Return on Investment*, Vol. 1. J. Phillips (Ed), Alexandria, VA: American Society for Training and Development, 1994, pp. 235-252.

[2] Ford, D., "Three Rs in the Workplace," *In Action: Measuring Return on Investment*, Vol. 1 J. Phillips (Ed), Alexandria, VA: American Society for Training and Development, 1994, pp. 85-104.

[3] Schmidt, F. L., Hunter, J. E., and Pearlman, K., "Assessing the Economic Impact of Personnel Programs on Workforce Productivity," *Personnel Psychology*, Vol. 35, p. 333-347, 1982.

[4] Schmidt, F. L., Hunter, J. E., and Pearlman, K., "Assessing the Economic Impact of Personnel Programs on Workforce Productivity," *Personnel Psychology*, Vol. 35, p. 333-347, 1982.

8

IDENTIFYING INTANGIBLE
MEASURES

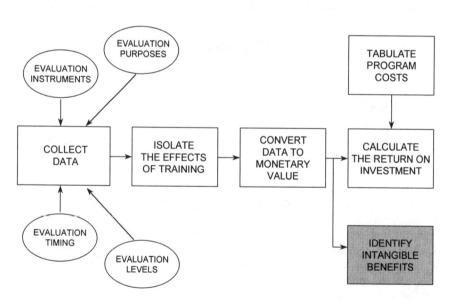

ROI Model

Intangible measures are the benefits or detriments directly linked to the training program, which cannot or should not be converted to monetary values.

These measures are often monitored after the training program has been conducted and, although not converted to monetary values, they are still very important in the evaluation process. While the range of intangible measures is almost limitless, this chapter describes the more common variables that are often linked with training. Table 8-1 lists these measures.

Table 8-1
Typical Intangible Variables Linked with Training

■ Attitude Survey Data	■ Employee Transfers
■ Organizational Commitment	■ Customer Satisfaction
■ Climate Survey Data	Survey Data
■ Employee Complaints	■ Customer Complaints
■ Grievances	■ Customer Response Time
■ Discrimination Complaints	■ Teamwork
■ Stress Reduction	■ Cooperation
■ Employee Turnover	■ Conflict
■ Employee Absenteeism	■ Decisiveness
■ Employee Tardiness	■ Communication

Key Issues

Importance

Not all measures can or should be converted to monetary values. By design, some are captured and reported as intangible measures. Although they may not be perceived as valuable as the measures converted to monetary values, intangible measures are critical to the overall evaluation process.[1] In some programs, such as interpersonal skills training, team development, leadership, communications training, and management development, the intangible or non-monetary benefits can be more important than monetary or tangible measures. Consequently, these measures should be monitored and reported as part of the overall evaluation. In practice, every training program, regardless of its nature, scope, and content, will have intangible measures associated with it.[2] The challenge is to efficiently identify and report them.

Identification of Measures

Intangible measures can be identified in several ways representing different time frames. First, they can be uncovered early in the process, during the needs assessment. Once identified, the intangible data is planned for collection as part of the overall data collection strategy. For example, a team leader training program has several hard data measures linked to the program. An intangible measure, employee satisfaction, is identified and monitored with no plans to convert it to a monetary value. Thus, from the beginning, this measure is destined to be a non-monetary benefit reported along with the ROI results.

A second way in which an intangible benefit is identified is to discuss with clients or sponsors the impact of training. Clients can usually identify intangible measures expected to be influenced by the program. For example, a management development program in a large multi-national company was conducted, and an ROI analysis was planned. Program developers, instructors, participants' managers, and senior executives identified potential intangible measures that were perceived to be influenced by the program.

The third way in which an intangible measure is identified is during an attempt to convert the data to monetary values. If the process used to convert the data to monetary value loses credibility, the measure should be reported as an intangible benefit. For example, in a selling skills program, customer satisfaction is identified early in the process as one of the measures of training success. A conversion to monetary values was attempted. However, the process of assigning a value to the data lost credibility; therefore, customer satisfaction was reported as an intangible benefit.

A fourth way in which an intangible measure is identified is during a follow-up evaluation. Although the measure was not expected nor anticipated in the initial program design, the measure surfaces on a questionnaire, in an interview, or during a focus group. Questions are often asked about other improvements linked to the training program. Several intangible measures are usually provided and there are no planned attempts to place a value on the actual measure. For example, in the evaluation of a customer service training program, participants were asked specifically what had improved about their work area and their relationship with customers as a result of the application of the skills acquired in the program. The participants provided over a dozen intangible measures, which managers perceived to be linked directly to the program.

Analysis

For most intangible data, no specific analysis is planned. Previous attempts to convert intangible data to monetary units results in aborting the entire process, thus no further data analysis was conducted. In some cases there may be attempts to isolate the effects of training using one or more of the methods outlined in Chapter 4. This step is necessary when there is a need to know the specific amount of change in the intangible measure that is linked to the program. In many cases, however, the intangible data reflect improvement. However, neither the precise amount of the improvement nor the amount of improvement related directly to the training will be clearly identified. Since the value of this data is not placed in the ROI calculation, intangible measures are not normally used to justify additional training or continuation of existing training. Consequently, a detailed analysis is not needed. Intangible benefits are viewed as supporting evidence of the programs success and are presented as qualitative data.

Employee Satisfaction

Employee satisfaction is perhaps one of the most important intangible measures. Almost any training program will improve job satisfaction if it is perceived to be successful by the participants, participants' employees, participants; customers, or peer group members. Some of the most influential employee satisfaction measures are briefly described here.

Attitude Survey Data

Many organizations conduct attitude surveys which reflect the degree to which employees are satisfied with the organization, their jobs, their supervisor, coworkers, and a host of other issues. Employee job satisfaction is closely correlated with absenteeism and turnover, both of which are linked with some training programs. Some attitude survey items focus on issues directly related to training programs such as satisfaction with the quality of leadership of managers and supervisors. Attitude survey data is usually linked to training results when specific issues on the survey are related to training. For example, in a diversity training program conducted for all employees at a television station, the annual attitude survey contained five questions directly tied to perceptions and attitudes influenced by the training program.

Because attitude surveys are usually taken annually, the results may not be in sync with the timing of the training program. When job satisfaction is one of the program objectives, some organizations conduct surveys at a prescribed timeframe after training and design the survey instrument around issues related to the training program. This approach, however, is very expensive.

Organizational Commitment

Measuring organizational commitment is perhaps a more important method for understanding the motivational state of employees. Similar to attitude surveys, organizational commitment instruments reflect the degree to which employees are aligned with company goals, values, philosophy, and practices. High levels of organizational commitment often correlate with high levels of productivity and performance; therefore, organizational commitment is an important intangible measure. Changes in survey data may reflect the success of the training program. The difficulty with this intangible measure is that it is not routinely measured in organizations.

Climate Survey Data

Some organizations conduct climate surveys, which reflect work climate changes such as communication, openness, trust, and quality of feedback. Climate surveys are similar to attitude surveys, but are more general and often focus on a range of workplace issues and environmental enablers and inhibitors. Climate surveys conducted before and after training may reflect the extent to which training has changed these intangible measures.

Employee Complaints

Some organizations record and report specific employees' complaints. A reduction of employee complaints is sometimes directly related to training, such as a team building program. Consequently, the level of complaints is used as a measure of the program's success and is reported as an intangible measure.

Grievances

In both union and non-union organizations, grievances often reflect the level of dissatisfaction or disenchantment with a variety of factors in their organization. Sometimes, training programs, such as labor management cooperation, are designed to reduce the number of grievances when they are excessive. An improvement in the grievance level reflects the success of the training program. This measure may be converted to a monetary value, although it may be reported as an intangible measure.

Discrimination Complaints

Employee dissatisfaction shows up in different types of discrimination complaints, ranging from informal complaints to external charges and even litigation. Training programs. such as a sexual harassment prevention workshop, may be designed to prevent complaints or to reduce the current level of complaint activity. The result of the program, in terms of complaint reduction, may not be converted to monetary values because of the various assumptions and estimations involved in the process. When this is the case, these measures are reported as intangible program benefits.

Stress Reduction

Occasionally, training programs reduce work-related stress by showing participants how to improve the job, accomplish more in a workday, and relieve tension and anxiety. The subsequent reduction in stress may be directly linked to the training program.

Employee Withdrawal

When job satisfaction deteriorates to the point where employees withdraw from work or the organization, either permanently or temporarily, the results can be disastrous. Several employee withdrawal measures are monitored and are often linked to training or performance programs. Additional information on employee withdrawal measures outlined in this section can be found in other resources.[3]

Employee Turnover

Perhaps the most critical employee withdrawal variable is employee turnover. An extremely costly variable, turnover, can have devastating consequences on organizations when it is excessive. Many supervisor and team leader training programs are designed to reduce employee turnover in their work units. In many situations, turnover is actually converted to monetary values, using one of the methods described in Chapter 5. However, because of the multitude of costs and assumptions involved in developing the value, some organizations prefer not to convert turnover to a monetary value. In this case, turnover should be reported as an intangible benefit, reflecting the success of the training program.

Employee Absenteeism

Absenteeism is another disruptive and costly variable. Many training programs are designed to reduce absenteeism, and the impact of training on absenteeism can usually be pinpointed. Although the cost of absenteeism can be developed, sometimes the conversion process is not credible enough for some audiences, and consequently, absenteeism changes are reported as intangible benefits.

Employee Tardiness

Many organizations actually monitor tardiness, especially with the use of electronic and computerized time reporting. Tardiness is an irritating work habit problem that can cause inefficiencies and delays. A few training programs are designed to reduce it. Tardiness is very difficult to convert to a monetary value. Consequently, when tardiness is presented as an improvement from a training program, it is listed as an intangible benefit.

Employee Transfers

A unique way for employees to withdraw is to request a transfer to another section, department, or division of the organization. Requests for transfers often reflect dissatisfaction with a variety of issues, including management, policies, and practices in the organization. Training programs are sometimes designed to reduce or remove these unpleasant environmental influences. In these situations, requests for transfers are monitored and reported as an intangible benefit of training. There is usually no attempt to assign monetary values to transfers.

Customer Service

Because of the importance of building and improving customer service, a variety of measures are often monitored and reported as a payoff of training. A variety of customer service training programs have a direct influence on these measures. Because of the difficulty of placing values on them, customer service measures are not usually converted to monetary values and are reported as intangible benefits. Several measures are described here.

Customer Satisfaction Survey Data

One of the most important measures is actual survey data showing the degree to which customers are pleased with the products and services. These survey values, reported as absolute data or as an index, represent important data from which to compare the success of a customer service training program. Although techniques are available to convert survey data to monetary values, in most situations, the conversion is rarely attempted. Consequently, customer service improvements are usually reported as intangible benefits.

Customer Complaints

Most organizations monitor customer complaints. Each complaint is recorded along with the disposition and the time required to resolve the complaint, as well as specific costs associated with the complaint resolution. Organizations sometimes design training programs to reduce the number of customer complaints. Because it is difficult to assign an accurate monetary value to a customer complaint, the measure usually becomes a very important intangible benefit.

Customer Response Time

Providing prompt customer service is a critical issue in most organizations. Consequently, the time it takes to respond to specific customer service requests or problems is recorded and monitored. Response time reduction is sometimes an objective of training programs, although the reduction is not usually converted to monetary values. Thus, customer response time becomes an important intangible benefit.

Other Customer Responses

A variety of other types of customer responses can be tracked such as creativity with customer response, responsiveness to cost and pricing issues, customer loyalty, and other important issues customers may specify or require. Monitoring these variables can provide more evidence of the training program's results when the program influences particular variables. And because of the difficulty of assigning values to the items, they are usually reported as intangible measures.

Team Effectiveness Measures

A variety of measures are often monitored to reflect how well teams are working. Although the output of teams and the quality of their work are often measured as hard data and converted to monetary values, other interpersonal measures may be monitored and reported separately. A few of these measures are represented here.

Teamwork

Sometimes organizations survey team members before and after training to see if the level of teamwork has increased. The monetary value of increased teamwork is rarely developed and consequently, it is reported as an intangible benefit.

Cooperation

The success of a team often depends on the cooperative spirit of team members. Some instruments measure the level of cooperation before and after training. Because of the difficulty of converting this measure to a monetary value, it is always reported as an intangible benefit.

Conflict

In team environments, the level of conflict is measured. A reduction in conflict may reflect the success of training. In most situations, a monetary value is not placed on conflict reduction, and it is reported as an intangible benefit.

Decisiveness

Teams make decisions, and the timing of the decision-making process often becomes an issue. Consequently, decisiveness is sometimes measured in terms of the speed at which decisions are made. Survey measures may reflect the perception of the team or in some cases, may monitor how quickly decisions are made. Some training programs are expected to influence this process, and improvements are usually reported as intangible benefits.

Communication

A variety of communication instruments reflects the quality and quantity of communication within a team. Changes in communications skills, or perceptions of skills, driven by a training program are not usually converted to monetary values and are reported as an intangible benefit.

Other Team Measures

While the previously listed measures are common, there are many other potential measures available that reflect the performance and functioning of teams. Table 8-2 shows a report of the intangible measures after a team building program had been undertaken. [4] These measures, obtained as part of a survey process, show the possibilities for reflecting team success.

Table 8-2
A Sample of Intangible Measures of Team Effectiveness

Item	# Of Resp.	Point Range	Total Points	Point Average	Rank (By Avg.)
Clearly states mission/goals	7	4 - 6	34	4.9	4
Operates creatively	7	3 - 7	37	5.3	2
Focuses on results	7	4 - 5	31	4.3	6
Clarifies roles and responsibilities	7	2 - 6	34	4.9	4
Is well-organized	7	4 - 6	36	5.1	3
Builds upon individual strengths	7	5 -7	41	5.9	1
Supports leadership/each other	7	4 - 6	37	5.3	2
Develops team climate	5	3 - 5	21	4.2	7
Resolves disagreements	6	2 - 5	20	3.3	9
Communicates openly	7	2 - 4	21	3.0	10
Makes objective decisions	7	3 - 6	33	4.7	5
Evaluates its own effectiveness	7	2 - 4	24	3.4	8

Source: Bader, G.E., Bloom, A.E., and Change, R.Y. *Measuring Team Performance.*
Irvine, CA: Richard Chang Associates, 1994.

Conclusion

A variety of available intangible measures reflect the success of the HRD program. Although they may not be perceived as valuable as specific monetary measures; nevertheless, they are an important part of an overall evaluation. Intangible measures should be identified, explored, examined, and monitored for changes when they are linked to the program. Collectively, they add a unique dimension to the overall program results since most, if not all, programs have intangible measures associated with them. While some of the most common intangible measures were covered in this chapter, the coverage was not meant to be complete. The number of intangible measures is almost unlimited.

Case Study - Part G
National Auto Products Company

Figure 8-1 shows the projected trend lines and the estimates for the trend line differences.

The tabulations of the benefits for the program for both participant estimates and trend line analysis differences are shown in Table 8-3.

Figure 8-1

Productivity

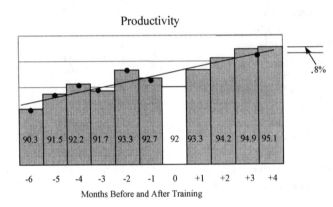

Percent of
On-Time
Production

.8%

| 90.3 | 91.5 | 92.2 | 91.7 | 93.3 | 92.7 | 92 | 93.3 | 94.2 | 94.9 | 95.1 |

-6   -5   -4   -3   -2   -1   0   +1   +2   +3   +4

Months Before and After Training

Figure 8-1 Cont'd.

Reject Rates

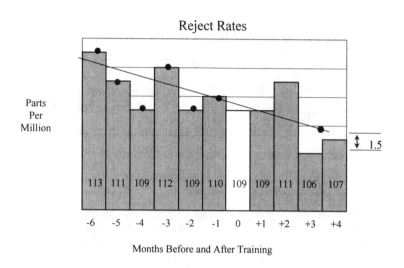

Parts
Per
Million

113 111 109 112 109 110 109 109 111 106 107

-6 -5 -4 -3 -2 -1 0 +1 +2 +3 +4

1.5

Months Before and After Training

Figure 8-1. Cont'd.

Turnover

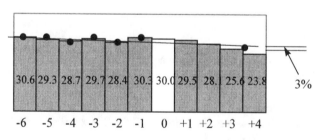

Annual
Turnover
Presented
As a Percent

30.6 29.3 28.7 29.7 28.4 30.3 30.0 29.5 28.1 25.6 23.8

3%

-6 -5 -4 -3 -2 -1 0 +1 +2 +3 +4

Months Before and After Training

Figure 8-1. Cont'd.

Absenteeism

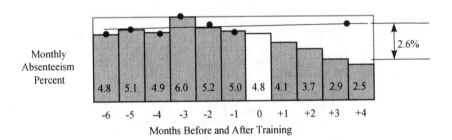

Monthly
Absenteeism
Percent

| 4.8 | 5.1 | 4.9 | 6.0 | 5.2 | 5.0 | 4.8 | 4.1 | 3.7 | 2.9 | 2.5 |

2.6%

-6   -5   -4   -3   -2   -1   0   +1   +2   +3   +4
Months Before and After Training

While participants' estimates (shaded above) were considered more accurate than the trend line estimates in this situation, they were recommended because they generated the lowest values for benefits. This is the conservative approach. The projected annual benefits for training 16 supervisors are as follows, using participants' estimates.

Productivity:
Savings = .96 x $21,000 = $20,160

Quality:
Savings = 1.55 x $3,100 $4,805

Turnover:
Change in number leaving in a year = 385 x 3.46% = 13.3
Savings = 13.3 x $5,000 = $66,500

Absenteeism:
Change in absences (Incidents) = 385 x 228 x 1.9% = 1668
Savings = 1668 x $98 $163,446

Table 8-3

	Pre-Training, 6 Month Average	Post-Training Months 3 and 4 Average	Pre-Post Differences	Participant's Estimate of Impact of Training	Annual Impact of Training (Estimates)	Trend Line Differences	Annual Impact of Training (Trend Line)
Productivity (% of Schedule)	92%	95%	3%	.96% (3% x 32%)	$20,160	.8%	$16,800
Quality (Parts Per Million)	110.7	106.5	4.2	1.55 (4.2 x 37%)	$4,805	1.5	$4,650
Turnover (Annualized)	29.5%	24.7%	4.8%	3.46% (4.8% x 72%)	$66,500	3%	$57,750
Absenteeism (% Absence)	5.2%	2.7%	2.5%	1.9% (2.5% x 76%)	$163,446	2.6%	$223,663

The trend line values are developed the same way except the trend line differences are used instead of the participant estimates.

Total Benefits Summary:

	Based on Estimates	Based on Trend Line
Increase in Productivity	$20,160	$16,800
Reduction in Rejects	$4,805	$4,650
Reduction in Employee Turnover	$66,500	$57,750
Reduction in Absenteeism	$163,446	$223,663
Total	$254,911	$302,863

ROI and BCR Calculations:

	Benefit to Cost Ratio:	Return on Investment:
Estimates	$BCR = \dfrac{\$254,911}{36,031} = 7.1$	$ROI\ (\%) = \dfrac{254,911 - 36,031}{36,031} \times 100 = 607\%$
Trend Line	$BCR = \dfrac{302,863}{36,031} = 8.4$	$ROI\ (\%) = \dfrac{302,863 - 36,031}{36,031} \times 100\% = 741\%$

Discussion Questions

1. Are your estimates of the trend line analysis different from those presented here? How do you account for these differences?
2. Which ROI would you report to management and why?
3. Are these numbers lower or higher than you expected? Comment.
4. How do you think these estimates would compare with the values at six months after the program is conducted? One year?
5. How could the ROI process be improved?
6. What are the potential intangible benefits from this program?

References

[1] Denzin, N.K., and Lincoln, Y. S. (Eds.), *Handbook of Qualitative Research*, Thousand Oaks, CA: Sage Publications, 1994.

[2] Gummesson, E., *Qualitative Methods and Management Research* (Revised Edition), Thousand Oaks, CA: Sage Publications, 1991.

[3] *Accountability in HRM*

[4] Bader, G.E., Bloom, A.E., and Chang, R.Y., *Measuring Team Performance*. Irvine, CA: Richard Chang Associates, 1994.

9

ROI AT MULTIPLE LEVELS

Sometimes there is confusion about when it is appropriate to develop the ROI, the types of data to collect, and the level of evaluation that is most appropriate for an ROI calculation. The traditional and recommended approach, described in the previous chapters of this book, is to base ROI calculations strictly on business results obtained from the program. Business performance measures (Level 4 data) are easily converted to a monetary value, which is necessary for an ROI calculation. Sometimes these measures are not available, and it is usually assumed that an ROI calculation is out of the question. This chapter will illustrate that ROI calculations are possible at all levels of evaluation.

ROI at Level 1: Reaction

When a Level 1 evaluation includes planned applications of training, the important data can ultimately be used in ROI calculations. With questions concerning how participants plan to use what they have learned and the results that they expect to achieve, higher level evaluation information can be developed. The questions presented in Figure 9-1 illustrate how this type of data is collected with an end-of-program questionnaire for a supervisory training program. Participants are asked to state specifically how they plan to use the program material and the results they expect to achieve. They are asked to convert their accomplishments to an annual monetary value and to show the basis for developing the values. Participants can moderate their responses with a level of confidence to make the data more credible while allowing them to reflect their uneasiness with the process.

Planned Improvements

■ As a result of this program what specific actions will you attempt as you
apply what you have learned?
1. _____
2. _____
3. _____

■ Please indicate what specific measures, outcomes, or projects will change as
a result of your actions.

1. _____
2. _____
3. _____

■ As a result of the anticipated changes in the above, please estimate (in
monetary values) the benefits to your organization over a period of one
year. _____

■ What is the basis of this estimate?
_____
_____

■ What confidence, expressed as a percentage, can you put in your estimate?
(0% = No Confidence; 100% = Certainty) _____%

Figure 9-1. *Important questions to ask on feedback questionnaires*

When tabulating data, managers multiply the confidence level by the annual
monetary value which results in a more conservative estimate for use in the data
analysis. For example, if a participant estimated that the monetary impact of the
program would be $10,000, but was only 50% confident, a $5,000 value is used
in the calculations.

To develop a summary of the expected benefits, several steps are taken.
First, any data that is incomplete, unusable, extreme, or unrealistic is discarded.
Next, an adjustment is made for the confidence estimate as previously described.
Individual data items are then totaled. Finally, as an optional exercise, the total

value is adjusted again by a factor that reflects the subjectivity of the process and the possibility that participants will not achieve the results they anticipate. This figure can be developed with input from management or can be established by the training and development staff. In one organization, the benefits are divided by 2 to develop a number to use in the equation. Finally, the ROI is calculated using the net program benefits divided by the program costs. This value, in essence, becomes the expected return on investment, after the two adjustments for accuracy and subjectivity.

Perhaps this process can be best described using an actual case. M&H Engineering and Construction Company is involved in the design and construction of large commercial projects such as plants, paper mills, and municipal water systems. Safety is always a critical issue at M&H and usually commands much management attention. To improve the current level of safety performance, a two-day safety awareness program was developed for project engineers and construction superintendents. The program focused on safety leadership, safety planning, safety training, safety meetings, accident investigation, safety policy and procedures, safety standards, and workers' compensation. After completing this training program, participants were expected to improve the safety performance of their specific construction projects. A dozen safety performance measures used in the company were presented and discussed during the program. At the end of the two-day program, participants completed a comprehensive Level 1 reaction questionnaire, which probed into specific action items planned as a result of this program and the monetary value of the completed items. In addition, participants explained the basis for estimates and placed a confidence level on their estimates. Table 9-1 presents data provided by the first group of participants. Only 18 of the 24 participants supplied data, (experience has shown that approximately 50-70% of participants will provide usable data on this series of questions). The total cost of the program, including participants' salaries was $29,000. Prorated development costs were included in this figure.

The monetary value of the planned improvements are extremely high, reflecting the participants' optimism and enthusiasm at the end of a very effective program. As a first step in the analysis, extreme data items are omitted. Data such as millions, unlimited, and $4 million are discarded, and each remaining value is multiplied by the confidence value and totaled. This adjustment is a way of reducing the very subjective estimates. The resulting tabulations yielded a total improvement of $655,125. Because of the subjectivity of the process, the values were adjusted by a factor of 2, an arbitrary

Table 9-1
Level 1 Data for ROI Calculations

Participant No.	Estimated Value	Basis	Confidence Level
1	$80,000	Reduction in Accidents	90%
2	90,000	OSHA Reportable Injuries	80%
3	50,000	Accident Reduction	100%
4	10,000	First Aid Visits/Visits to Doctor	100%
5	50,000	Reduction in Lost Time Injuries	95%
6	Millions	Total Accident Cost	100%
7	75,000	Workers' Compensation	80%
8	7,500	OSHA Citations	75%
9	50,000	Reduction in Accidents	100%
10	30,000	Workers Compensation	80%
11	150,000	Reduction in Total Accident Costs	90%
12	20,000	OSHA Fines/Citations	70%
13	40,000	Accident Reductions	100%
14	4,000,000	Total Cost of Safety	95%
15	65,000	Total Workers' Compensation	50%
16	Unlimited	Accidents	100%
17	45,000	Injuries	90%
18	2,000	Visits to Doctor	100%

number suggested by the HRD manager, but supported by the management group. This "adjusted" value is $327,563 or $328,000 with rounding. The projected ROI, based on the end of program questionnaire is as follows:

$$ROI = \frac{\$328,000 - \$29,000}{\$29,000} \times 100 = 1,031\%$$

The HRD manager communicated these projected values to the CEO but cautioned that the data was very subjective, although it had been twice adjusted downward. The HRD manager also emphasized that the forecasted results were generated by the participants in the program, who should be aware of what they could accomplish. In addition, she mentioned that a follow-up was planned to determine the results that were actually delivered by the group.

A word of caution is in order when using Level 1 ROI data. These calculations are highly subjective and may not reflect the extent to which participants will apply what they have learned to achieve results. A variety of influences in the work environment can enhance or inhibit the participants' attainment of performance goals. Having high expectations at the end of the program is no guarantee that those expectations will be met. Disappointments are documented regularly in programs throughout the world and are reported in research findings.[1]

While this process is subjective and possibly unreliable, it does have some usefulness. First, if evaluation must stop at this level, this approach provides more insight into the value of the program than the data from typical reaction questionnaires. Managers will usually find this data more useful than a report stating that "40% of participants rated the program above average." Unfortunately, there is evidence that a high percentage of evaluations stop at this first level of evaluation.[2] The majority of HRD programs do not enjoy rigorous evaluations at Level 3 and 4. Reporting Level 1 ROI data is a more useful indication of the potential impact of the program than the alternative which is to report attitudes and feelings about the program and instructor.

Second, this data can form a basis for comparison of different presentations of the same program. If one program forecasts an ROI of 300% whereas another projects 30%, then it appears that one program may be more effective than the other. The participants in the first program have more confidence in the planned application of the program material.

Third, collecting this type of data causes increased attention to program outcomes. Participants leave the program with an understanding that specific behavior change is expected, which produces results for the organization. This issue becomes very clear to participants as they anticipate results and convert them to monetary values. Even if this projected improvement is ignored, the exercise is productive because of the important message sent to participants.

Fourth, if a follow-up is planned to pinpoint post-program results, the data collected in the Level 1 evaluation can be very helpful for comparison. This end of program data collection helps participants plan the implementation of what they have learned. Incidentally, when a follow-up is planned, participants are more conservative with these estimates.

The use of Level 1 ROI is increasing, and some organizations have based all of their ROI calculations on Level 1 data.[3] Although it may be very subjective, it does add value, particularly when it is included as part of a comprehensive evaluation system.

ROI at Level 2: Testing

Testing for changes in skills and knowledge in HRD programs is a very common technique for Level 2 evaluation. In many situations, participants are required to demonstrate their knowledge or skills at the end of the program, and their performance is expressed as a numerical value. When this type of test is developed, it must be reliable and valid. A reliable test is one that is stable over time with consistent results. A valid test is one that measures what it purports to measure. Since a test should reflect the content of the HRD program, successful mastery of program content should be related to improved job performance. Consequently, there should be a relationship between test scores and subsequent on-the-job performance. Figure 9-2 illustrates the potential relationship between test scores and job performance in a perfect correlation. This relationship, expressed as a correlation coefficient, is a measure of validity of the test.

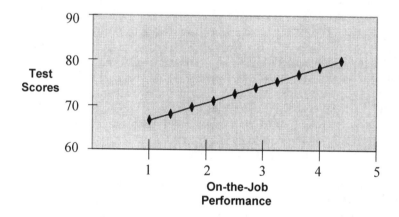

Figure 9-2. *Relationship between test scores and performance*

This testing situation provides an excellent opportunity for an ROI calculation with Level 2 data using test results. When there is a statistically significant relationship between test scores and on-the-job performance, and the performance can be converted to monetary units, then it is possible to use test scores to estimate the ROI from the program, using the following steps:

■   Ensure that the program content reflects desired on-the-job performance.
■   Develop an end-of-program test that reflects program content.

- Establish a statistical relationship between test data and output performance for participants.
- Predict performance levels of each participant with given test scores.
- Convert performance data to monetary value.
- Compare total predicted value of program with program costs.

An example will illustrate this approach. Consumer Products Marketing (CPM) is the marketing division of a large consumer products company. Sales representatives for CPM make frequent sales calls to large retail food and drug companies with the objective of increasing sales and market share of CPM products. Sales representatives must ensure that retailers understand the advantages of CPM products, provide adequate space for their products, and assist in promotional and advertising efforts.

CPM has developed a very strong sales culture and recruits highly capable individuals for sales representative assignments. Newly recruited sales representatives rotate through different divisions of the company in a two-month assignment to learn where and how the products are made and their features and benefits, as well as specific product marketing strategies. This initial assignment culminates with an intensive one-week Professional Marketing Training Program, which focuses on sales techniques, marketing strategies, and customer service skills. At the end of the one-week program, participants complete a comprehensive exam which reflects the knowledge and skills taught in the program. As part of the exam, participants analyze specific customer service and sales situations and decide on specific actions. Also, the test covers product features, policies, and marketing practices.

To validate the test, CPM developed correlations between test scores and actual on-the-job performance measured by sales volumes, sales growth, and market shares for sales representatives. The correlations were statistically significant with each variable. As a quick way of calculating the expected ROI for a program, CPM estimates output levels for each item using the test scores, converts them to monetary values, and calculates the ROI.

As with the previous ROI estimate with end of program questionnaires, some cautions are in order. This is a forecast of the ROI and not the actual value. Although participants acquired the skills and knowledge from the program it is no guarantee that they will apply the techniques and processes successfully and that the results will be achieved. This process assumes that the current group of participants has the same relationship to output performance as previous groups. It ignores a variety of environmental influences, which can alter the situation.

And finally, the process requires calculating the initial correlation coefficient which may be difficult to develop for most tests.

Although this approach develops an estimate, based on historical relationships, it can be useful in a comprehensive evaluation strategy and it has several advantages. First, if post-program evaluations (Level 4) are not planned, this process will yield more information about the projected value of the program than what would be obtained from the raw test scores. This process represents an expected return on investment based on the historical relationships involved.   Second, by developing individual ROI measurements, and communicating them to participants, the process has reinforcement potential. It communicates to participants that increased sales and market share are expected through the applications of what was learned in the program. Third, this process can have considerable credibility with management and can preclude expensive follow-ups and post program monitoring. If these relationships are statistically sound, the estimate should have credibility with the target group.

ROI at Level 3: Skills and Competencies

In almost every HRD program, participants are expected to change their on-the-job behaviors by applying of the program materials. On-the-job applications are very critical to program success. Although the use of the skills on the job is no guarantee that results will follow, it is an underlying assumption for most programs that if the knowledge and skills are applied, then results will follow. Some of the most prestigious training organizations, such as Motorola University, base their ultimate evaluation on this assumption.[4]   A few organizations attempt to take this process a step further and measure the value of on-the-job behavior change and calculate the ROI. In these situations, estimates are taken from individual participants, their supervisors, the management group, or experts in the field. The following steps are used to develop the ROI:

1. Develop competencies for the target job.
2. Indicate percentage of job success that is covered in the training program.
3. Determine monetary value of competencies using salaries and employee benefits of participants.
4. Compute the worth of pre- and post-program skill levels.
5. Subtract post-program values from pre-program values.
6. Compare the total added benefits with the program costs.

Perhaps an example will illustrate one technique to measure the value of on-the-job applications. The United States government redesigned its Introduction to Supervision course, a five-day training program for newly appointed supervisors. [5] The program focuses on eight competencies:

1. role and responsibilities of the supervisor;
2. communications;
3. planning, assigning, controlling, and evaluating work;
4. ethics;
5. leadership and motivation;
6. analyzing performance problems;
7. customer service; and
8. managing diversity

The immediate managers of the new supervisors indicated that these eight competencies accounted for 81% of first-level supervisors' jobs. For the target group being evaluated, the average annual salary plus benefits for the newly appointed supervisors was $42,202. Thus, multiplying this figure by the amount of job success accounted for by the competencies (81%), yielded a dollar value of $34,184 per participant. If a person was performing successfully in these eight competencies for one year, the value to the agency would be $34,184. Of course, this assumes that employees are paid an amount equal to their contribution, when they are fully competent.

Using a scale of 0-9, managers rated the skills for each of the competencies before the program was conducted. The average level of skills required to be successful in the job was determined to be 6.44. The skill ratings, prior to the job, was 4.96, which represented 77% of the 6.44 (i.e., participants were performing at 77% of the level to be successful in the competencies). After the program, the skill rating was 5.59, representing 87% of the level to be successful.

Monetary values were assigned based on the participants' salaries. Performance at the required level was worth $34,184. At a 77% proficiency level, the new supervisors were performing at a contribution value of $26,322. After training, this value had reached 87%, representing a contribution value of $29,740. The difference in these values, $3,418, represents the gain per participant attributable to training. The program cost was $1,368 per participant. Thus, the ROI is:

$$ROI = \frac{\$3,418 - \$1,368}{\$1,368} = \frac{2,050}{1,368} \times 100 = 150\%$$

As with other estimates, a word of caution is in order. These results are subjective because the rating systems used are subjective and may not necessarily reflect an accurate assessment of the value of the program. Also, since training is usually implemented to help the organization achieve its objectives, some managers insist on tangible changes in hard data such as quantity, quality, cost, and time. For them, Level 3 evaluation is not always a good substitute for Level 4 data, if it is available.

Although this process is subjective, it has several useful advantages. First, if there are no plans to track the actual impact of the program in terms of specific measurable business results (Level 4), then this approach represents a credible substitute. In many programs, particularly skill-building programs for supervisors, it is difficult to identify tangible changes on the job. Therefore, alternate approaches to determine the worth of a program are needed. Second, this approach results in data that are usually credible with the management group if they understand how it is developed and the assumptions behind it. An important point is that the data on the changes in competence level came from the managers who have rated their supervisors. In this specific project, the numbers were large enough to make the process statistically significant.

ROI at Level 4: Business Results

For most programs that develop ROI calculations, the focus is on the business results (Level 4 data) that have been influenced by the HRD program. These output variables are usually expressed in terms of cost reduction, productivity increases, improved quality, increased customer service, or reduced response times. It is relatively easy to convert them to monetary values for an ROI calculation. Earlier chapters focused on this type of data for ROI calculations. A brief explanation is presented here to contrast with ROI at other levels.

There are two critical issues involved in this Level 4 ROI development. The first is isolating the effect of training. When a program has been conducted and the output variables have changed, the first step for the evaluator is to determine the extent to which the training program changed the output variables. As presented in Chapter 4, at least 10 strategies can be used to isolate these variables. Each of these strategies varies in terms of their ability to provide reliable estimates of the program's influence.   The second challenge is to convert business results to a monetary unit using one or more of the strategies covered in Chapter 5. This step involves converting output data, such as a reduction in error rates, improvement in customer service, or a decrease in response times, to actual monetary units so that a monetary value can be developed. For some situations this is a relatively easy task. For example, cost reductions usually can be moved directly to the benefit side of the equation without a conversion. Productivity measures can be converted to units of profit from the additional productivity. It is more difficult to assign monetary values to quality improvements, response times, and customer satisfaction levels. There are at least ten strategies for making this conversion, each of which provides a reliable process for developing the value.

An example illustrates the process involved.   The Magnavox Electronic Systems Company's mechanical and electrical assemblers lacked basic skills.[6] On a trial basis, the company implemented a workplace basic skills (literacy) training program to improve verbal and mathematical skills.   The company evaluated the program at all four levels. The Level 4 evaluation resulted in the reduction of scrap rates, rework costs, and productivity improvements. Management estimated the amounts of these variables that were attributed to the program and then converted the resulting values to monetary units. Overall, the program netted annualized improvements of $321,600 when compared to the program cost of $38,233. This yields an ROI value of 741%.

ROI calculations on business results are very credible and reliable if appropriate processes have been used to isolate the effect of training and to accurately convert the results to monetary units. When ROI data are needed, this level of evaluation should always be sought if it is at all possible. ROI with Level 4 thus becomes the fifth level of evaluation, the ultimate level of accountability.

Conclusion

This chapter illustrates that ROI calculations can be developed at different levels of evaluation, although most practitioners and researchers focus only on Level 3 and 4 data for ROI calculations. While post-program data are desired, there are situations when Level 3 and Level 4 data are not available or evaluations at those levels are not attempted or planned. ROI estimates, developed at Level 1 and 2, can be very useful and helpful to management and the HRD staff, while at the same time focusing the program participants' attention on the economic impact of training. Using ROI estimates at Level 1 and 2 may give a false sense of accuracy. Figure 9-3 shows the relationship of ROI at the different levels. As would be expected, ROI calculations with Level 1 data are at the lowest in credibility and accuracy, but have the advantage of being inexpensive and relatively easy to conduct. However, ROIs using Level 4 data are high in credibility and accuracy, but are very expensive and difficult to develop.

ROI with:	Data Collection Timing-(Relative to Program)	Credibility	Accuracy	Cost to Develop	Difficulty
Pre-Program Forecast	Before				
Level 1 Data	During				
Level 2 Data	During				
Level 3 Data	After				
Level 4 Data	After				

Figure 9-3. *ROI at different levels*

Although ROI calculations at Level 4 are preferred, ROIs at other levels are an important part of a comprehensive and systematic evaluation process. This usually means that targets for evaluation should be established as illustrated in Table 9-2.

The first set of targets are the percent of courses evaluated at a particular level. Level 1 is usually very high, in the 90-100% range, whereas Level 5 is extremely low, usually in the 5% range. The next target is the percent of courses in which ROI is developed at that level. The ROIs at Level 1 would usually have the highest percent, whereas ROI at Level 4 is much lower. These targets are very specific to the organization and reflect the desires of the staff to develop ROI calculations and the resources available to pursue them.

Table 9-2
Targets for ROI Calculations

Level of Evaluation	Evaluated at this Level	Target Percent of ROI
1. Reaction/Planned Action	90%	15%
2. Learning	50%	10%
3. Job Application	25%	10%
4. Business Results	10%	5%
5. ROI	5%	N/A

Case Study - Part H
National Auto Products Company

Trend Line Analysis

To illustrate the simplicity of this technique, the trend line projection for this project was developed using a ruler. While this approach provided enough accuracy for this situation, it can result in varying training impact estimates. If more accuracy is needed, a computer program or calculator can be used to forecast the actual values. If the freehand technique is used, it is best to attempt the process three or four times and use an average of the lines. Having midpoint values instead of bars is sometimes helpful. Also, if there is not enough spread between the numbers on the vertical axis, perhaps the scale can be adjusted to help estimate the trend line.

ROI Analysis

Because the participants were primed to provide estimates after the program and had ample time to think through the issues during the follow-up period, they felt very comfortable in providing estimates. Consequently, the evaluation team felt that the participant's estimates were perhaps more reliable than the trend line analysis and thus favored the estimates in the actual analysis. Also, because the ROI from the participant-estimating process was lower than the trend line analysis, this value became the preferred choice to present to management. It should be noted, however, that the trend line analysis, when applicable, can usually provide a more reliable and accurate method for isolating the effects of training, making it the preferred choice. Because the evaluation team developed both values, they presented both items to management to illustrate the process in two different ways. This was particularly helpful in building senior management's confidence in the estimating process.

The values presented in this study were much higher than management anticipated, even higher than the consulting firm anticipated. In discussions held before implementation, the senior management team (president, director of manufacturing, and plant manager) agreed that for the program to be successful, the payoff would have to be in productivity and quality. This senior management group even suggested that absenteeism and turnover be considered intangible data and reported as additional improvements without a conversion to monetary values. Thus, in early discussions, absenteeism and turnover, although linked directly to the skills training, were considered to be potentially low impact variables using improvements in productivity and quality alone. If the original suggestion had been followed, the program would have generated a negative ROI. An important lesson was learned. Behaviorally based Level 4 data, although considered to be soft in nature, can have a tremendous impact in the organization. And in this situation, the impact would have been considerably enhanced if more appropriate values were used for the monetary conversion of absenteeism and turnover.

An important issue evolved concerning the projection of output data six months to one year after the program. It was clear that the output was moving in the right direction and it appeared that further improvement was in store. While it is tempting to assume the variables will continue to improve, in reality, other variables usually enter the analysis and a deterioration of the output variables may be realized, unless additional training or interventions are implemented. However, this is what happened. Each data item continued to improve for the six months. Absenteeism tapered off and then increased slightly, turnover remained fairly constant, while productivity and quality continued to improve, perhaps driven by the TQM and team building sessions.

As part of the evaluation process, the evaluation team (consultant, facilitators, HRD manager, and department heads) explored ways in which the process could be improved. The team discussed several issues. First, because the control group strategy most accurately isolates the effects of training, the team thought it would have been better to initiate this program in a plant that could be compared to another location in a control group arrangement. This strategy will often develop more confidence in the process and will build a more convincing case for the high impact ROI.

A second issue was the needs assessment. The team thought it was important to have sufficient evidence of a direct connection between the Level 4 measures and the planned training program. However, some team members wanted to see more evidence of how this was accomplished so that they would be more convinced about the direct linkage.

The third issue was the early follow-up. The consultants wanted to wait six months to capture the improvement, although management insisted on making a decision in four months. Perhaps a compromising solution is to capture data at four months, make the decision based on the apparent high impact level, and continue to capture data for another two months and develop an ROI impact study with six months of data, which would then be communicated to the target audience.

The fourth issue involved the apparent lack of a comprehensive evaluation at Level 3. Some team members wanted a more comprehensive assessment of actual behavior changes, which would convince them that the supervisors were actually operating differently. While this is an important issue, it was a tradeoff process. A comprehensive Level 3 evaluation is time consuming and costly. When a Level 4 evaluation was planned with two specific techniques to isolate the effects of training, team members felt that a more comprehensive Level 3 was unnecessary.

Overall, the evaluation team perceived this to be an excellent ROI analysis. The process was credible with an acceptable level of accuracy.

Intangible Benefits

Other potential intangible benefits were identified including improved supervisor morale, improved employee morale, reduction in stress for supervisors, and an increase in the bonus for supervisors (bonus pay is linked to productivity and quality). While these items were considered to be important benefits of the program, they were not measured because of the additional effort required for monitoring and analysis. When intangible benefits are important and influential to the target audience, they should be monitored and analyzed, and an attempt should be made to isolate the impact of the program on those intangible measures. Interestingly, the management group initially proposed absenteeism and turnover measures as intangible benefits. If this suggestion had been followed, the improvements in absenteeism and turnover would have been presented as intangible benefits, resulting in a negative ROI. The team learned a valuable lesson. There should be an attempt to convert each intangible measure that is monitored and isolated. If the conversion process becomes unmanageable, inaccurate, or not very credible, then a data item is listed as an intangible benefit and reported without any further analysis.

Discussion Questions
1. Although the ROI analysis plan (Figure 2-2) is usually completed prior to pursuing the evaluation process, please take a few minutes to complete the plan shown in Figure 9-4.
2. Could the ROI be developed with Level 1 data in this case? Please explain.
3. Would an ROI at Level 2 or 3 be possible? Please explain.
4. How should the results of this study be communicated? Please explain.
5. How could this process be implemented with other programs?

References

[1] Dixon, N.M., "The Relationship Between Trainee Responses on Participant Reaction Forms and Posttest Scores," *Human Resource Development Quarterly*, 1(2), pp. 129-137.

[2] Industry Report, *Training*, 1996, 33(10), pp. 36-79.

[3] Phillips, J., "Return on Investment-Beyond the Four Levels," *Academy of HRD 1995 Conference Proceedings*, E. Holton (Ed.), 1995.

[4] Geber, B., "Does Training Make a Difference? Prove It!" *Training*, March 1995, pp. 27-34.

[5] Broad, M., "Built-in Evaluation," *In Action: Measuring Return on Investment*, Vol. 1, J. Phillips (Ed.), Alexandria, VA: American Society for Training and Development, 1994, pp. 55-70.

[6] Ford, D., "Three Rs in the Workplace," *In Action: Measuring Return on Investment*, Vol. 1, J. Phillips (Ed.), Alexandria, VA: American Society for Training and Development, 1994, pp. 85-104.

Program:_____   Responsibility_____   Date:____

Evaluation Strategy: ROI Analysis

Data Items	Methods of Isolating the Effects of the Program	Methods of Converting Data	Cost Categories	Intangible Benefits	Other Influences/Issues	Communication Targets

Figure 9-4. *Evaluation strategy: ROI analysis*

10

IMPLEMENTATION ISSUES

The best designed process model or technique will be worthless unless it is integrated efficiently and effectively in the organization. Although the ROI process is presented in this book as a step-by-step, methodical, and simplistic procedure, it will fail even in the best organizations if it is not integrated into the mainstream of activity and fully accepted and supported by those who should make it work in the organization. This chapter focuses on the critical issues involved in implementing the ROI process in the organization.

Planning the Implementation

Few initiatives will be effective without proper planning and the ROI process is no exception. Planning is synonymous with success. Several issues are presented in this chapter that show how the organization should plan for the ROI process and position it as an essential component of the training and development process.

Identifying a Champion

As a first step in the process, one or more individual(s) should be designated as the internal leader or champion for the process. As in most change efforts, someone must take the responsibility for ensuring that the process is implemented successfully. This leader serves as a champion for ROI and is usually the one who understands the process best and sees the vast potential for the contribution of the process. More importantly, this leader is willing to show and teach others.

The ROI leader is a member of the HRD training staff who usually has this responsibility full time in larger organizations or part-time in smaller organizations. The typical job title for a full time ROI leader is manager of measurement and evaluation. Some organizations assign this responsibility to a team and empower them to lead the ROI effort. For example, one company selected five individuals to lead this effort as a team. All five received certification in the ROI process.

Developing the ROI Leader

In preparation for this assignment, individuals usually obtain special training that builds specific skills and knowledge in the ROI process. The role of the implementation leader is very broad and serves a variety of specialized duties. In some organizations, the implementation leader can take on as many as 14 roles:

1. technical expert,
2. consultant,
3. problem solver,
4. initiator,
5. designer,
6. developer,
7. coordinator,
8. cheerleader,
9. communicator,
10. process monitor,
11. planner,
12. analyst,
13. interpreter, and
14. teacher

It is a difficult and challenging assignment that will need special training and skill building. In the past there have been only a few programs available that help build these skills. Now there are many available and some are quite comprehensive. For example, one program is designed to certify the individuals who are assuming a leadership role in the implementation of ROI.[1] This certification is built around ten specific skill sets identified with success of an ROI implementation. These are:

1. planning for ROI calculations;
2. collecting evaluation data;
3. isolating the effects of training;
4. converting data to monetary values;
5. monitoring program costs;
6. analyzing data, including calculating the ROI;
7. presenting evaluation data;
8. implementing the ROI process;
9. providing internal consulting on ROI; and
10. teaching others the ROI process

This process is quite comprehensive, but may be necessary to build the appropriate skills to tackle this challenging assignment.

Assigning Responsibilities

Determining the specific responsibilities is a critical issue because there can be confusion when individuals are unclear of their specific assignments in the ROI process. Responsibilities apply to two groups. The first is the measurement and evaluation responsibility for the entire training and development staff. It is important for all of those involved in developing and delivering programs to have some responsibility for measurement and evaluation. These responsibilities include providing input on the design of instruments, planning a specific evaluation, analyzing data, and interpreting the results. Typical responsibilities include:

- Ensuring that the needs assessment includes specific business impact measures.
- Developing specific application objectives (Level 3) and business impact objectives (Level 4) for each program.
- Focusing the content of the program on the performance improvement, ensuring that exercises, case studies, and skill practices relate to the desired objectives.
- Keeping participants focused on application and impact objectives.
- Communicating rationale and reasons for evaluation.

- Assisting in follow-up activities to capture application and business impact data.
- Providing technical assistance for data collection, data analysis, and reporting.
- Designing instruments and plans for data collection and analysis.
- Presenting evaluation data to a variety of groups.

While it may be inappropriate to have each member of the staff involved in all of these activities, each individual should have at least one or more responsibilities as part of their routine job duties. This assignment of responsibility keeps the ROI process from being disjointed and separate from major training and development activities. More importantly, it brings accountability to those who develop and deliver the programs.

The second issue involves the technical support function. Depending on the size of the training and development staff, it may be helpful to establish a group of technical experts who provide assistance with the ROI process. When this group is established, it must be clear that the experts and are not there to relieve others of evaluation responsibilities, but to supplement technical expertise. Some firms have found this approach to be effective. For example, Andersen Consulting has a measurement and evaluation staff of 32 individuals who provide technical support for the education and training function.[2] When this type of support is developed, responsibilities revolve around six key areas:

1. designing data collection instruments;
2. providing assistance for developing an evaluation strategy;
3. analyzing data, including specialized statistical analyses;
4. interpreting results and making specific recommendations;
5. developing an evaluation report or case study to communicate overall results; and
6. providing technical support in any phase of the ROI process.

The assignment of responsibilities for evaluation is also an issue that needs attention throughout the evaluation process. Although the training and development staff must have specific responsibilities during an evaluation, it is not unusual to require others in support functions to have responsibility for data collection. These responsibilities are defined when a particular evaluation strategy plan is developed and approved.

Developing Evaluation

As presented earlier, establishing specific targets for evaluation levels is an important way to make progress with measurement and evaluation. Targets enable the staff to focus on the improvements needed with specific evaluation levels. In this process, the percent of courses planned for evaluation at each level is developed. The first step is to assess the present situation. The number of all courses, including repeated sections of a course, is tabulated along with the corresponding level(s) of evaluation presently conducted for each course. Next, the percent of courses using Level 1 reaction questionnaires is calculated. The process is repeated for each level of the evaluation.

After detailing the current situation, the next step is to determine a realistic target within a specific time frame. Many organizations set annual targets for changes. This process should involve the input of the entire HRD staff to ensure that the targets are realistic and that the staff is committed to the process. If the training and development staff does not develop ownership for this process, targets will not be met. The improvement targets must be achievable, while at the same time, challenging and motivating. Table 10-1 shows the targets established for Andersen Consulting for four levels.[3] Andersen indicates that many of the Level 4 evaluations are taken to ROI. In some organizations, half of the Level 4 calculations are taken to Level 5 while in others, every one of them are taken. Table 10-2 shows current percentages and targets for five years in another organization, a large multinational company. Table 10-2 shows the gradual improvement of increasing evaluation activity at Levels 3, 4, and 5. Year 0 is the current status in Table 10-2.

Table 10-1

Evaluation Targets in Arthur Andersen & Co.

Level	Target
Level 1, Reaction	100%
Level 2, Learning	50%
Level 3, Job Application	$\approx 30\%$
Level 4, Business Results	10%

Table 10-2
Percentages and Targets for Five Years in a Large Multinational Company

	Percent of Courses Evaluated at Each Level					
	Year 0	Year 1	Year 2	Year 3	Year 4	Year 5
Reaction and Planned Action	85%	90%	95%	100%	100%	100%
Learning	30%	35%	40%	45%	50%	60%
Job Application	5%	10%	15%	20%	25%	30%
Business Results	2%	4%	5%	9%	12%	15%
ROI	0%	2%	4%	6%	8%	10%

Target setting is a critical implementation issue. It should be completed early in the process with full support of the entire HRD staff. Also, if practical and feasible, the targets should have the approval of the key management staff, particularly the senior management team.

Developing a Project Plan for Implementation

An important part of the planning process is to establish timetables for the complete implementation process. This document becomes a master plan for the completion of the different elements presented in this chapter, beginning with assigning responsibilities and concluding with meeting the targets previously described. From a practical basis, this schedule is a project plan for transition from the present situation to a desired future situation. The items on the schedule include, but are not limited to, developing specific ROI projects, building staff skills, developing policy, teaching managers the process, analyzing ROI data, and communicating results. The more detailed the document, the more useful it will become. The project plan is a living long-range document that should be reviewed frequently and adjusted as necessary. More importantly, it should always be familiar to those who are working on the ROI process. Figure 10-1 shows an ROI implementation project plan for a large petroleum company.

Revising/Developing Policies and Procedures

Another key part of planning is revising (or developing) the organization's policy concerning measurement and evaluation, often a part of policy and practice for developing and implementing training and development programs. The policy statement contains information developed specifically for the measurement and evaluation process. It is frequently developed with the input of the HRD staff and key managers or clients. Sometimes policy issues are addressed during internal workshops designed to build skills with measurement and evaluation. The policy statement addresses critical issues that will influence the effectiveness of the measurement and evaluation process. Typical topics include adopting the five-level model presented in this book, requiring Level 3 and 4 objectives in some or all programs, and defining responsibilities for training and development. Figure 10-2 shows the topics in the measurement and evaluation policy for a large firm in South Africa.

Policy statements are very important because they provide guidance and direction for the staff and others who work closely with the ROI process. They keep the process clearly on focus and enables the group to establish goals for evaluation. Policy statements also provide an opportunity to communicate basic requirements and fundamental issues regarding performance and accountability. More than anything else, they serve as a learning tool to teach others, especially when they are developed in a collaborative and collective way. If policy statements are developed in isolation and do not have the ownership of the staff and management, they will not be effective or useful.

Guidelines for measurement and evaluation are important to show how to utilize the tools and techniques, guide the design process, provide consistency in the ROI process, ensure that appropriate methods are used, and place the proper emphasis on each of the areas. The guidelines are more technical than policy statements and often contain detailed procedures showing how the process is actually undertaken and developed. They often include specific forms, instruments, and tools necessary to facilitate the process. Figure 10-3 shows the table of contents of evaluation guidelines for a multinational company. As this table of contents reveals, the guidelines are comprehensive and include significant emphasis on ROI and accountability.

Task	J	F	M	A	M	J	J	A	S	O	N	D	J	F	M	A	M	J	J	A	S	O	N
Team Formed	█																						
Policy Developed		█	█																				
Targets Set			█																				
Workshops Developed			█		█	█	█																
ROI Project (A)							█	█	█														
ROI Project (B)									█	█	█	█											
ROI Project (C)												█	█	█									
ROI Project (D)								█	█	█	█	█	█	█	█	█	█	█	█	█			
HRD Staff Trained														█									
Vendors Trained																							
Managers Trained															█	█	█	█	█	█			
Support Tools Developed					█												█	█					
Evaluation Guidelines Developed					█	█																	

Figure 10-1. *ROI implementation project plan for a large petroleum company*

Assessing the Climate

As a final step in planning the implementation, some organizations assess the current climate for achieving results. One useful tool, presented in Appendix 1, shows a results-based test. This test instrument, or some version of it, can serve as an initial assessment of how the full training and development staff, and others whom they support, perceive the status of training results. This instrument, which is provided with more detailed analysis in other publications, is an excellent tool to determine the current status.[4] In some organizations, annual assessments are taken to measure progress as this process is implemented. Others take the assessment instrument to the management group to determine the extent managers perceive training and development to be effective. Still others use an instrument designed specifically for management input, as shown in Appendix 2. Collectively, the use of an assessment process provides an excellent understanding of current status. Then the organization can plan for significant changes, pinpointing particular issues which need support as the ROI process is implemented.

Preparing the HRD Staff

One group that will often resist the ROI process is the training and development staff who must design, develop, and deliver training. These staff members often see evaluation as an unnecessary intrusion into their responsibilities, absorbing precious time, and stifling their freedom to be creative. The cartoon character Pogo perhaps characterizes it best when he said "We have met the enemy and he is us." This section outlines some important issues that must be addressed when preparing the staff for the implementation of ROI.

Involving the Staff

On each key issue or major decision, the staff should be involved in the process. As policy statements are prepared and evaluation guidelines developed, staff input is absolutely essential. It is difficult for the staff to be critical of something they helped design and develop. Using meetings, brainstorming sessions, and task forces, the staff should be involved in every phase of developing the framework and supporting documents for ROI.

1. Purpose
2. Mission
3. Evaluate all programs which will include the following levels:
    a. Participant satisfaction (100%)
    b. Learning (no less than 70%)
    c. Job applications (50%)
    d. Results (usually through sampling) (10%) (highly visible, expensive)
4. Evaluation support group (corporate) will provide assistance and advice in Measurement & Evaluation, Instrument Design, Data Analysis, and Evaluation Strategy.
5. New programs are developed following logical steps beginning with needs analysis and ending with communicating results.
6. Evaluation instruments must be designed or selected to collect data for evaluation. They must be valid, reliable, economical, and subject to audit by evaluation support group.
7. Responsibility for HRD program results rests with trainers, participants, and supervisors of participants.
8. An adequate system for collecting and monitoring HRD costs must be in place. All direct costs should be included.
9. At least annually the management board will review the status and results of HRD. The review will include HRD plans, strategies, results, costs, priorities, and concerns.
10. Line management shares in the responsibility for HRD programs. Evaluation through follow-up, pre-program commitments, and overall support.
11. Managers/Supervisors must declare competence achieved through training and packaged programs. When not applicable, HRD staff should evaluate.
12. External HRD consultants must be selected based on previous evaluation. Central data/resource base should exist. All external HRD programs of over one day in duration will be subjected to evaluation procedures. In addition, the quality of external programs will be assessed by participants.
13. HRD program results must be communicated to the appropriate target audience. As a minimum, this includes management (participants' supervisor), participants, and all HRD staff.
14. HRD staff should be qualified to do effective needs-analysis and evaluation.
15. Central database for program development to prevent duplication and serve as program resource.
16. Union involvement in total Training and Development plan.

Figure 10-2. *Results-based internal HRD policy (excerpts from actual policy for a large firm in South Africa)*

Section 1: Policy
1.1   The Need for Accountability
1.2   The Bottom Line: Linking Training with Business Needs
1.3   Results-Based Approach
1.4   Implications
1.5   Communication
1.6   Payoff

Section 2: Responsibilities
2.1   Training Group Responsibilities: Overall
2.2   Training Group Responsibilities: Specifics for Selected Groups
2.3   The Business Unit Responsibilities
2.4   Participant Manager Responsibilities
2.5   Participants Responsibilities

Section 3: Evaluation Framework
3.1   Purpose of Evaluation
3.2   Levels of Evaluation
3.3   Process Steps for Training Implementation
3.4   Evaluation Model

Section 4: Level 1 Guidelines
4.1   Purpose and Scope
4.2   Areas of Coverage - Standard Form
4.3   Optional Areas of Coverage
4.4   Administrative Issues
4.5   How to Use Level 1 Data

Section 5: Level 2 Guidelines
5.1   Purpose and Scope
5.2   Learning Measurement Issues
5.3   Techniques for Measuring Learning
5.4   Administration
5.5   Using Level 2 Data

Section 6: Level 3 Guidelines
6.1   Purpose and Scope
6.2   Follow-Up Issues
6.3   Types of Follow-Up Techniques
6.4   Administrative Issues
6.5   Using Level 3 Evaluation

Figure 10-3. *Evaluation guidelines for a multinational company*

Section 7: Level 4 and 5 Guidelines
7.1   Purpose and Scope
7.2   Business Results and ROI Issues
7.3   Monitoring Performance Data
7.4   Extracting Data from Follow-Up Evaluation
7.5   Isolating the Effects of the Learning Solution
7.6   Converting Data to Monetary Values
7.7   Developing Costs
7.8   Calculating the ROI
7.9   Identifying Intangible Benefits
7.10   Administrative Issues
7.11   Using Business Impact and ROI Data

Figure 10-3. *Cont'd.*

Using ROI as a Learning Tool

One reason the HRD staff may resist the ROI process is that the effectiveness of their programs will be fully exposed, putting their reputation on the line. They may have a fear of failure. To overcome this, the ROI process should clearly be positioned as a tool for learning and not a tool to evaluate training staff performance, at least during its early years of implementation. HRD staff members will not be interested in developing a process that will be used against them.

Evaluators can learn as much from failures as successes. If the program is not working, it is best to find out quickly and understand the issues first hand - not from others. If a program is ineffective and not producing the desired results, it will eventually be known to clients and/or the management group, if they are not aware of it already. A lack of result will cause managers to become less supportive of training. If the weaknesses of programs are identified and adjustments are made quickly, not only will effective programs be developed, but the credibility and respect for the function will be enhanced.

Removing Obstacles

Several obstacles to the implementation of the ROI process will usually be encouraged. Some of these are realistic barriers, while others are often based on misconceptions. Each should be explored and addressed. The most common are:

- **ROI is a complex process**. Many of the HRD staff will perceive ROI as too complex a process to implement. To counter this, the staff must understand that by breaking the process down into individual components and steps, it can be simplified.
- **Staff members often feel they do not have time for evaluation**. They need to understand that the evaluation efforts can save more time in the future. An ROI study may show that the program should be changed, modified, or even terminated altogether. Also, up front planning with evaluation strategy can save additional follow-up time for the overall evaluation.
- **The staff must be motivated to pursue evaluations, even when senior executives are not requiring it**. Most staff members will know when top managers are pushing the accountability issue. If they do not see that push, they are reluctant to take the time to make it work. They must see the benefits of pursuing the process even if not required or encouraged at the top.
- **The staff may be concerned that ROI results will lead to criticism**. Many staff members will be concerned about the use of ROI study information. If the results are used to criticize or assess the performance of program designers or facilitators, there will be a reluctance to embrace the concept. ROI should be considered as a learning process, at least in the early stages of implementation.

These and other obstacles can thwart an otherwise successful implementation. Each must be removed or reduced to a manageable issue.

Teaching the Staff

The training staff will usually have inadequate skills in measurement and evaluation and thus will need to develop some expertise in the process. Measurement and evaluation is not always a formal part of their preparation to become a trainer or instructional designer. Consequently, each staff member must be provided training on the ROI process to learn how the overall ROI process works, step-by-step. In addition, staff members must know how to develop an evaluation strategy and specific plan, collect and analyze data from the evaluation, and interpret results from data analysis. Sometimes a one-to-two day workshop is needed to build adequate skills and knowledge to understand the process, appreciate what it can do for the organization, see the necessity for it, and participate in a successful implementation. Perhaps the two most useful ROI documents are the Data Collection Plan and ROI Analysis Plan discussed in an earlier chapter. These plans show what data will be collected, at what time, by whom, and how specific analyses will be conducted, including isolating the effects of training and converting data to monetary values. Each staff member should know how to develop, understand, and use these plans.

Initiating the ROI Process

The first tangible evidence of the ROI process may be initiation of the first project in which the ROI is calculated. This section outlines some of the key issues involved in identifying the projects and keeping them on track.

Selecting Initial Programs

Selecting a program for ROI analysis is an important and critical issue. Only specific types of programs should be selected for a comprehensive, detailed analysis. Typical criteria for identifying programs for analysis are to select programs that:

- involve large target audiences,
- are expected to be viable for a long time,
- are important to overall strategic objectives,
- are expensive,
- have high visibility, and
- have a comprehensive needs assessment.

Using these criteria, or similar criteria, the staff must select the appropriate courses to consider for an ROI project. Ideally, management should concur with, or approve, the criteria.

The next major step is to determine how many projects to undertake initially and in which particular areas. A small number of initial projects are recommended, perhaps two or three programs. The selected programs may represent the functional areas of the business such as operations, sales, finance, engineering, and information systems. Another approach is to select programs representing functional areas of training such as sales training, management and supervisor training, computer-based training, and technical training. It is important to select a manageable number so the process will be implemented.

Reporting Progress

As the projects are developed and the ROI implementation is underway, status meetings should be conducted to report progress and discuss critical issues with appropriate team members. For example, if a supervisory training program for operations is selected as one of the ROI projects, all of the key staff involved in the program (design, development, and delivery) should meet regularly to discuss the status of the project. This keeps the project team focused on the critical issues, generates the best ideas to tackle particular problems and barriers, and builds a knowledge base to implement evaluation in future programs. Sometimes this group is facilitated by an external consultant, an expert in the ROI process. In other cases, the internal ROI leader may facilitate the group.

In essence, these meetings serve three major purposes: reporting progress, learning, and planning. The meeting usually begins with a status report on each ROI project, describing what has been accomplished since the previous meeting. Next, the specific barriers and problems encountered are discussed. During the discussions, new issues are interjected in terms of possible tactics, techniques, or tools. Also, the entire group discusses how to remove barriers to success and focuses on suggestions and recommendations for next steps, including developing specific plans. Finally, the next steps are determined.

Establishing Discussion Groups

Because the ROI process is considered to be difficult to understand and apply, it is sometimes helpful to establish discussion groups designed to teach the process. These groups could supplement formal workshops and other training processes and are often very flexible in their format. Groups are usually facilitated by an external ROI consultant or the internal ROI leader. In each session a new topic is presented and discussed thoroughly. Concerns and issues about the topic are discussed including how it is applies to the organization. The process can be very flexible and adjusted to different topics as the needs of the group drive the issues. Ideally, if the participants in group discussions should have an opportunity to apply, explore, or research the topics between sessions. Assignments such as reviewing a case analysis or reading an article are also appropriate between sessions to continue the development of knowledge and skills associated with the process.

Training the Management Team

Perhaps no group is more important to the ROI process than the management team who must allocate resources for training and development and support the programs. In addition, they often provide input and assistance in the ROI process. Specific actions to train and develop the management team should be carefully planned and executed.

A critical issue that must be addressed before training the managers is the relationship between the training and development staff and key managers. A productive partnership is needed which requires each party to understand the concerns, problems, and opportunities of the other. Developing this type of relationship is a long-term process that must be deliberately planned and initiated by key HRD staff members. Sometimes the decision to commit resources and support for training is often based on the effectiveness of this relationship.

Workshop for Managers

One effective approach to prepare managers for the ROI process is to conduct a workshop for managers, "Training for Non-Training Managers." Varying in duration from one half to two days, this practical workshop shapes critical skills and changes perceptions to enhance the support of the ROI process. Managers leave the workshop with an improved perception of the impact of training and a clearer understanding of their roles in the training process. More importantly, they often have a renewed commitment to make training work in their organization.

Due to the critical need for this topic in management training, this workshop should be required for all managers, unless they have previously demonstrated strong support for the training function. Because of this requirement, it is essential for top executives to be supportive of this workshop and, in some cases, take an active role in conducting it. To tailor the program to specific organizational needs, a brief needs assessment may be necessary to determine the specific focus and areas of emphasis for the program.

Target Audiences. While the target audience for this program is usually middle-level managers, the target group may vary with different organizations. In some organizations, the target may be first-level managers and in others, the target may begin with second-level managers. Three important questions help determine the proper audience:

Questions to Help Determine the Proper Audience

Which group has the most direct influence on the training and development function?

Which management group is causing serious problems with lack of management support?

Which group has the need to understand the ROI process so they can influence training transfer?

The answer to both questions is often middle-level managers.

Timing. This workshop should be conducted early in the management development process before non-supportive habits are delivered. When this program is implemented throughout the organization, it is best to start with higher level managers and work down the organization. If possible, a version of the program should be a part of a traditional management training program provided to supervisors when they are promoted into managerial positions.

Selling Top Management. Because convincing top management to require this program may be a difficult task, three approaches should be considered:

1. Discuss and illustrate the consequences of inadequate management support for training. For example, the statistics are staggering in wasted time and money.

2. Show how current support is lacking. An evaluation of an internal training program will often reveal the barriers to successful application of training. Lack of management support is often the main reason, which brings the issue close to home.

3. Demonstrate how money can be saved and results can be achieved with the ROI process.

The endorsement of the top management group is very important. In some organizations, top managers actually attend the program to explore first hand what is involved and what they must do to make the process work. At a minimum, top management should support the program by signing memos describing the program or by approving policy statements. They should also ask provoking questions in their staff meetings from time to time. This will not happen by chance. The HRD manager must tactfully coach top executives.

Workshop Content

The program will usually cover the topics outlined next. The time allotted for each topic and specific focus will depend on the organization, the experience of the managers, the needs of the managers, and the preparation of the management group. The program can be developed in separate modules where managers can be exempt from certain modules based on their previous knowledge or experience with the topic. This module concept is recommended.

The Overall Importance of Training. Managers need to be convinced that training and development is a mainstream responsibility which is gaining in importance and influence in the organizations. They need to understand the results-based approach of today's progressive training and development organization. After completing this module, managers should perceive training as a critical process in their organization and be able to describe how the process contributes to strategic and operational objectives. Data from the organization is presented to show the full scope of training in the organization. Tangible evidence of top management commitment should be presented in a form such as memos, directives, and policies signed by the CEO or other appropriate top executive. In some organizations, the invitation to attend the program comes from the CEO, a gesture which shows strong top management commitment. Also, external data should be included to illustrate the growth of training budgets and the increasing importance of training and development. Perhaps a case showing the linkage between HRD and strategy would be helpful.

The Impact of Training. Too often, managers are unsure about the success of training. After completing this module, managers will be able to identify the steps to measure the impact of training on important output variables. Reports and studies should be presented showing the impact of training using measures such as productivity, quality, cost, response times, and customer satisfaction. Internal evaluation reports, if available, are presented to managers showing convincing evidence that training is making a significant difference in the organization. If internal reports are not available, other success stories or case studies from other organizations can be utilized. To meet this need, The American Society for Training and Development has published a casebook on measuring the return on investment in training and development.[5] Managers need to be convinced that training is a successful, results-based tool, not only to help with change, but to meet critical organizational goals and objectives.

The Training and Development Process. Managers usually will not support activities or processes that they do not fully understand. After completing this module, managers should be able to describe how the training process works in their organization and understand each critical step from needs assessment to ROI calculation. Managers need to be aware of the effort that goes into developing a training program and their role in each step of the process. A short case, illustrating all the steps, is helpful in this module. This discussion also reveals various areas of the potential impact of training and development.

Responsibility for Training. Defining who is responsible for training is important to the success of training. After completing this module, managers should be able to list their specific responsibilities for training and development. Managers must see how they can influence training and the degree of responsibility they must assume in the future. Multiple responsibilities for training are advocated, including managers, participants, participant supervisors, and trainers (developers and instructors). Case studies are appropriate in this module to illustrate the consequences when responsibilities are neglected or when there is failure to follow-up by managers. One specific case is available which was designed for this purpose.[6] In some organizations, job descriptions are revised to reflect training responsibility. In other organizations, major job-related goals are established to highlight management responsibility for training. Overall, this session leaves participants with a clear understanding of how their responsibility is linked to the success of training and development.

Active Involvement. One of the most important ways to enhance manager support for training and development is to get them actively involved in the process. After completing this module, managers will actually commit to one or more ways of active involvement in the future. Table 10-3 shows twelve ways for manager involvement identified for one company. The information in the table was presented to managers in the workshop with a request for them to commit to at least one area of involvement. After these areas are fully explained and discussed, each manager is asked to select one or more ways in which he or she will be involved in training and development in the future. A commitment to sign up for at least one involvement role is required.

If used properly, these commitments are a rich source of input and assistance from the management group. There will be many offers for involvement, and the training and development department must follow through with the offers. A quick follow-up on all offers is recommended.

Monitoring Progress and Communicating Results

A final part of the implementation process is to monitor the overall progress made and communicate the results of specific ROI projects. Although it is an often overlooked part of the process, an effective communication plan can help keep the implementation on target and let others know what the ROI process is accomplishing for the organization.

Monitoring Progress

The initial schedule for implementation of ROI provides a variety of key events or milestones. Routine progress reports need to be developed to present the status and progress of these events or milestones. Reports are usually developed at six-month intervals. Two target audiences, the training and development staff and senior managers, are critical for progress reporting. The entire training and development staff should be kept informed on the progress, and senior managers need to know the extent to which ROI is being implemented and how it is working in the organization.

Table 10-3
Management Involvement in Training and Education

The following are areas for present and future involvement in the Training and Education Process. Please check your areas of planned involvement.

	In Your Area	Outside Your Area
■ Attend a Program Designed for Your Staff	❑	❑
■ Provide Input on a Training Needs Analysis	❑	❑
■ Serve on a Training Advisory Committee	❑	❑
■ Provide Input on a Training Program Design	❑	❑
■ Serve as a Subject Matter Expert	❑	❑
■ Serve on a Task Force to Develop a Program	❑	❑
■ Volunteer to Evaluate an External T&E Program	❑	❑
■ Assist in the selection of a Vendor Supplied T&E Program	❑	❑
■ Provide Reinforcement to Your Employees After They Attend Training	❑	❑
■ Coordinate a Training Program	❑	❑
■ Assist in Program Evaluation or Follow-Up	❑	❑
■ Conduct a Portion of the Program, as a Facilitator	❑	❑

Developing Evaluation Reports

The results from an ROI impact study must be reported to a variety of target audiences. One of the most important documents for presenting data, results, and issues is in an evaluation report. Figure 10-4 shows a table of contents from a typical evaluation report at the ROI level. This specific study was conducted for a large financial institution and involved an ROI analysis on relationship selling skills and financial consulting skills. The typical report provides background information, explains the processes used, and most importantly, presents the results. Recognizing the importance of on-the-job behavior change, Level 3 results are presented first. Business impact results are presented next, which include the actual ROI calculation. Finally, other issues are covered along with the intangible benefits. While this report is an effective and professional way to present ROI data, several cautions need to be followed. Since this document is reporting the success of a training and development program involving a group of employees outside of the training function, the complete credit for all of the success and results must go to the participants and their immediate supervisors. Their performance has generated the success. Also, another important caution is to avoid boasting about the results. Although the ROI process may be accurate and credible, it still may have some subjective issues. Huge claims of success can quickly turn off an audience and interfere with the delivery of the desired message.

A final caution concerns the structure of the report. The methodology should be clearly explained along with the assumptions made in the analysis. The reader should readily see how the values were developed and how the specific steps were followed to make the process more conservative, credible, and accurate. Detailed statistical analyses should be relegated to the appendix.

Preparing a Case

Case studies are an effective way to communicate the results from an ROI impact study. Consequently, it is recommended that a few ROI projects be developed in a case format. A typical case study will describe the situation, provide appropriate background information, including the events that led to the program, present the techniques and strategies used to develop the ROI, and highlight the key issues in the project. These cases tell an interesting story of how the ROI was developed and the problems and concerns identified along the way.

The ROI case studies have many useful applications in an organization. First, they can be used in group discussions where interested individuals can react to the material, offer different perspectives, and draw conclusions about approaches or techniques. Second, the case study can serve as a self-teaching guide as individuals try to understand how the ROI process is developed and utilized in the organization. Finally, case studies provide appropriate recognition for those who were involved in the actual case. More importantly, it recognizes the participants who achieved the results, and the managers of participants who allowed them to attend the program. The case study format has become one of the most effective ways to learn the ROI process.

- **General Information**
  - Background
  - Objectives of Study
- **Methodology for Impact Study**
  - Levels of Evaluation
  - ROI Process
  - Collecting Data
  - Isolating the Effects of Training
  - Converting Data to Monetary Values
  - Costs
- **Results: General Information**
  - Response Profile
  - Success with Objectives
  - Relevance of Materials
- **Results: Use of Skills/Knowledge**
- **Results: Business Impact**
  - General Comments
  - Linkage with Business Measures
  - ROI Calculation
- **Results: Intangible Benefits**
- **Barriers and Participants Recommendations**
  - Barriers
  - Positive Comments
  - Suggestions from Participants
- **Conclusions and Recommendations**
  - Conclusions
  - Recommendations
- **Exhibits**

Figure 10-4. *Impact study (report format)*

Communicating Results to a Variety of Audiences

While several potential audiences could receive ROI evaluation data, four audiences should always receive the data. A senior management team (however it may be defined) should always receive information about the ROI project because of their interest in the process and their influence to allocate additional resources for HRD and evaluation. The supervisors of program participants need to have the ROI information so they will continue to support programs and reinforce specific behavior taught in the program. The participants in the program who actually achieved the results should receive a summary of the ROI information so they understand what was accomplished by the entire group. This also reinforces their commitment to make the process work. The training and development staff must understand the ROI process and consequently, need to receive the information from each ROI project. This is part of the continuing educational process. Collectively, these four groups should always receive ROI information. In addition, other groups may receive information based on the type of program and the other potential audiences.

Conclusion

In summary, the implementation of the ROI process is a very critical part of the process. If not approached in a systematic, logical, and planned way, the ROI process will not become an integral part of training and development and consequently, the accountability of the programs will be lacking. This final chapter presented the different elements that must be considered and issues that must be addressed to ensure that implementation is smooth and uneventful. The result would be a complete integration of ROI as a mainstream activity in the ROI process.

Case Study - Part I
National Auto Products Company

ROI Analysis Plan

Figure 10-5 shows the ROI analysis plan for NAPCo. Each decision and strategy outlined in the various parts of this case is reflected on this form. This document is a decision making tool for the ROI analysis and is used to make specific plans for the analysis to be complete. It is completed before beginning the evaluation process.

Level 1 ROI Analysis

Although it was not attempted in this case, it is possible and perhaps instructive to develop a Level 1 ROI analysis. With this process, a series of potential impact questions could be asked where participants anticipate potential changes and estimate the particular impact of changes for each of the four variables (productivity, quality, turnover, and absenteeism). First year values would be developed, along with a confidence percentage obtained from participants reflecting their level of certainty with the process. The data could be adjusted with this confidence level to provide a forecast of the benefit and the calculation of the ROI. Although this ROI value is subjective and often inflated, this analysis would provide some insight into the relationship between the projections at the end of the program and the actual performance four months later. Also, it may actually enhance the results because participants who make projections of performance may be motivated to meet those projections.

ROI with Level 2 and 3 Data

At NAPCo, it was impossible to capture data for a Level 2 ROI. For this calculation to be possible, a validated instrument must be developed to measure the performance of supervisors in the program and have it correlated with subsequent on-the-job performance. This was not feasible in this situation. A Level 3 ROI was not considered because of the concern over the subjective assessments that must be made using Level 3 data. Also, the client was very bottom-line oriented and preferred to discuss performance in terms of Level 4 measures (productivity, quality, turnover, and absenteeism, etc.). While management recognized that skills must be acquired and behavior must be changed, they were less interested in discussing the extent to which changes have occurred and the value of the change. Thus, an ROI at Level 3 would have provided little value for the client.

Date: _____

Evaluation Strategy: ROI Analysis

Data Items	Methods of Isolating the Effects of the Program	Methods of Converting Data	Cost Categories	Intangible Benefits	Other Influences/Issues	Communication Targets
Productivity % of Shipments Met	• Trendline Analysis • Participant Estimates	• Direct Conversion - Company Standard Value	• Program Fee from Consulting Company • Program Materials • Food and Refreshments	• Improved Supervisor Morale • Improved Employee Morale • Stress Reduction	• Team building was in process • Total Quality Management program has been launched	• Participants • Managers of Participants • Senior Management • Training and HR Staff
Quality - Rejects Per Million Units of Production	• Trendline Analysis • Participant Estimates	• Expert Estimate	• Facilities • Evaluation Costs • Salaries and Benefits of Participants	• Increase in Bonus Pay	• Management support is good • Management is very anxious to see results	• Other Plant Managers • Potential Clients
Turnover (Quits and Discharges)	• Trendline Analysis • Participant Estimates	• External Studies • Senior Management Estimate				
Absenteeism	• Trendline Analysis • Participant Estimates	• External Studies • Participant Estimate				

Figure 10-5. *Evaluation strategy: ROI analysis*

Communication of Results

Communication of results from an ROI impact study is very crucial to the process, almost as important as obtaining the actual calculation. Although there can be many target audiences, six target audiences received the study results at NAPCo:

1. The participants themselves were provided copies of the study results to show what they had accomplished, collectively. In this case, supervisors were sent a summary of the impact study showing the ultimate ROI and how the values were developed.
2. The managers of the supervisors (participants) received copies of the study with appropriate explanation. These department heads for the various production and support departments were aware of the ROI impact study and were anticipating the results.
3. Senior management received executive summaries and copies of the detailed study. At NAPCo, this group included the president, director of manufacturing (for all plants), and the plant manager. In addition, this group received a briefing on the study results and discussed how it was developed and what it actually meant. This step is important to ensure that there is a complete understanding of the process.
4. The training and HR staff received copies of the study so that they could understand how the ROI process is applied to this type of program. This ROI study was part of an ongoing effort to build skills and develop strategies to increase accountability of HR programs.
5. Plant managers for the other locations received copies of the study to show what can be accomplished with this type of training. Essentially, this communication served as an internal marketing tool to convince others that using supervisory training can improve their plants.
6. Potential clients for the consulting firm received summary copies of the study. This target group was unique to the consulting firm. With permission of the company, the impact study was used by the consulting firm to convince other prospective clients that supervisory training can produce high impact. The name of the organization was disguised and sensitive data was slightly altered to protect the company.

Collectively, these six target audiences received information on the ROI impact study, ensuring that all important audiences understand the results and the process.

Implementation Issues

A variety of implementation issues emerged at NAPCo:

- One individual was appointed as coordinator for measurement and evaluation and was asked to leader the process. This action ensures that the ROI process has a champion and a leader to ensure that it works properly, is executed timely, and is supported appropriately.
- To ensure that the study can be replicated, the internal leader participated in all phases of the ROI development process. The consulting firm worked closely with this individual to ensure that each step of the ROI process was understood and could be applied in other situations.
- To help accomplish the transfer of technology, the consulting firm provided the evaluation leader with additional training to develop skills in the ROI process and to provide additional practice with ROI calculations.
- To help improve management support, a 2 1/2 hour briefing was scheduled with the management team (department managers and above) at the next quarterly meeting to discuss the results of this study, and the potential opportunity for significant returns from training. The program also underscored the manager's responsibility to make training effective in the company.
- Specific targets were set where a few courses were identified for planned ROI calculations. This provided some guidance for the HRD director to focus on high priority programs.
- A policy statement was developed to capture the basic requirements for measurement and evaluation. This document described the responsibilities for training and evaluation, outlined how ROI studies would be conducted, and indicated how the results would be communicated.

Collectively, these six actions provided adequate ROI mechanisms to implement the process internally and make it a routine activity at NAPCo.

References

[1] *Certification Process for Measuring the Return on Investment in Training and Development Workshop* Brochure, Birmingham, AL 35238-0637: Performance Resources Organization, P O Box 380637, 1996.

[2] Geber, B., "Does Training Make a Difference? Prove It!" *Training*, March 1995, pp. 27-36.

[3] Geber, B. "Does Training Make a Difference? Prove It!" *Training*, March 1995, pp. 27-36.

[4] Phillips, J.J., *Handbook of Training Evaluation and Measurement Methods*, 2nd ed. Houston: Gulf Publishing, 1991.

[5] Phillips, J.J. (ed.) *In Action: Measuring Return on Investment*, Alexandria, VA: American Society for Training and Development, 1994.

[6] Phillips, J.J., *International Electric*. Birmingham, AL 5238-0637: Performance Resources Organization, P O Box 380637, 1994.

Appendix 1

How Results-Based Are Your HRD Programs?

A Quick Test for the HRD Staff

Select the most correct response.

1. HRD programs are:
   a. Activity-oriented (all supervisors attend the "Performance Appraisal Workshop").
   b. Individual results-based (the participant will reduce his or her error rate by at least 20%).
   c. Organizational results-based (the cost of quality will decrease by 25%).

2. The investment in HRD is measured primarily by:
   a. Accident; there is no consistent measurement.
   b. Observations by management, reactions from participants.
   c. Dollar return through improved productivity, cost savings, or better quality.

3. The concern for the method of evaluation in the design and implementation of an HRD program occurs:
   a. When the program is completed.
   b. When the program is developed; before it is conducted.
   c. Before the program is developed.

4. HRD efforts consist of:
   a. Usually one-shot, seminar-type approaches.
   b. A full array of courses to meet individual needs.
   c. A variety of training and education programs implemented to bring about change in the organization.

5. Cost/benefits comparisons of HRD programs are:
    a. Never developed.
    b. Occasionally developed.
    c. Frequently developed.

6. HRD programs, without some formal method of evaluation, are implemented:
    a. Regularly
    b. Seldom
    c. Never

7. The results of HRD programs are communicated:
    a. When requested, to those who have a need to know.
    b. Occasionally, to members of management only.
    c. Routinely, to a variety of selected target audiences.

8. The HRD staff involvement in evaluation consists of:
    a. No specific responsibilities in evaluation, with no formal training in evaluation methods.
    b. Part of the staff has responsibilities for evaluation, with some formal training.
    c. All members of the staff have some responsibilities in evaluation, even if some are devoted full time to the effort; all staff members have been trained in evaluation.

9. In an economic downturn the HRD function will:
    a. Be the first to have its staff reduced.
    b. Be retained at the same staffing level.
    c. Go untouched in staff reductions and possibly beefed up.

10. Budgeting for HRD is based on:
    a. Last year's budget.
    b. Whatever the department head can "sell."
    c. A zero-based system.

11. HRD is funded through:

    a. The training department budget.
    b. The administrative budget.
    c. Line operating budgets.

12. The principal group that must justify HRD expenditures is:
   a.   The training department.
   b.   Various staff areas, including human resources.
   c.   Line management.

13. Over the last two years, the HRD budget as a percent of operating expenses has:
   a.   Decreased
   b.   Remained stable
   c.   Increased

14. The CEO interfaces with the manager responsible for HRD:
   a.   Never; it is a delegated responsibility.
   b.   Occasionally, when someone recommends it.
   c.   Frequently, to know what is going on.

15. The CEO's involvement in the implementation of HRD programs is:
   a.   Limited to sending invitations, extending congratulations, passing out certificates, etc.
   b.   Monitoring progress, opening/closing speeches, presentation on the outlook of the organization, etc.
   c.   Program participation to see what's covered, conducting major segments of the program, requiring key executives to be involved, etc.

16. On the organization chart, the HRD manager:
   a.   Is more than two levels removed from the top executive.
   b.   Is two levels below the top executive.
   c.   Reports directly to the top executive.

17. Line management involvement in implementing HRD programs is:
   a.   Very minor; only HRD specialists conduct programs.
   b.   Limited to a few specialists conducting programs in their area of expertise.
   c.   Significant; on the average, over half of the programs are conducted by key line managers.

18. When an employee completes an HRD program and returns to the job, his or her supervisor usually:
    a. Makes no reference to the program.
    b. Asks questions about the program and encourages the use of the material.
    c. Requires use of the program material and gives positive rewards when the material is used successfully.

19. When an employee attends an outside seminar, upon return, he or she is required to:
    a. Do nothing.
    b. Submit a report summarizing the program.
    c. Evaluate the seminar, outline plans for implementing the material covered, and estimate the value of the program.

20. With the present HRD organization and attitude toward results, the HRD function's impact on profit:
    a. Can never be assessed accurately.
    b. Can be estimated but probably at a significant cost.
    c. Can be estimated (or is being estimated) with little cost.

Analysis of Test Scores

Score the test as follows. Allow:

    1 point for each (a) response.
    3 points for each (b) response.
    5 points for each (c) response.

The total should be between 20 and 100 points.

The score can reveal much about HRD in an organization and in particular the attitude toward evaluation and measurement. A perfect score of 100 is probably unachievable. It represents utopia and is an ultimate goal of many HRD departments. Conversely, a score of 20 reveals an ineffective organization with inappropriate methods. The test has been administered to several hundred HRD staff members and managers. The scores can be analyzed by examining four ranges.

Score Range	Analysis of Score
81-100	This organization represents results-based education and training in action. There is little room for improvement and little need to take any additional concentrated efforts to improve evaluation of the HRD function. Management support is great. Departments with this rating are leaders in this important field of evaluation and setting examples for others. This organization should be extremely effective with this attitude toward HRD and evaluation.
61-80	This organization is probably better than average in HRD evaluation. There is room for improvement, but present efforts appear to be headed in the right direction. There is some attention to obtaining results and evaluation of programs. Some methods appear to be appropriate, but additional emphasis is needed to position HRD to contribute more in the future. Management support is moderate.
41-60	Improvement is needed in this organization. The attitude and approach to HRD evaluation are less than desirable. Present methods are ineffective. Emphasis needs to be placed on securing the appropriate management support to change the philosophy of the organization.
20-40	In this organization there is little or no concern for measuring results of the HRD function. The HRD function is ineffective and needs improvement if it is to survive. Urgent attention is needed from top management to change the approach of the HRD function.

Appendix 2

How Results-Based Are Your Training and Development Programs?

A Survey for Managers

Instructions. For each of the following statements, please circle the response that best matches the Training and Development function at your organization. If none of the answers describe the situation, select the one that best fits. Please be candid with your responses.

Select the most correct response.

1. The direction of the Training and Development function at your organization:
   a. Shifts with requests, problems, and changes as they occur.
   b. Is determined by Human Resources and adjusted as needed.
   c. Is based on a mission and a strategic plan for the function.

2. The primary mode of operation of the Training and Development function is:
   a. To respond to requests by managers and other employees to deliver training programs and services.
   b. To help management react to crisis situations and reach solutions through training programs and services.
   c. To implement many training programs in collaboration with management to prevent problems and crisis situations.

3. The goals of the Training and Development function are:
   a. Set by the training staff based on perceived demand for programs.
   b. Developed consistent with your organization's human resources plans and goals.
   c. Developed to integrate with operating goals and strategic plans of the organization.

240

4. Most new training programs are initiated:
   a. By request of top management.
   b. When a program appears to be successful in another organization.
   c. After a needs analysis has indicated that the program is needed.

5. When a major organizational change is made:
   a. We decide only which presentations are needed, not which skills are needed.
   b. We occasionally assess what new skills and knowledge are needed.
   c. We systematically evaluate what skills and knowledge are needed.

6. To define training plans:
   a. Management is asked to choose training from a list of canned, existing courses.
   b. Employees are asked about their training needs.
   c. Training needs are systematically derived from a thorough analysis of performance problems.

7. When determining the timing of training and the target audiences:
   a. We have lengthy, nonspecific training courses for large audiences.
   b. We tie specific training needs to specific individuals and groups.
   c. We deliver training almost immediately before its use, and it is given only to those people who need it.

8. The responsibility for results from training:
   a. Rests primarily with the training staff to ensure that the programs are successful.
   b. Is a responsibility of the training staff and line managers, who jointly ensure that results are obtained.
   c. Is a shared responsibility of the training staff, participants, and managers all working together to ensure success.

9. Systematic, objective evaluation, designed to ensure that trainees are performing appropriately on the job,:
   a. Is never accomplished. The only evaluations are during the program and they focus on how much the participants enjoyed the program.
   b. Is occasionally accomplished. Participants are asked if the training was effective on the job.
   c. Is frequently and systematically pursued. Performance is evaluated after training is completed.

10. New training programs are developed:
    a. Internally, using a staff of instructional designers and specialists.
    b. By vendors. We usually purchase programs modified to meet the organization's needs.
    c. In the most economical and practical way to meet deadlines and cost objectives, using internal staff and vendors.

11. Costs for training and developing are accumulated:
    a. On a total aggregate basis only.
    b. On a program by program basis.
    c. By specific process components such as development and delivery, in addition to a specific program.

12. Management involvement in the training process is:
    a. Very low with only occasional input.
    b. Moderate, usually by request, or on an as needed basis.
    c. Deliberately planned for all major training activities, to ensure a partnership arrangement.

13. To ensure that training is transferred into performance on the job, we:
    a. Encourage participants to apply what they have learned and report results.
    b. Ask managers to support and reinforce training and report results.
    c. Utilize a variety of training transfer strategies appropriate for each situation.

14. The training staff's interaction with line management is:
    a. Rare. We almost never discuss issues with them.
    b. Occasional; during activities such as needs analysis or program coordination.
    c. Regular; to build relationships, as well as to develop and deliver programs.

15. Training and Development's role in major change efforts is:
    a. To conduct training to support the project, as required.
    b. To provide administrative support for the program, including training.
    c. To initiate the program, coordinate the overall effort, and measures its progress, in addition to providing training

16. Most managers in your organization view the Training and Development function as:
    a.   A questionable function that wastes too much time of employees.
    b.   A necessary function that probably cannot be eliminated.
    c.   An important resource that can be used to improve the organization.

17. Training and Development programs are:
    a.   Activity-oriented (All supervisors attend the "Performance Appraisal Workshop").
    b.   Individual results-based (The participant will reduce his or her error rate by at least 20%).
    c.   Organizational results-based (The cost of quality will decrease by 25%).

18. The investment in Training and Development is measured primarily by:
    a.   Subjective opinions.
    b.   Observations by management, reactions from participants.
    c.   Dollar return through improved productivity, cost savings, or better quality.

19. The Training and Development effort consists of:
    a.   Usually one-shot, seminar-type approaches.
    b.   A full array of courses to meet individual needs.
    c.   A variety of training and development programs implemented to bring about change in the organization.

20. New Training and Development programs, without some formal method of evaluation, are implemented at my organization:
    a.   Regularly.
    b.   Seldom.
    c.   Never.

21. The results of training programs are communicated:
    a.   When requested, to those who have a need to know.
    b.   Occasionally, to members of management only.
    c.   Routinely, to a variety of selected target audiences.

22. Management involvement in training evaluation:
    a.   Is minor, with no specific responsibilities and few requests.
    b.   Consists of informal responsibilities for evaluation, with some requests for formal training.
    c.   Very specific. All managers have some responsibilities in evaluation.

23. During a business decline at my organization, the training function will
   a. Be the first to have its staff reduced.
   b. Be retained at the same staffing level.
   c. Go untouched in staff reductions and possibly beefed up.

24. Budgeting for training and education is based on:
   a. Last year's budget.
   b. Whatever the training specialist can "sell".
   c. A zero-based system.

25. The principal group that must justify Training and Development expenditures is:
   a. The Training and Development department.
   b. The human resources function.
   c. Line management.

26. Over the last two years, the Training and Development budget as a percent of operating expenses has:
   a. Decreased.
   b. Remained stable.
   c. Increased.

27. Top management's involvement in the implementation of Training and Development programs:
   a. Is limited to sending invitations, extending congratulations, passing out certificates, etc.
   b. Includes monitoring progress, opening/closing speeches, presentation on the outlook of the organization, etc.
   c. Includes program participation to see what's covered, conducting major segments of the program, requiring key executives to be involved, etc.

28. Line management involvement in conducting training and development programs is:
   a. Very minor; only HRD specialists conduct programs.
   b. Limited to a few specialists conducting programs in their area of expertise.
   c. Significant. On the average, over half of the programs are conducted by key line managers.

29. When an employee completes a training program and returns to the job, his or her manager is likely to:
    a. Make no reference to the program.
    b. Ask questions about the program and encourage the use of the material.
    c. Require use of the program material and give positive rewards when the material is used successfully.

30. When an employee attends an outside seminar, upon return, he or she is required to:
    a. Do nothing.
    b. Submit a report summarizing the program.
    c. Evaluate the seminar, outline plans for implementing the material covered, and estimate the value of the program.

Interpreting the Training and Development Programs' Assessment

Score the assessment instrument as follows. Allow:

> 1 point for each (a) response.
> 3 points for each (b) response.
> 5 points for each (c) response.

The total will be between 30 and 150 points

The interpretation of scoring is provided below. The explanation is based on the input from dozens of organizations and hundreds of managers.

Score Range	Analysis of Score
120 - 150	**Outstanding Environment** for achieving results with Training and Development. Great management support. A truly successful example of results-based Training and Development.
90-119	**Above Average** in achieving results with Training and Development. Good management support. A solid and methodical approach to results-based Training and Development.
60-89	**Needs Improvement** to achieve desired results with Training and Development. Management support is ineffective. Training and Development programs do not usually focus on results.
30-59	**Serious Problems** with the success and status of Training and Development. Management support is non-existent. Training and Development programs are not producing results.

INDEX

A

Absenteeism, 179, 186
Action plans, 68-77
    Sample, 70
Advertising and sales, 94
American Society for Training and
    Development (ASTD), 2, 3,
    12, 88
Analysis plan, 36-38
Andersen Consulting, 210, 211
Annualized values, 153-154, 159
Applications of ROI, 23-24

B

Benefits of ROI, 18-19
    Intangible
    (*see also* Intangibles),
    34, 204-205
Benefit/Cost Ratio, 11-12, 33
    154-155, 156-160, 188

C

Calculating effects of training,
    108
Calculating ROI, 33
    Sample data for, 207
Case studies, 12-13
    National Auto Products
        Company (NAPCo) 39-42,
        82-85, 110-112,
        133-134, 147-151,
        167-172, 184-188,
        202-206, 229-233

CIGNA, 107
Coca-Cola, 14
Consumer Products Marketing
    (CPM), 196
Control groups, 30, 89-92
Converting data to monetary
    benefits (*see* Monetary
    benefits)
Costs, 32-33
    Fully loaded, 138-139
    Tabulating, 136-151
        Case study, 147-151
        Categories, 141-144
        Estimation, 144-147
        Strategies, 137-140
    Sample summary, 159
    Sample worksheet, 148-149
Customer input, 104-109
Customer satisfaction, 180
Customer service, 180-181

D

Data collection (*see also* Post-
    program), 35-37
    Sample, 112
Data, converting to monetary
    benefits (*see* Monetary
    benefits)
Data credibility, 129-132
Data, hard vs. soft, 115-117
Data, historical, 32, 123-124
Data, soft, 125
Databases, external, 125
Definitions, 10-12
    HRD, 11
Discounted cash flow, 161

E

EEO, 163
Employee
    Attitude, 176-177
    Commitment, 177
    Complaints, 177-178
    Satisfaction, 176-178
    Stress reduction, 178
    Withdrawal, 178-180
Estimation (*see also* Cost),
    30, 32
    Monetary
        HRD staff, 128
        Management, senior,
        127-128
        Participant, 126
        Supervisor, 126-127
    Program cost, 144-147
    Training effects
        Expert, 106
        Management, 104
        Participant, 95-99
        Subordinate, 107-108
        Supervisor, 99-104
Evaluation
    Data collection, sample, 95
    Guidelines, 217-218
    Instruments, 27
    Levels, definitions, 27
    1: Reaction and Planned
        Action, 9, 190-194
    2: Learning, 9, 195-197
    3: Job Applications, 9,
        197-199
    4: Business Results, 9,
        199-200
    5: ROI, 9
    Purposes, 26
    Timing, 28
    Strategy, 206, 231

F

Fair Labor Standards Act
    (FLSA), 138
Federal Express, 89
Focus groups, 61-63
Follow-up session, 78-79
Forecasting, 30, 93-95
Formulas, 11-12
    Benefit/cost ratio, 154-155
    ROI, 155-156

H

Historical data, 31, 123-124

I

Impact study, sample, 228
Implementation, 34-35
    Barriers to, 13-18
    Case study, 229-233
    Initiating, 220-221
    Monitoring results, 226-229
    Planning, 207-215
    Preparing staff
        HRD, 215-220
        Management, 222-225
Intangibles, 173-189, 204-205
    Case study, 202-206
    Customer service, 180-181
    Employee satisfaction, 176-
    178
    Employee withdrawal, 178-180
    Issues, 174-176
    List, 174
    Team effectiveness, 181-183
        Sample, 183
Internal rate of return, 161

International Federation of
   Training and Development
   Organizations, 4
Interviews, 60-61
Issues, trends, 1-19

L

Litton, 16, 104

M

M&H Engineering, 192
Magnavox, 17, 155-156, 200
Management involvement, 165, 226
Measuring ROI, 1-24
   Applications, 23-24
   Issues, trends, 1-19
   Barriers to
      implementation, 13-18
      Benefits, 19
      Case studies, 12-13
      Characteristics of
         evaluation levels, 10
      Concerns, 5-7
      Criteria, 7-8
      Definitions, formulas,
         10-12
      Evaluation levels, 9-10
      Progress, 2-5
   Strategy, 19-23
Model, 25-42
   Calculating ROI, 33
   Cost of program, 32-33
   Evaluation, preliminary, 26-28
   Implementation, 34-35
   Intangible benefits, 34
   Isolating the effects of training,
      29-31
   Monetary values, 31-32
   Planning, 35-38
   Post-program data, 28-29

Monetary benefits, 114-135
   Accuracy, 129-132
   Case study, 133-134
   Contribution, 119-121
   Conversion sample, 120
   Databases, external, 125
   Employee time, 122-123
   Estimates
      HRD staff, 128
      Management, senior,
         127-128
      Participant, 126
      Supervisor, 126-127
   Historical costs, 123-124
   Issues, 115-119
   Quality, cost of, 121-122
   Strategies, 119, 128-129
Monetary values, 23, 31-32
Motorola, 197
Multi-Marques, 16

N

Nadler, L., 10
National Auto Products Company
   (NAPCo), 39-42, 82-85,
      110-112, 133-134,
      147-151, 167-172,
      184-188, 202-206,
      229-233
Needs assessment, 164-165

O

Obstacles, 218-219
Omega Consultants, 106
On-the-job-observation, 63-66
OSHA, 123
Overhead, 144

P

Participant input, sample, 100, 105
Payback period, 160
Penske, 16
Performance
    Contracts, 77-78
    Monitoring, 66-68
    Relationship with test scores,
        195
Planning, 35-38
Post-program
    Data collection, 28-29, 43-85
        Action plans, 68-77
            Sample, 70
        Focus group, 61-63
        Follow-up session, 78-79
        Interviews, 60-61
        Method selection, 79-81
        On-the-job observation,
            63-66
        Performance contracts,
            77-78
        Performance monitoring,
            66-68
        Questionnaires, surveys,
            45-59
        Sources, 44-45
    Control groups, 89-92
    Evaluation methods, 21
Productivity, 92-93, 169, 172, 184,
    186
Project plan, 212
    Sample, 214
Profitability analysis, of a loan, 121

Q

Questionnaires, surveys, 45-59
    Response rate, 57-59
    Sample, 50-54, 191

R

Restaurant managers, 103
Results, 14-17
    Sample, 102
Retail Merchandise Company
    (RMC), 156
Return, calculating, 152-172
    Case study, 167-172
    Discounted cash flow, 161
    Internal rate of return, 161
    Issues, 153-154
    Benefit/cost ratio, 154-155
        Case application, 156-160
    Payback period, 160
    ROI formula, 155-156
    Utility analysis, 161-162
ROI
    Calculation (*see* Benefit/cost
    ratio)
        Sample targets, 202
    Case study, 202-205
    Cautions, 164-166
    Complexity, 163-164
    Definition, 153
    Formula, 155-156
    Issues, 163-166
    Levels, 27, 190-206
        1: Reaction and Planned
            Action, 9, 190-194
        2: Learning, 9, 195-197
        3: Job Applications, 9,
            197-199
        4: Business Results, 9,
            199-200
        5: ROI, 9

S

Sexual harassment, 178
Sources of data, 44-45
Strategy, 19-23
Supervisor input, sample, 105

T

Tardiness, employee, 179
Team effectiveness, 181-183
    Sample, 183
TQM, 106
Training, magazine, 3
Training effects,
    Case study, 110-112
    Calculating impact, 108
    Control groups, 89-92
    Customer input, 104, 106
    Estimates
        Expert, 106
        Management, 104
        Participants, 95-99
        Subordinate, 107-108
        Supervisor, 99-104
    Forecasting methods, 93-95
    Isolating, 29-31, 86-113
    Strategies, 109
    Trend line analysis, 92-93
Training evaluation
    Paradigm shift in, 6
    Status of, 3
Transfers, employee, 180
Trend line analysis, 30, 92-93
    202
Turnover, employee, 179, 185, 186,
    188

Y

Yellow Freight Systems,
17, 132

U

United States Government, 22, 198
Utility analysis, 161-162

W

*William and Mary Business
    Review*, 4
Workshops, for managers, 217-218